Boxing, Narrative and Culture

Boxing, Narrative and Culture: Critical Perspectives is the first interdisciplinary response to the dominant boxing narratives that are produced, performed, and circulated in commercial boxing culture.

This collection includes global perspectives on boxing. It highlights the diverse range of bodies and communities that engage with boxing practices but are oftentimes overlooked and overwritten by popular narrative tropes and misconceptions of the sport. These interdisciplinary and global perspectives engage with boxing's shared narrative resources, offering new readings and insights on how and what boxing performs and for whom. The contributors to this collection are academics, artists, amateur boxers, and/or coaches who provide a culture critique of boxing. The work shows how boxing practices are performed and channelled by individuals and communities who access and utilise boxing culture as a means of physical enquiry, political statement, and community building. These contributions challenge the notion that boxing is a sport reserved for masculine bodies adorned as heroes, warriors, or victims of the sport.

Exploring key themes in socio-cultural studies including gender, race, community, media, and performance, this book is fascinating reading for anybody with an interest in physical culture, sport studies, cultural studies, gender studies, cultural geography, critical race theory, labour studies, performance studies, or media studies.

Sarah Crews is a performance and media studies scholar and senior lecturer at the University of South Wales whose research centres on vectors of power as they relate to gender, activism, sport, and performance making practices. Sarah's recent research projects are concerned with how female boxers are represented in sport and popular media, and how their work challenges stereotypes of female bodies. Sarah is in the process of developing an archive of female contributions to Welsh boxing in collaboration with People's Collection Wales.

P. Solomon Lennox is the head of the Department of Arts at Northumbria University. His research explores the relationships between physical performance practices, theories of performance space, and narrative identity. Solomon has published in the area of combat sports, specifically boxing. His work examines the connections between narrative tropes and physical performance practices. Solomon is currently developing work on the power of memetic performance, memetic haunting, and activism.

Routledge Research in Sport, Culture and Society

Sport, Physical Activity and Criminal Justice
Politics, Policy and Practice
Edited by Haydn Morgan and Andrew Parker

Sport Stadiums and Environmental Justice
Edited by Timothy Kellison

Sport, Performance and Sustainability
Edited by Daniel Svensson, Erik Backman, Susanna Hedenborg and Sverker Sörlin

The Future of Motorsports
Business, Politics and Society
Edited by Hans Erik Næss and Simon Chadwick

Experiencing the Body in Yoga Practice
Meanings and Knowledge Transfer
Krzysztof T. Konecki, Aleksandra Płaczek, and Dagmara Tarasiuk

Boxing, Narrative and Culture
Critical Perspectives
Edited by Sarah Crews and P. Solomon Lennox

Cricket, Capitalism and Class
From the Village Green to the Cricket Industry
Chris McMillan

For more information about this series, please visit: www.routledge.com/routledgeresearch insportcultureandsociety/book-series/RRSCS

Boxing, Narrative and Culture

Critical Perspectives

Edited by Sarah Crews
and P. Solomon Lennox

LONDON AND NEW YORK

First published 2024
by Routledge
4 Park Square, Milton Park, Abingdon, Oxon OX14 4RN

and by Routledge
605 Third Avenue, New York, NY 10158

Routledge is an imprint of the Taylor & Francis Group, an informa business

© 2024 selection and editorial matter, Sarah Crews and
P. Solomon Lennox; individual chapters, the contributors

The right of Sarah Crews and P. Solomon Lennox to be identified as the authors of the editorial material, and of the authors for their individual chapters, has been asserted in accordance with sections 77 and 78 of the Copyright, Designs and Patents Act 1988.

All rights reserved. No part of this book may be reprinted or reproduced or utilised in any form or by any electronic, mechanical, or other means, now known or hereafter invented, including photocopying and recording, or in any information storage or retrieval system, without permission in writing from the publishers.

Trademark notice: Product or corporate names may be trademarks or registered trademarks, and are used only for identification and explanation without intent to infringe.

British Library Cataloguing-in-Publication Data
A catalogue record for this book is available from the British Library

ISBN: 978-1-032-32056-4 (hbk)
ISBN: 978-1-032-32055-7 (pbk)
ISBN: 978-1-003-31263-5 (ebk)

DOI: 10.4324/9781003312635

Typeset in Optima
by Apex CoVantage, LLC

Contents

List of Contributors   vii

Introduction   1

PART 1
Serious Athletes and the Politics of Community   7

1   Increasing Visibility and the (Re)presentation of Female Boxers in Print Media   9
PAIGE SCHNEIDER

2   Influencer Boxing: Authenticity and the Quest for Redemption   24
P. SOLOMON LENNOX

3   Ducking and Diving: Why Boxing Clubs Hit the Targets Other Sports Cannot Reach in Deprived Communities   40
DAVID BARRETT, LEE EDMONDSON, ROBBIE MILLAR, AND P. SOLOMON LENNOX

4   Narratives of Struggle: Boxing, Gender, and Community   55
SUPRIYA CHAUDHURI

5   Practicing Otherwise: Feminist Boxing Challenges Mainstream Narratives of Combat Sports   72
ELISA VIRGILI

6   Reflections on the Empowerment of Women in Boxing from Athletes and Coaches in Norway Female Box   87
ANNE TJØNNDAL

PART 2
(De)constructing Self, to Be Somebody 103

7 Trans Boxing: A Boxing Club, an Art Project 105
   NOLAN HANSON AND ZAC EASTERLING

8 Katie Taylor: Complicating a Boxing Identity 116
   EMMA CALOW

9 Letting Down the Team? Individualism, Selfishness, and Kinship in Women's Boxing 128
   SARAH CREWS

10 Alfonso 'Mosquito' Zvenyika and the Dominant Narratives on Boxing in Post-Colonial Zimbabwe 148
   MANASE KUDZAI CHIWESHE AND GERALD DANDAH

11 Political Symbolism of Mary Kom from the Manipuri Autobiography to the Indian Blockbuster 164
   MYRIAM MELLOULI

12 Turn the Volume Up! Boxing Hearts and Beats 179
   KRISTÍNA ORSZÁGHOVÁ

13 Gender Transgression in the (Trans)National Domain: Laura Serrano and Women's Boxing in Mexico 194
   MARJOLEIN VAN BAVEL

Afterword: Boxing and Cultural Value *207*
Index *210*

Contributors

David Barrett, Lee Edmondson, and Robbie Millar (Sheffield Hallam University) The authors are part of the Sport Industry Research Group, working with National Governing Bodies of sport (NGBs) to understand motivations and behaviours which influence participation. In 2019, they were commissioned by England Boxing to investigate the reasons why Community Boxing Clubs (CBCs) are considered to be successful in engaging with young people in deprived communities which are traditionally thought of as hard to reach in sport development terms. Nearly 75% of all affiliated CBCs are located in the most deprived 20% of neighbourhoods in England, underlining the importance of the clubs to their host communities.

Emma Calow was born and bred in Northern Ireland and is currently a Ph.D. candidate in the American Culture Studies program at Bowling Green State University, Ohio. Specializing in ethnicity, gender, and social identity, Emma's research predominantly lies in the sociocultural studies of sport, women and girls in/and sport, and athlete activism through a feminist cultural studies lens. Her experiences as a former elite athlete in Northern Ireland/Ireland informs the kind of work she does. Emma has recently published in the *European Journal for Sport and Society* and in *Kinesiology Review*.

Supriya Chaudhuri is an emeritus professor of English at Jadavpur University, Kolkata, India. Her research fields include Renaissance literature, cultural history, modernism, critical theory, and the cultures of sport. She engages publicly with issues concerning the arts, politics, and gender. Among relevant publications are her co-edited books *Fields of Play: Sport, Literature and Culture* (University of Toronto Press 2015); *Sport, Literature, Society: Cultural Historical Studies* (Routledge 2013); chapters in *Sporting Cultures, 1650–1850* (University of Toronto Press 2018) and *Women Contesting Culture: Changing Frames of Gender Politics in India* (Stree/Samya 2012); and articles in the *International Journal of the History of Sport*.

Manase Kudzai Chiweshe is a senior lecturer in the Department of Social and Community Development, University of Zimbabwe. He is the winner of the 2015 Gerti Hesseling Prize for Best Paper Published in African

Studies. His work revolves around the sociology of everyday life in African spaces with a special focus on promoting African ways of knowing with specific interest in gender, urban sociology, agrarian studies, identity land, and livelihoods.

Sarah Crews is a performance and media studies scholar and senior lecturer at the University of South Wales whose research centres on vectors of power as they relate to gender, activism, sport, and performance making practices. Sarah's recent research projects are concerned with how female boxers are represented in sport and popular media, and how their work challenges stereotypes of female bodies. Sarah is in the process of developing an archive of female contributions to Welsh boxing in collaboration with People's Collection Wales.

Gerald Dandah is a PhD candidate in the Sociology Department at the University of Johannesburg (South Africa). His research interests include sport sociology; sport, gender, and the media; sport for development; as well as social inclusion and sport. He is also currently a practising freelance sport journalist and a FIFA-certified sports manager.

Zac "Sweet Tea" Easterling (they/them) is a second-year PhD student in the Department of Performance Studies at NYU. The North Carolina native leverages their background in anthropology, philosophy, African American studies, performance studies, and boxing in order to generate illuminations about being. Today, their work most deals with boxing as an expression of human virtuosity and public intimacy, with the main takeaway being how boxing gestures towards possibilities of being as being-together.

Nolan "Evil" Hanson (they/he) is an artist based in New York City. Their practice includes independent and collaborative socially engaged projects. Much of their work uses boxing to explore identity, embodiment, and relationality. Nolan is the founder of Trans Boxing, an ongoing and co-authored art project in the form of a boxing club which was founded in 2017. Nolan holds an MFA in art and social practice from Portland State University.

P. Solomon Lennox is the head of the Department of Arts at Northumbria University. His research explores the relationships between physical performance practices, theories of performance space, and narrative identity. Solomon has published in the area of combat spots, specifically boxing. His work examines the connections between narrative tropes and physical performance practices. Solomon is currently developing work on the power of memetic performance, memetic haunting, and activism.

Myriam Mellouli specializes in research on artistic expressions and representations of boxing. She obtained a master's degree in literature (ENS Lyon) thanks to a master's thesis in comparative literature on the aesthetics of survival in boxing literature and started film studies with a master's thesis on spaces in boxing films. Since 2019, she has pursued her specialization on "the Noble Art" by preparing a Ph.D. dissertation in film studies entitled "Le film de boxe: le combat d'un genre" (Le Mans Université, Laboratoire 3L.AM).

Kristína Országhová is a PhD student in sociology at Charles University in Prague. Kristína's research interests include senses and the body, gender identities and space, and boxing and physical culture in housing estates in the city peripheries.

Paige Schneider (PhD, Emory University) holds a joint appointment in the departments of Politics, and Women's and Gender Studies at the University of the South (Sewanee). Her research focuses on gender and sport in the Global South, and gender and political violence with a specialization in violence against women political actors. Most recently, her work has appeared in the *Journal of Gender Studies*; *Policy Studies*; the book *Building Inclusive Elections*, eds. T. James and H. Garnett (Routledge 2020); and in the forthcoming volume *Gender and Violence against Political Actors*, eds. E. Bjarnegård and P. Zetterberg (Temple University Press 2015).

Anne Tjønndal is the head of the Department of Leadership and Innovation and a research group leader for RESPONSE – Research Group for Sport and Society, Nord University, Bodø, Norway. She is also a visiting professor at the Norwegian University of Science and Technology (NTNU). Tjønndal is a former Olympic boxer and national champion. She is currently a member of the IBA Coaches Committee and head coach for Norway Female Box.

Marjolein Van Bavel is a postdoctoral fellow at the Department of History of the University of Antwerp (UA). Her work is characterised by the continuous search for the voices of women in history. Van Bavel is a member of the organisational team of the Cátedra 'Miguel León-Portilla' of the UA Centre for Mexican Studies and she collaborates with the Institute of Historical Research at the National Autonomous University of Mexico (UNAM). She is board member of the Association for Gender History in the Dutch-language area (*Vereniging voor Gendergeschiedenis*) and member of the Belgian Forum for Gender History and of the A* Antwerp Gender and Sexuality Studies Network.

Elisa Virgili is an independent researcher in the field of political philosophy, gender studies, and queer theories, and is part of the Politesse Research Center of the University of Verona. One of her main areas of research is the relationship between language and gender between public spaces and bodies. She also wrote a book and several articles on gender and sport, focusing on combat sports. She is part of a weird family that is a pack, a grassroot gym, and a transfeminist collective.

Introduction

Boxing, Narrative and Culture: Critical Perspectives is the first interdisciplinary response to the dominant boxing narratives that are produced, performed, and circulated in commercial boxing culture. This collection includes global perspectives on boxing. It highlights the diverse range of bodies and communities that engage with boxing practices but are oftentimes overlooked and overwritten by popular narrative tropes and misconceptions of the sport. These interdisciplinary and global perspectives engage with boxing's shared narrative resources, offering new readings and insights on how and what boxing performs and for whom. The contributors to this collection are academics, artists, amateur boxers, and/or coaches who provide a culture critique of boxing. The work shows how boxing practices are performed and channelled by individuals and communities who access and utilise boxing culture as a means of physical enquiry, political statement, and community building. These contributions challenge the notion that boxing is a sport reserved for masculine bodies adorned as heroes, warriors, or victims of the sport.

Boxing is a form of mass entertainment haunted by a troubled history and besieged by scandal. At the institutional level, organised crime has long played a part in the sport's evolution. Historically, the mob controlled professional boxing in the USA between 1930–1970. More recently (2021), a BBC Panorama investigation explored the involvement of the alleged head of one of Europe's biggest drug cartels, Daniel Kinahan, in a proposed heavyweight title fight between Tyson Fury and Anthony Joshua. For International Boxing Hall of Fame trainer Angelo Dundee, organised crime has long been boxing's hidden secret sin (see Dundee, 2008, p. 39). However, criminality, scandal, and ill-intent seep into the sport in a myriad of other ways. Individual boxers have faced suspensions from the sport for cheating (Antonio Margarito's 'loaded gloves' in 2009) and abusing drugs (Shane Mosley PEDs in 2003; Shane Mosely Jr PEDs in 2015; Tyson Fury cocaine in 2016, to name but a few), and one of the sport's governing bodies, the Amateur International Boxing Association (AIBA), was not permitted to participate in 2020 Olympics by the International Olympic Committee (IOC) after years of financial chaos and

DOI: 10.4324/9781003312635-1

allegations of corrupt judging. The sport is unlikely to feature at the Olympic games in 2028 and risks being banned from the competition for good. Boxing's detractors suggest that the risks (moral, legacy, and health-related) are sufficient reasons to call for it to be severely modified and restricted or banned completely (Brayne et al., 1998; White, 2007).

Nevertheless, the sport maintains a pervasive hold on contemporary culture. As Benita Heiskanen (2012) accurately observes, boxing occupies a spatial and temporal position between 'society's margins and centers' (Heiskanen, 2012, p. 8). Scholarship on boxing strongly affirms that despite its troubled identity, the sport is a cause for good, helping provide transformative purpose to individuals otherwise forgotten, excluded, or overlooked by society. However, the sport remains 'poorly understood in the literature and reduced to stereotypes in the popular imagination' (Lewandowski, 2022, p. 1). Because boxing is a global sport, it contributes to globalising trends, is itself globalising, and is subject to the forces of globalisation (Woodward, 2014, p. 20). For this reason, it is important to understand how boxing works in a global context, and what it means for individuals and groups. Boxing, like all other sports, is a site where claims of legitimacy and authenticity ring loud. But, perhaps unlike other sports, it is one in constant need of asserting this.

Authenticity and legitimacy may be claimed by individuals through their engagement with boxing practices, including in training and competition. Boxing's sites, such as the boxing gym, play an important role for boxers and feature heavily within this collection. Loïc Wacquant (2005) observes that the 'factory' of the gym is where the fighting self is 'forged' (Wacquant, 2005, p. 145). For Wacquant, 'the anonymous and prosaic obscurity of the training gym', with its specific sounds, smells, and atmosphere, 'impregnate' the male body, moulding it 'for combat' (ibid). Similarly, for Woodward (2004), the 'work' of boxing takes place in the gym, a site where fantasy and fiction are 'reconstructed and transformed' through the 'rhythmic, staccato punches and pulsating beat of dance music' (Woodward, 2004, p. 14). Boxing works bodies, both the boxing ring and the gym provide a space for bodies to *work out* their identity. If, through Wacquant's reference to factories and forges, the metaphors of industrialisation are invoked, boxing can be understood as a sport that shapes particular bodies for particular purposes (private, communal, and national). However, Woodward's reading of the work carried out by boxing bodies foregrounds a more socio-cultural lens through which to examine the crafting of boxing identity.

In section one, 'Serious Athletes', Paige Schneider examines the changing representations of female AIBA boxers in the print and digital publication *Boxing!* between 2007–2017. The chapter recognises the importance of traditional media's role in documenting social phenomena, but also emphasises the power of media to actively shape what and how phenomena are (re)presented to the public through selective coverage. Schneider's analysis reveals a dramatic increase in AIBA coverage of women boxers over time and a transformation in the representation of female boxers. Schneider argues that the changing nature of traditional media coverage and representation of female boxers may reflect, in part, important societal changes in the gendered social order and more tolerance for flexibility in conceptions of masculinity. P. Solomon Lennox writes about the phenomenon of influencer boxing, focusing on the recruitment of the shared narrative resources of boxing as a legitimising practice. Using the *celebrity capital lifecycle framework* proposed by François Carrillat and Jasmina Ilicic (2019), the chapter examines the role traditional boxing is playing in its own evolution. It raises questions about the formation of narrative identity, specifically *who* can lay claim to a boxing identity and *when*. Influencer boxing has a potentially significant impact on how narrative identity is performed and legitimised, particularly as it pertains to the relationship between the recruitment of shared narrative resources and habitual, repeated, and rehearsed physical practices. The chapter argues for greater consideration of the relationship between shared narrative resources and the physical actions associated with identity work to better understand how identities are formed and legitimised.

Similarly, David Barrett, Lee Edmondson, Robbie Millar, and P. Solomon Lennox argue that access to the social cultural rewards associated with boxing are possible for individuals who engage with boxing clubs, not just those who identify as boxers. The qualitative work conducted by Barrett, Edmondson, and Millar includes narrative testimony of 56 boxing leaders at amateur clubs in England. The chapter explores how boxing clubs function as important sites in areas suffering from multiple deprivations. Supriya Chaudhri's work also focuses on the importance of boxing spaces as sites for change, particularly in extremely religious social conditions. Chaudhri's focus on a group of Muslim women boxers from an extremely underprivileged section of society in the city of Kolkata, India, argues that boxing sites become repositories of individual and community aspirations.

Drawing on ethnographic research in two community boxing gyms in Italy, Elisa Virgili explores how queer and feminist subjectivities find boxing gyms productive spaces to challenge and subvert hegemonic masculinity. Anne Tjønndal reflects on her own experiences of boxing as an empowering practice for women. Tjønndal's analysis highlights the Norway Female Box project as good practice ('what works'), as well as its impact on the issues and challenges facing athletes and coaches. A central argument made in the chapter is that a double strategy consisting of formal regulations, such as the introduction of gender quotas for coaches on national teams, and women-centered approaches with preferential treatment are needed to recruit and empower women in boxing. This section of the book, 'Serious Athletes', addresses what it means to be taken seriously in the highly regulated and codified global sport of boxing. At the heart of each of the chapters is a claim that to be taken seriously is to be read as legitimate and authentic.

Section two, '(De)constructing Self', opens with Nolan Hanson's and Zac Easterling's 'In the Funk: Trans Boxing and American Pragmatism'. This chapter considers the possibilities of boxing as an 'on-going co-authored art project', which foregrounds boxing practice (and spaces demarcated for the sport) as a form of community-building and social engagement that welcomes trans and gender-variant individuals. Trans Boxing challenges established codes of practice in boxing, offering original insight that views 'trans' as a 'sense of co-authorship: a movement beyond the discrete individualized body'. This chapter orients the reader towards the potential of boxing bodies (individual and institutional) to push back against received ideas about gender performance. The contributors open up space and opportunities to confront traditional, hegemonic perspectives of boxing. Emma Calow's chapter on Irish Olympian and Two-weight World Champion boxer Katie Taylor offers a focused analysis on Taylor's experiences in boxing, including Taylor's capacity to expand assumptions of what it means to be a boxer. Drawing on feminist cultural studies, Calow analyses a number of key texts pertaining to Taylor's career in boxing and identity as a boxer, demonstrating how narratives attributed to Taylor politicise her national identity and her position within the broader landscape of mainstream boxing. For Calow, Taylor *complicates* three common misconceptions of boxing bodies, conceived by Wacquant (1992): '1. boxing is exclusively for men; 2. boxers are "near-illiterate . . . raised in broken homes" and 3. boxing is a sport through which boxers "parlay anger at the world" as they seemingly crave violence'. Alongside these new insights from Hanson, Easterling, and Calow, several other authors in this section counter normative readings of boxing bodies and 'selves'. Sarah Crews interrogates historical misconceptions of femininity in boxing, developing ideas about how femininity and *feminism* are performed and understood in relation to female boxing bodies that occupy professional women's boxing in the West. Highlighting the work of Australian boxer and IBF Super Bantamweight World Champion Ebanie Bridges, Crews's 'Letting Down the Team?' provides a feminist analysis of women's boxing between 2012–2022, accounting for female boxers who subvert dominant ideas about individualism, competitiveness, and societal perceptions of women. For Crews, Ebanie 'Blonde Bomber' Bridges actively resists recent attempts to crudely group female boxers together or isolate them from their broader athletic communities and/or histories. Instead, using her popularity and commercial appeal, Bridges evokes alternative forms of kinship in women's boxing, which, Crews argues, indicates opportunities for where the projects of 'inclusivity and equality' in boxing can serve a diverse range of individuals and communities.

Popularity in boxing is inextricably linked with cultural practices that bind individual boxers to particular socio-cultural groups. A boxer's value and worth are qualified by their *reach* and their ability to establish a sense of connection with audiences. Authors Manase Kudzai Chiweshe, Gerald Dandah, and Myriam Mellouli explore how broader socio-political narratives are mapped onto individual boxing bodies in an attempt to respond to dynamic changes in cultural heritage, identity, and perceptions of gender in sport and media. Chiweshe and Dandah study how the prevalent and pervasive idea of 'rags-to-riches' (and back to rags again) applies to Zimbabwean boxer Alfonso 'Mosquito' Zvenyika. Their chapter questions how boxers are positioned as role models, in which individuals are upheld as 'exceptional', aspirational figures who demonstrate 'good' and proper codes of moral conduct. For Chiweshe and Dandah, there is a danger that such boxers become docile bodies utilised for broader socio-political and cultural endeavours. Addressing tensions that exist between 'glamourised' representations of struggle, will, and sacrifice in boxing, Chiweshe and Dandah unpack the narratives around Zvenyika in a bid to explore how media commentaries on his life and career have impacted the image of boxing and Black athletes from poor backgrounds. Myriam Mellouli also pays attention to how media interpretations of boxers mask more complex readings of boxing identity and overwrite important issues facing individuals and communities. In her analysis of Olympic boxer Mangte Chungneijang 'Mary Kom', Mellouli argues that the Hollywood version of Kom overlooks her Manipuri origins and presents instead a 'highly conformist' image of how Kom's identity intersects with broader socio-political ideas about gender in India. This contribution draws strong links with the final two chapters in this section: Kristina Országhová's empirical analysis of Slovakian identities in community boxing gyms and Marjolein Van Bavel's textual analysis of the status of Mexican boxer Laura Serrano (the first WIBF Lightweight Boxing Champion and the first Mexican or Latin American woman to win a world boxing title) within her home nation. Specifically, Országhová's 'Turn the Volume Up! Boxing Hearts and Beats' explores how the soundscapes of boxing gyms invoke Yugo-nostalgia in the Czech Republic. More generally though, Országhová offers a perspective on female boxing bodies that confronts popular assumptions of boxing as the last bastion of masculinity and male virility. As Van Bavel's chapter on Laura Serrano indicates, gender is both problematic and contested within boxing. However, through a range of intersectional issues, this section shows how individuals and communities *challenge* the oppositional dynamics of binary gendered norms (Clymer, 2004; Dunn, 2009; Matthews, 2016), undoing gender stereotypes and those attributed to boxing bodies. The chapters in this section gesture towards where boxing spaces and practices have the potential to embrace gender variance and transgress socio-cultural norms. Authors explore the relations between self, space, and place, positioning boxing as both a sense-making and meaning-making activity that provides individuals with cross-spatiotemporal kinaesthetic and reflective connections to other bodies, places, histories, and futures.

Bibliography

Brayne, H., Sergeant, L. and Brayen, C. (1998) 'Could boxing be banned? A legal and epidemiological perspective', *BMJ*, 316, pp. 1813–1815.

Carrillat, F. and Ilicic, J. (2019) 'The celebrity capital life cycle: a framework for future research directions on celebrity endorsement', *Journal of Advertising*, 48(1), pp. 61–71.

Clymer, J.A. (2004) 'The market in male bodies: Henry James's The American and late nineteenth-century boxing', *The Henry James Review*, 25, pp. 127–145.

Dunn, K. (2009) *One ring circus: dispatches from the world of boxing*. Tucson, AZ: Schaffner Press, Inc.

Dundee, A., with Sugar, B.R. (2008) *My view from the corner: a life in boxing*. New York: McGraw-Hill.

Heiskanen, B. (2012) *The urban geography of boxing: race, class and gender in the ring*. Oxon: Routledge.

Lewandowski, D.J. (2022) *On boxing: critical interventions in the bittersweet science*. Oxon: Routledge.

Matthews, C.R. (2016) 'The tyranny of the male preserve', *Gender & Society*, 30(2), pp. 312–333.

Wacquant, L.J.D. (1992) 'The social logic of boxing in Black Chicago: toward a sociology of pugilism', *Sociology of Sport Journal*, 9, pp. 221–254.

Wacquant, L.J.D. (2005) 'Men at work', in Gattuso, J. (ed.) *Shadow boxers: sweat, sacrifice & the will to survive in American boxing gyms*. Milford, NJ: Stone Creek Publications, pp. 145–148.

White, C. (2007) 'Mixed martial arts and boxing should be banned, says BMA', *BMJ*, 335, p. 469.

Woodward, K. (2004) Rumbles in the jungle: boxing, racialization and the performance of masculinity." *Leisure Studies*, 23(1), pp. 5–17.

Woodward, K. (2014) *Globalizing boxing*. London: Bloomsbury Academic.

Part 1

Serious Athletes and the Politics of Community

Image 1 Boxer Zainab, at Kidderpore School of Physical Culture, Kolkata, India, 2022

Chapter 1

Increasing Visibility and the (Re)presentation of Female Boxers in Print Media

Paige Schneider

In 2007 at the closing of the women's world boxing championship in Delhi, India, International Boxing Association (IBA)[1] executive committee member Bettan Andersson was quoted as saying, 'To see these girls giving it their all against the best in the world is proof that there is a strong future ahead for women's boxing. All we need now is to hold these world championships consistently every two years'.[2] On the one hand, Andersson's message was one of encouragement for women in the sport, and it acknowledged the lack of institutional support from the IBA. Conversely, he referred to some of the best women boxers in the world as 'girls', a patronising label that infantilises women and undermines their legitimacy as serious athletes on equal footing with men (Crews and Lennox, 2020). In a medium established to promote the sport of boxing, in this instance, women were represented as neophytes despite their athletic accomplishments. Andersson's slight was likely unintentional. Nonetheless, because he was quoted in the major print publication of the IBA, his statement was amplified to a global audience of boxers, fans, and other stakeholders in the sport.

Over the last 20 years, the number of girls and women learning to box and participating in sanctioned amateur boxing competitions has risen globally (Schneider, 2021). Female boxers upend patriarchal notions of women's physical vulnerability and emotional fragility and, in doing so, challenge what has historically been a male preserve (Matthew, 2016). Protecting heteronormative masculinity has been central to the sport of boxing and, as Dunning concludes, boxing has been one of the 'categorically unacceptable sports' for women precisely because it is perceived as incompatible with feminine gender norms. Mass media – especially sport media – plays an instrumental role in constructing and reinforcing societal gender norms when reporting on male and female athletes (Dunning, 1999, p. 231).

Engaging the central themes of this volume, this chapter investigates how sport media cover and represent female boxers. Content analysis of the International Boxing Association's print publication, *Boxing!*, shows considerable change over time in the association's (re)presentation of female amateur boxers.[3] In the early years of the publication, there is very little coverage of

DOI: 10.4324/9781003312635-3

women in the sport. By the end of the period under study, coverage of women in the sport is extensive, and women boxers are portrayed as authentic, skilled athletes at home in the boxing ring. To what can we attribute this marked change? To provide theoretical context to the discussion, I begin by reviewing existing scholarship on gender and sport media. Then, I turn to documenting the evolution of the representation of women boxers by the IBA and consider its implications in light of the growing popularity of the sport among women, globally.

Gendered Sport Media and the Representation of Women Athletes

Mass media has the power to actively shape what and how phenomena are (re)presented to the public. *Sport* media is pervasive, one of the most widely consumed forms of journalism, and an integral part of sport cultures. In her work on women, sport, and media, Creedon argues that sport media serves as a socializing agent engaged in 'creating and reflecting gender values' through the editorial decisions of gatekeepers who determine how women athletes will be represented in comparison to their male counterparts (1994, p. 3). Scholars have demonstrated the importance of media effects in a number of ways.[4] How female athletes are represented by sport media can either reinforce women's marginalisation or advance the project of dismantling gendered hierarchies in sport cultures.

Scholars working at the intersections of gender, sport, and media have documented gender disparities in media coverage and exposed the mechanisms by which sport media may feminise, sexualise, and trivialise female athletes (Kane, 2013; Cooky, Messner and Hextrum, 2013; Godoy-Pressland, 2014; Cooky, Mears and Messner, 2015; Sherry et al., 2016; Cooky, Council and Messner, 2021). Mechanisms include the prominence or placement of stories about women relative to men, passive vs. active representations of female athletes, the sexualisation or feminisation of women athletes (for instance, dress, hair, passive or suggestive poses), or emphasising women's traditional gender roles in the private sphere of home and family (Sherry, Osborne and Nicholson, 2016, p. 300). Media practices are important because content and images speak to the worth, status, and legitimacy of women athletes.

Biscomb's and Matheson's (2019) research tracks changes over time in the media's representation of women athletes across a number of these mechanisms. With some media practices, they find gender-based inequities exist over decades of reporting on women athletes. One example is found in the media practice of othering female athletes by framing their accomplishments in relation to assistance from parents, or focusing on social roles and interpersonal relationships (such as romantic partners). (Biscomb and Matheson, 2019, p. 274). Another example is found in the use of the prefix *women's* but not *men's* when reporting on athletic competitions, reinforcing the gender hierarchy by positioning men's sports as the default (Biscomb and Matheson, 2019, p. 269).

A number of scholars find ongoing gender disparities between male and female athletes in the magnitude of coverage, with male athletes and teams dominating coverage even as women's participation rates have skyrocketed. For instance, Courtney, Breen, and McGing found that over the period of time in which women's numerical representation on Ireland's national Olympic team increased, media coverage declined. They hypothesise that both a failure to recognise implicit journalistic bias and to institutionalise mechanisms to ensure gender equity in coverage explain this worrisome pattern (Courtney, Breen and McGing, 2020). There is some encouraging news emerging from studies of how media represent women in sport. For instance, MacKay and Dallaire (2016) find little evidence of gender discrimination in student-produced college sport publications, other than some inequities in story prominence and placement. A 2016 study of gendered patterns of reporting on ESPN found that while men still received significantly more coverage than did women, journalists focused first and foremost on aspects of athleticism in descriptions of both male and female athletes. This is noteworthy in light of decades of media coverage that represented (especially white) women athletes in overly sexualised ways Shifflett et al., 2016, p. 111).

In Godoy-Pressland's (2015) examination of the media's representation of British boxing champion Nicola Adams, they conclude that coverage of Adams during the 2012 Olympic Games broke new ground. The discriminatory and subordinating coverage of women athletes prevalent in the past was less apparent in the case of Adams. Because Adams is a Black woman, Godoy-Pressland's findings require close scrutiny.[5] Black feminist scholars have documented and interrogated the many ways in which controlling negative images of Black women has been deployed as punishment for resisting oppression (Hill Collins, 1991, pp. 67–90). The historical record is replete with negative stereotypes of Black women as aggressive and overly masculine. Scholars note that these stereotypes have been activated in coverage of Black athletes in traditionally white-dominated sports like tennis or gymnastics, with Black women positioned as suspect (Douglas, 2005, p. 262). Sport media may tap into these very same stereotypes to subtly de-gender Black women boxers and naturalise their participation in this violent sport.

Imaging Women Athletes in Sport Media

Images commonly augment the media's reporting on athletes and sporting events, and are thus an important source of data. Goffman's classic work on gendered advertisements theorises that media images do much more than reflect reality. Images, like language, evoke cognitive frames or ways of knowing and understanding phenomena and hold semiotic importance in the construction of gender difference and gender hierarchies (Sherry, 2016, p. 301).

Sport cultures have long served as sites for constructing and reinforcing masculine privilege, and a half century of women's rights activism has worked to challenge this privilege. Left uncontested, the underrepresentation or misrepresentation of women athletes in media images may act to undermine the tremendous progress women athletes have made in garnering respect and legitimacy.

Scholars such as Sherry, Osbourne, and Nicholson have found that images of female athletes in sport media are less numerous than those of male athletes. They do find more gender-equal coverage during the Olympic Games, but only when women are pictured in individual rather than team sports, or in 'socially acceptable' and more feminised sports, such as tennis (Sherry, 2016, p. 302). Biscomb and Matheson find that, over time, media images of women athletes focused less on appearance and more on gender-neutral performance characteristics (except in the sport of tennis) (Biscomb and Matheson, 2019, pp. 274–275). However, studies consistently find that female athletes are more likely than male athletes to be pictured in passive, rather than active, poses (Godoy-Pressland and Griggs, 2014).

Research suggests that coverage of women athletes today is more gender equal than in the past, yet discriminatory practices persist. The following analysis contributes to this body of research by examining how amateur female boxers are represented in stories and images in the International Boxing Association's print publication, *Boxing!* I document changes over time in the volume, range, nature, and tone of the stories and images. The implications of the findings in light of ongoing challenges for women in the sport is discussed.

Method of Inquiry and Analytical Framework

Data for this project is drawn from the International Boxing Association print and digital archive of the publication *Boxing!*. The IBA organizes amateur regional and world championship boxing competitions, and the qualifying events for the Olympic Games. During the period under study (2007 to 2016), the IBA publication was one of the primary official sources of news on amateur boxers, competitions, and match results worldwide, releasing 20 volumes comprised of over 875 pages of stories, profiles of individual boxers and coaches, images, competition tables, and other information relevant to the amateur boxing world.[6] Stories of one paragraph or more that covered females in the sport, and images picturing one or more females, were coded for the analysis.[7] Stories are coded by *length* of the article as a measure of the level of commitment that the federation demonstrates towards gender-inclusive coverage. *Short* stories comprise content less than one page in length, *medium-length* stories are those of more than one page but less than two, and *long* stories are feature articles of two pages or more.

Forms of gendered coverage that are documented and analysed include such mechanisms as placement of stories about women relative to those of men; the use of prefixes (men; women) in titles or story headings; the sexualization, feminization, or trivialization of women boxers; and coverage of highwater marks or 'firsts' for women in boxing. The quantity and nature of photographic images of women are also investigated in the analysis. Images are coded as either representing females in active/fight mode or in passive poses. Documenting changes over time in the imaging of women boxers is important, especially the ratio of active to passive poses. Images that portray women boxers as active agents in fight mode challenge disempowering stereotypes of women as physically weak, vulnerable, and in need of protection from men. Active images include acts of punching or other physical contact between boxers, boxers in a fight stance, and post-bout expressions of victory in the ring. Examples of passive poses include formal or casual group or individual photos outside of the ring, such as at an award ceremony.

The continuous publication of *Boxing!* provides a unique documentary source to analyse change over time in the visibility and representation of amateur female boxers by the very organisation tasked with encouraging participation in the sport and marshalling financial and other types of resources to sustain the sport globally. As such, the content reflects the choices and perspectives of individuals working for the IBA organisation, rather than the opinions of sport reporters working for independent news organisations. For this reason, the content of *Boxing!* may not be representative of the larger body of sports commentary on women boxers in print or broadcast news during this time period.

Evolving (Re)presentations of Female Boxers

A tabulation of stories and images covering female amateur boxers from 2007 to 2016 in *Boxing!* is reported in Table 1.1. In 2007, female boxers received little overall coverage. The first two volumes from this year contained only three stories of short to medium length, and a table of the medallists in each of three weight classes from the 2006 Fourth Women's World Championship in Delhi, India. Any news about women's boxing was overshadowed by the far more numerous stories and features about male competitions, male boxers, and the male-dominated IBA executive committee.

The few stories about women included several examples of gendered reporting. For instance, a women's world championship was referred to as 'the colourful competition', and India's champion boxer Mangte Chungneijang (popularly known as Mary Kom) was referred to as a 'diminutive 25 year old' (*Boxing News*, 2007, p. 9). A medium-length *Women's Profile* interview with Canadian boxer Ariane Fortin included a query about how her parents view her decision to box. Biscomb and Matheson argue that attributing the success of an athlete to others (such as one's parents) is more common in media coverage of female athletes and is thus a gendered mechanism that undermines women's athletic accomplishments. Another common gendered

Table 1.1 Increasing Coverage of Females in *Boxing!* 2007–2016

Year	2007	2008*	2009	2010	2012*	2013	2014	2015	2016*
Number of volumes per year	2	4	1	2	2	1	2	3	3
Stories									
Short (less than 1 page)	1	3	0	1	3	2	4	2	11
Medium (1 full page)	2	5	3	2	0	1	3	3	11
Long (2 + pages)	0	0	0	2	2	1	3	4	11
Total stories per year	3	8	3	5	5	4	10	9	33
Stories per volume	1.5	2	3	2.5	2.5	4	5	3	11
Images Active/fight	2	10	2	3	5	2	7	6	28
Passive	1	3	3	2	8	4	13	10	32
Front cover	0	1	0	0	2	0	2	2	2
Total images per year	3	14	5	5	15	6	22	18	62
Images per volume	1.5	3.5	5	2.5	7.5	6	11	6	20.6

* Denotes Olympic-year coverage. Women's boxing became an Olympic sport at the 2012 Games.

practice is failing to use gender prefixes in reporting, thereby reinforcing the assumption that stories about sports are naturally stories about male athletes or teams. Alternatively, media may use a prefix to designate only women's events. Both practices were exhibited in the early years of *Boxing!*. Coverage of men in the sport clearly predominates during this time.

Another pattern that emerges in the early years of the publication is the dearth of images of women. In part, this was because there were far fewer female boxing competitions and thus fewer female boxers to photograph. For instance, in one volume from 2007, there were 33 images of male boxers in the ring and no images of women. In the second volume from that year, only three images of women are featured, although two of the three were active/fight poses.

In 2008, the number of volumes doubled to four, and stories about women increased to an average of two per volume, for a total of eight stories. The number of images of women increased to a total of 14, or an average of 3.5 per volume, compared to 1.5 from the previous year. The stories were short to medium in length, and the images of women were primarily in active poses, but the very few images of women fighting are juxtaposed with images of women in formal attire (dresses) at award ceremonies. Two of the four volumes included no images of women at all. As 2008 was an Olympic year and women's boxing was not yet an Olympic sport, stories and images of male boxers qualifying for or competing in the Olympics predominated. In fact, in over 100 pages of published material, one of the few stories concerning women's boxing was an interview with China's *male* women's national team boxing coach. Another story included only an image of male Chinese officials at the signing ceremony for the 2008 Women's World Championships in Ningbo.

The last volume in 2008 showed some improvement in gender equity. Ireland's champion Katie Taylor was featured on the cover (along with male counterparts) at the IBA annual award ceremony where she was honoured as female boxer of the year. There was some coverage of the Fifth Women's World Championships in Podolsk, Russia, including a two-page spread on medal winners. It is noteworthy that ten of the 14 images of females were in fight mode, throwing punches at their opponents. To the credit of the editors of Boxing!, there was no noticeable sexualization or feminization of the boxers. Yet, in one story covering the IBA application to include women's boxing in the 2012 Olympics, the IBA president notes: 'the momentum behind women's boxing [is] gathering great speed', but this was followed by the ambivalent comment, 'whatever the result, we know that the IOC will be acting in the best interests of boxing' (Boxing News, 2008. p. 36).

In 2009 there was only one volume of Boxing!, with only three stories referencing women in the sport. One story was noteworthy in that it called attention to the dearth of competition for high-level women boxers, the lack of female coaches and officials, and the public controversy surrounding the proposal to require amateur women boxers to wear skirts in competitions. There were references to both men's and women's Continental Championships, but no use of gender prefixes in the coverage of the junior and youth championships. As for images, women were represented in only five of the 40 images, with two of the five in active poses.

The two volumes of the 2010 edition displayed small changes in a positive direction in coverage and representation of women compared to previous years. Whilst there were still few stories or images of women in the 66 pages of content, we do see, for the first time, longer feature articles about women. For instance, one article with the headline 'Magnificent Mary Makes It Five' provided an in-depth exposé on Indian boxer and five-time champion Mary Kom (Boxing News, 2010, vol. 7, pp. 10–11). There were statements of support for women's boxing, highlighting the growth in the number of boxers representing an increasing array of countries in successive women's world championships. Descriptions of female boxers included that they are 'fierce competitors', and India's Mary Kom was referred to as a 'living legend' and 'one of history's strongest boxing competitors' (Boxing News, 2010, vol. 6, pp. 20–21). One other notable story is a half-page description of the work of the IBA Women's Commission, including a group photo of the 11 women on the commission. This is one of the earliest images picturing the increased presence of women officials in the sport (Boxing News, 2010, vol. 7, p. 6).

After many years of lobbying, women's boxing became an Olympic sport in 2012. Nonetheless, the two volumes from this year disappointed in the quantity of coverage of the women's debut. On the upside, for the first time in the publications short history, women appeared on the front covers of both volumes in the edition, including the first time a woman boxer (Katie Taylor) was the sole and prominent boxer featured on a cover (*Boxing News*, 2012, vol. 10, cover). In a nod to more gender-equitable coverage, Olympic results were presented by national team, rather than by gender, interweaving commentary about both male and female medallists in the article. In a show of support, one writer stated that 'the women's boxing tournament was one of the major highlights of the London Games' (*Boxing News*, 2012, vol. 10, p. 12). Overall, the coverage was fairly gender neutral in tone until the discussion of the 'shocking' underperformance of team USA, which brought home 'only' two medals. However, the two medallists happened to be women, including Clarissa Shields, one of the best female boxers in the world.

Returning to the question of how intersecting social identities of race and gender might influence the media's coverage of Black women boxers, the IBA's coverage of boxers Clarissa Shields and Nicola Adams did not appear to be notably different from that of non-Black identified powerhouses such as Katie Taylor and Mary Kom. This is perhaps not too surprising, given that the number of 'elite' amateur women boxers is quite small, and many of these women are women of colour. There is a large body of scholarship interrogating the racialised coverage of sports,[8] however the scholarship that examines the role of race and ethnicity in the sport of boxing focuses almost exclusively on men (Woodward, 2004, pp. 5–17; Boddy, 2008).

As for story placement, an image of a woman boxer was found on the first page of the Olympic story spread, but that was followed by seven pictures of male boxers and the men's results before returning to images of women and the women's results. Because so few weight classes were included for women (3) compared to men (10) in the Games, there were many more male boxers to feature and many more male bouts to cover. Another 'first' appeared in reporting on the 2012 Women's World Championship in China, where participation reached an all-time high of 305 women boxers representing 70 countries.

Although the IBA failed to provide much coverage of women's participation in the 2012 Olympics relative to men, the International Olympic Committee's decision to include women's boxing was pivotal, nonetheless. It was the culmination of years of organizing and lobbying by and on behalf of female boxers. The enormous momentum behind this victory resulted in an increase in regional competitions (Schneider, 2021, p. 890) and in the number of women participating in these events from 2012 onward (Schneider, 2021, p. 891). Additional women's qualifying competitions provided more opportunities for the IBA to meaningfully cover women's participation in the sport. After 2013, there is a noticeable change in the IBA's coverage of women in the sport. Stories are more numerous, extensive, and the range of subject matter covered is broader. Examples include cameos of female coaches, IBA female executive committee members, and female referees who judge male bouts. One story profiled the only 'five star' woman referee and judge, Algerian Kheira Sidi Yahoub and another story covered the well-regarded referee Jennifer Huggins. Feature stories about individual women champions covered a more diverse group of boxers, including Brazil's Adriana Araujo and American-born Jennifer Chieng, who fights for Micronesia.

Over time, as more regional boxing competitions in the Global South opened their doors to women, the IBA included more stories about women in sub-Saharan Africa, Asia, the Commonwealth countries, and Latin America. Beginning in the 2009 volume, we find a story that highlighted the success of several South American female boxers in the American Women's Continental Championships in Guayaquil, Ecuador. In 2010, the IBA newsletter featured a story on the first African Confederation Boxing Championship to include women, noting that 20 women competed in the regional competition with medallists from four different countries. IBA's coverage of the 2012 women's world championship in China made a point of recognizing women who 'made history' as the first women from their respective countries (Philippines, Azerbaijan, and Tajikistan) to medal in a world championship. After 2013, coverage of women boxers from countries in the Global South increased even more and was routinely integrated into reporting about women in the sport.

Another notable change occured in the length and tenor of coverage of women's major regional and international competitions. Prior to 2014, stories about women's championships were 1–2 pages in length, and rather perfunctory and bland. After that, we find detailed features such as a 16-page spread in the run up to the 2016 women's world championships in Astana, Turkey, and a 12-page spread of post-event coverage. Descriptions of women's bouts were more compelling and interesting, resembling the coverage afforded to men's events (*Boxing!*, 2016, vol. 18, pp. 20–23). Coverage of women's participation in the Olympic Games in Rio in 2016 was much more extensive and gender equal than Olympic coverage in 2012. For instance, the Olympic boxing schedule was presented as a single chart, rather than in separate charts for men and women, and stories about women medallists were positioned before stories about men. There was a special feature, 'Olympic Facts', that included the use of the term '*both genders*', with *both* in bold, and the use of the female symbol was displayed prominently on the page (*Boxing!*, 2016, vol. 18, p. 74).

The three volumes published in 2016 show a much more balanced distribution of coverage between male and female boxers, and much more visibility for women overall. There were even more boxing equipment advertisements featuring women. The diversity of women represented continued to expand, and women were portrayed across a greater variety of roles in the sport. Stories were more likely to interweave male and female results, and gender prefixes were used more frequently (but not consistently) across editions. Coverage exhibited no discernible sexualisation or feminisation of women boxers.

As for images, in 2014, the average number of images per volume increased to 11, and peaked in 2016 at an average of 21 images per volume (63 images in total). *Boxing!* demonstrated a commitment to presenting women in fight mode early on, and this continued in later years. However, by 2016, not only the volume of images, but also the range of poses and stances in which women boxers are captured, more closely aligned with that of male boxers. There was greater diversity by race, ethnicity, nationality, and world region reflected in the images of women, highlighting the global reach of women's boxing.

Over time, more females were featured on the front cover of the publication. Up to and including 2013, only three female boxers were included on the covers. Between 2014 and 2016, this number doubled to six, including a 2016 volume highlighting the Women's World Championship in Turkey, in which all three boxers featured on the cover were well-known women champions. The transformation in women's representation on front covers of the magazine is striking and important. Prior to 2014, cover photos reflected a traditional boxing magazine reporting on a male-dominated sport, punctuated by the occasional image of a woman boxer. From 2014 on, women have been pictured authentically as skilled athletes, rather than novelties in the sport, reflecting a greater commitment to gender inclusivity in the public face of the IBA.

Conclusion

Findings from this chapter show a significant increase over time in the International Boxing Association's coverage of women in the sport of boxing, adding to the body of research demonstrating greater gender equity in sport media reporting. Over the course of the decade under study, story placement becomes more gender equal, gender prefixes are used more consistently, and there is little in the way of overt sexualisation or feminisation of female boxers. There is more coverage devoted to women boxers of different racial and ethnic identities, and from a wide array of countries in the Global South. References to the growth in women's participation, to increasing interest and participation among female youth, and the IBA's explicit statements of support for women in the sport become more numerous over time.

In the earlier years of the publication *Boxing!*, there were few images of women. By 2016, the number of images capturing women and girls in the ring, sweating, punching, and in classic boxing poses, predominated. The range of subjects in the photos expanded over time, with greater representation for female officials, referees, coaches, and executive committee members. National team photos represented a broader range of countries, including more from the Global South.

Even with documented changes in coverage over time, there is still work to be done to achieve gender equity in the representation of women in the sport.

Coverage of male boxing competitions and male boxers is still more numerous. The overwhelming male dominance in coaching and leadership in the sport is ongoing. A listing in 2013 of the 23 newly elected presidents of IBA country federations were all male (*Boxing!*, 2013, vol. 11, p. 19). In the final volumes of the publication the IBA began to include coverage of the short-lived and all male World Series of Boxing. Coverage was placed at the back of the publication, but nonetheless, the editorial decision to include coverage of the professional bouts skewed content back towards male boxers and events. In some of this coverage, there were images of scantily clad women serving as hosts and entertainers, harkening back to a time when this was the primary role for women in the sport.

To what can we attribute change over time? The changes in representation of women in *Boxing*! may be attributable in part to the diffusion of gender equality norms worldwide that have contributed to increasing rates of participation of women and girls in a wide range of sports.[9] Change over time in gendered patterns of participation in sports like boxing reflect broader cultural shifts around constructions of masculinity and femininity, gender roles in society, and the entire gender order or regime (Connell, 1987; Woodward, 2014, p. 108). The changing nature of media coverage and representation of female boxers may reflect, in part, important societal changes in the gendered social order, and more tolerance for flexibility in conceptions of masculinity – even in boxing and other combat sports.

The IBA's decision to embrace and heighten the visibility of female boxers and competitions may reflect the financial exigencies of a sport that has declined in popularity in many markets, including the U.S. This is in part a function of the growing interest in playing and watching other sports, such as European football. Moreover, boxing must now compete against other combat sports such as mixed martial arts and the Muay Thai boxing style for athletes, fans, and media investment. Hence, the IBA's decision to target more resources towards females in the sport may be primarily driven by the fact that interest in boxing among women and girls is global, growing, and appears quite robust.[10]

One shortcoming of investigating change over time by relying upon official association publications is that editors are unlikely to air dirty laundry or to report on conflictual topics like gender discrimination within an organisation. It is difficult to know without asking women boxers directly how much of what is reported by the IBA aligns with their experiences and interactions with association officials and other gatekeepers in the sport.

Interest among girls and women in boxing and other combat sports is clearly increasing, yet there are important gaps in the study of this phenomenon. Research that examines sport media coverage of women boxers from an intersectional perspective has not kept up with the increasing diversity of female boxers in the ring. Studying media effects from an intersectional perspective with a focus on the social identities of the gender and race of boxers is especially needed. There is also a dearth of scholarship on mainstream media's coverage of women boxers, making it difficult to discern if patterns found in the present study are generalizable to the much more extensive coverage found in other print and broadcast platforms.[11]

Women continue to fight for equity in the sport of boxing, and there have been some recent and notable victories. Back in 2015, women lobbied for more qualifying spots for the 2016 Rio Games, but received only 36 spaces to men's 240, and still had only three weight classes to men's ten. Recently, it was announced that for the 2024 Paris Games, there would be six weight classes for women and seven for men.[12] Also, in 2019 the IBA changed the rules around boxing attire to allow women to compete in hijab, opening the doors for more observant Muslim women to participate in the sport. Important advances for women in the sport appear to be occurring more rapidly than in the past. Whether this is due to less resistance on the part of men, more determination on the part of women, or perhaps a bit of both, the future looks bright for the next generation of female pugilists.

Notes

1 In 2021 the AIBA voted to change its name to the International Boxing Association (IBA).
2 *Boxing News*, no. 1 (February-March 2007): 10. The IBA changed the name of *Boxing News* to *Boxing!* in 2015.
3 The Association Internationale de Boxe Amateur (AIBA), now the International Boxing Association (IBA), produced a newsletter intermittently between 1999–2016. Originally titled *Boxing News*, the publication name was changed in 2015 to simply *Boxing!*. Digital editions were accessed from the AIBA/IBA website archive and retrieved in 2018 and 2019. In 2021, the IBA reconfigured the website with a new URL, www.iba.sport/. The old website is now password protected, but most digitized editions can be found on the YouTube channel of IBA boxing coach Jonathon Bochner. The internet archive search engine the Wayback Machine has some older editions of the newsletter published between 1999–2004, but these do not inform the present research.
4 Studies by Daniels and others have documented the negative effects of media's gendered representation of female athletes on both the perceptions of adolescent girls and boys. See Daniels, E.A. (2009) 'Sex objects, athletes, and sexy athletes', *Journal of Adolescent Research*, 24(4), pp. 399–422. And, Daniels, E.A. and Wartena, H. (2011) 'Athlete or sex symbol: what boys think of media representations of female athletes', *Sex Roles: A Journal of Research*, 65(7–8), pp. 566–579.
5 Nicola Adams is also an out lesbian. Tropes about lesbian athletes and Black lesbians abound, however Adams' sexual orientation was not widely discussed until after her gold medal performance in the 2012 Games, so it is unclear if her sexual orientation would have influenced the nature or content of media coverage leading up to and including the 2012 Games.
6 The number of pages per volume across years varied quite dramatically, with some volumes from earlier years having as few as 16 pages, while others covering the Olympics comprise over 100 pages. The modal length of the volumes is 44 pages. Digital editions were accessed from the AIBA/IBA website archive and retrieved in 2018 and 2019. In 2021, the IBA reconfigured the website with a new URL,

www.iba.sport/. The old website is now password protected. Most digitized editions can be found on the YouTube channel of IBA boxing coach Jonathon Bochner. The internet archive search engine the Wayback Machine was utilized to search for some volumes missing from the IBA site. I was unable to locate 2011, volume 8, on any platform.
7 Quantity of coverage of men and women is measured as the absolute numbers of stories and images of female boxers, coaches, and officials per volume, rather than as a numerical ratio. Some scholarship reports ratios as a measure of gender disparities in coverage, however, prior to 2014, coverage by the IBA was so skewed towards male boxers that reporting ratios would be of dubious interpretive value.
8 See Leonard, D.J. (2017) '(White) women and sports: selling white femininity', in Leonard, D.J. (ed.) *Playing while white: privilege and power on and off the field*. Seattle: University of Washington Press, pp. 159–179.
9 For scholarship on global diffusion of norms, see Htun and Weldon, 2010.
10 For an extensive survey of women's participation globally, see Channon, A. and Matthews, C.R. (eds.) (2015) *Global perspectives on women in combat sports*. London: Palgrave Macmillan.
11 Scholarly attention to women's participation in mixed martial arts has grown, however. See McClearen, J. (2021) *Fighting visibility: sports media and female athletes in the UFC*. Champaign, IL: University of Illinois Press.
12 See, www.boxingnewsonline.net/olympic-weight-classes-confirmed/.

Bibliography

Biscomb, K. and Matheson, H. (2019) 'Are the times changing enough? Print media trends across four decades', *International Review for the Sociology of Sport*, 54(3), pp. 259–281.

Boddy, K. (2008) *Boxing: a cultural history*. London: Reaktion Books.

Boxing News (2007) https://issuu.com/aiba_boxing/docs/aiba_no20_mag_2017__10__preview

Boxing News (2008) https://issuu.com/aiba_boxing/docs/aiba_no20_mag_2017__10__preview

Boxing News (2010) https://issuu.com/aiba_boxing/docs/aiba_no20_mag_2017__10__preview

Boxing News (2012) https://issuu.com/aiba_boxing/docs/aiba_no20_mag_2017__10__preview

Boxing! (2013) https://issuu.com/jonathanbochner/docs/aiba_boxing_news_magazine_review07

Boxing! (2016) https://issuu.com/jonathanbochner/docs/aiba_boxing_news_magazine_review07

Buysse, J.A. and Embser-Herbert, S.M. (2004) 'Constructions of gender in sport: an analysis of intercollegiate media guide cover photographs', *Gender & Society*, 18(1), pp. 66–81.

Collins, P.H. (1991) *Black feminist thought*. New York: Routledge.

Connell, R.W. (1987) *Gender and power*. Redwood City, CA: Stanford University Press.

Cooky, C., Council, D.L. and Messner, M.A. (2021) 'One and done: the long eclipse of women's televised sports, 1989–2019', *Communication & Sport*, 9(3), pp. 347–371.

Cooky, C., Mears, M. and Messner, M.A. (2015) ' "It's dude time!": a quarter century of excluding women's sports in televised news and highlight shows', *Communication & Sport*, 3(3), pp. 261–287.

Cooky, C., Messner, M.A. and Hextrum, H.R. (2013) 'Women play sport, but not on TV: a longitudinal study of televised news media', *Communication & Sport*, 1(3), pp. 203–230.

Courtney, M., Breen, M. and McGing, C. (2020) 'Underrepresenting reality? Media coverage of women in politics and sport', *Social Science Quarterly*, 101(4), pp. 1282–1302.

Creedon, J.P. (1994) *Women, media and sport: challenging gender values*. Thousand Oaks: SAGE Publications.

Crews, S. and Lennox, P.S. (2020) *Boxing and performance: memetic hauntings*. New York, NY: Routledge.

Daniels, A.E. (2009) 'Sex objects, athletes, and sexy athletes', *Journal of Adolescent Research*, 24(4), pp. 399–422.

Daniels, A.E. and Wartena, H. (2011) 'Athlete or sex symbol: what boys think of media representations of female athletes', *Sex Roles: A Journal of Research*, 65(7–8), pp. 566–579.

Douglas, D.D. (2005) 'Venus, Serena, and the Women's Tennis Association (WTS): when and where "race" enters', *Sociology of Sport Journal*, 22(3), pp. 255–281.

Dunning, E. (1999) *Sport matters: sociological studies of sport, violence, and civilization*. London, UK: Routledge.

Godoy-Pressland, A. (2014) 'Nothing to report: a semi-longitudinal investigation of the print media coverage of sportswomen in British Sunday newspapers', *Media, Culture & Society*, 36(5), pp. 595–609.

Godoy-Pressland, A. (2015) 'Moral guardians, miniskirts and Nicola Adams: the changing media discourse on women's boxing', in Channon, A. and Matthews, R.C. (eds.) *Global perspectives on women in combat sports*. London: Palgrave Macmillan, pp. 25–40.

Godoy-Pressland, A. and Griggs, G. (2014) 'The photographic representation of female athletes in the British print media during the London 2012 Olympic Games', *Sport in Society*, 17(6), pp. 808–823.

Goffman, E. (1979) *Gender advertisements*. London: Macmillan.

Hanke, R. (1998) 'Theorizing masculinity with/in the media', *Communication Studies*, 8(2), pp. 183–203.

Hargreaves, J. (1997) 'Women's boxing and related activities: introducing images and meanings', *Body and Society*, 3(4), pp. 33–49.

Htun, W.M. and Weldon, S.L. (2010) 'When do governments promote women's rights? A framework for the comparative analysis of sex equality policy', *Perspectives on Politics*, 8(1), pp. 207–216.

Kane, M.J. (2013) 'The better sportswomen get, the more media ignore them', *Communication & Sport*, 1(3), pp. 231–236.

Leonard, D.J. (2017) *Playing while white: privilege and power on and off the field*. Seattle: University of Washington Press.

MacKay, S. and Dallaire, C. (2009) 'Campus newspaper coverage of varsity sports: getting closer to equitable and sports-related representations of female athletes?', *International Review for the Sociology of Sport*, 44(1), pp. 25–40.

Matthews, R.C. (2016) 'The Tyranny of the male preserve', *Gender & Society*, 30(2), pp. 312–333.

McClearen, J. (2021) *Fighting visibility: sports media and female athletes in the UFC*. Champaign, IL: University of Illinois Press.

Schneider, P. (2021) 'Sparring with patriarchy: the rise of female boxers in the Global South', *Journal of Gender Studies*, 30(8), pp. 887–900.

Sherry, E., Osborne, A. and Nicholson, M. (2016) 'Images of sports women: a review', *Sex Roles*, 74, pp. 299–309.

Shifflett, B., Murphy, D., Ghiasvand, F., Carlton, M. and Cuevas, M. (2016) 'Gender bias in sports-media analytics', *Journal of Sports Media*, 11(2), pp. 111–128.

Woodward, K. (2004) 'Rumbles in the jungle: boxing, racialization and the performance of masculinity', *Leisure Studies*, 23(1), pp. 5–17.

Woodward, K. (2014) *Globalizing boxing*. London, UK: Bloomsbury Academy.

Chapter 2

Influencer Boxing
Authenticity and the Quest for Redemption

P. Solomon Lennox

The story of boxing ... from the early nineteenth century onwards has been one of gradual transformation into mass-market entertainment.
(Boddy, 2008, p. 140)

The masses are asses.... There are no connoisseurs. The way most of these guys fight, you'd think they were two fellows having a fight in a barroom.
(Al Thoma in Liebling, 2004, p. 166)

What does a 'real' boxer mean? I mean anyone can go down the street and get a professional boxing licence, you know?
(Jake Paul, 2023, BT Sport Boxing, 13:45–13:50)

Boxing has a pervasive hold on contemporary popular culture. It is prevalent because of the stories it tells and the cultural capital ascribed to them. At its most rudimentary, boxing is about binaries – good versus bad – and the appetite for these types of stories told by and through the sport remains 'undiminished' (Boddy, 2008, p. 391). The stories told about the sport form the shared narratives resources of boxing. These resources, when performed, have the potential to bind the storyteller's individual self to a group identity. In this case, binding the individual to the sport of boxing and, potentially, to the identity of a boxer. Typically, narrative resources are combined with 'the habitual, rehearsed and repetitive patterns of identity work people do' to construct their personal embodied narrative biography (Smith and Sparkes, 2008, p. 17). Therefore, to perform a legitimate and credible social identity of a boxer, the expectation is that an individual would have access to and recruit from the shared narrative resources of boxing whilst being engaged in the habitual and repetitive patterns of boxing, such as training and/or competing. To be part of the social group of boxing is potentially advantageous to certain members of society on account of what being part of that group legitimises. Access to a boxing identity has the potential to bestow publicly recognised sociocultural rewards on an individual, enabling the performance

DOI: 10.4324/9781003312635-4

of a specific type of masculine heroism, and the promise of redemption and salvation from whatever evils plague their lives. However, because boxing is not a neat, homogenous, or contained activity, and because the public narratives of the sport permeate popular culture (from pop music, literature, fine art, sculpture, cinema, politics, and the worlds of business and enterprise), there is significant bleed between who has access to boxing's narrative resources and the type of habitual and repetitive physical practices that might be expected of someone seeking to embody the identity of a boxer. This poses an existential threat for a sport that struggles to assert its own legitimacy. For example, the professional arm of the sport has four major sanctioning bodies. Based on how champions are awarded by these bodies, it is possible at any one time for six different men to lay claim to being the legitimate heavyweight world champion.[1] The codification, commercialisation, and mass appeal of the sport exacerbates these threats. At the time of writing, these threats are best experienced through the creation of influencer boxing. If boxing's long-term viability resides in its continued mass-appeal it will need to continue to engage in practices to define what it is to be a boxer and to legitimise *who* might be considered a boxer. However, this is something boxing purists and traditional boxing will not have sole purview over. The evolution of the sport will materialise based on who has access to and performs the shared narrative resources of boxing and the embodied physical practices of the sport. This evolution will be managed through a multitude of legitimising practices orchestrated from within the sport and beyond. Over time, what it means to be a boxer and who identifies as a boxer is liable to change. This chapter examines the shared narrative resources of boxing as they play out through influencer boxing. It identifies the legitimising practices at play as they pertain to influencer boxing. The chapter draws upon the *celebrity capital lifecycle framework* proposed by François Carrillat and Jasmina Ilicic to examine the active role traditional boxing is playing in its own evolution (Carrillat and Ilicic, 2019). It argues that this analysis leads to new understandings of the relationship between shared narrative resources and repeated physical practices as they pertain to identity formation in boxing. It demonstrates that the threshold for assuming a specific identity and being accepted within a particular social group may be lower than previously expected. This is important for the sport of boxing as it navigates and understands its identity crisis. It could also lead to new insights into the field of narrative identity more broadly.

When two British social media stars, KSI and Joe Weller, fought in an amateur bout in 2018, they instigated a phenomenon known as influencer boxing. In the last five years, influencer boxing has grown in popularity and visibility, with all signs suggesting the phenomenon is here to stay.[2] An influencer boxer is typically a micro-celebrity who elects to 'crossover' and compete in boxing bouts. These individuals are likely to have large online followings and make their living from social media, reality television shows, and/or sex work. Due to its relative infancy, influencer boxers are likely to be debutant or novice fighters with limited exposure to boxing training. As such, the activity shares similarities with white collar boxing and celebrity boxing. White collar boxing is an amateur entity, marketed to white collar professionals with no prior boxing experience who, after an eight-week training period, compete in a boxing bout to raise money for charity. Celebrity boxing operates under many guises, but typically sees traditional celebrities from the world of politics, television, film, music, or sport compete against other traditional celebrities to settle a grudge and/or for charity. Whilst there is significant belled between the three different endeavours, I argue that influencer boxing must be considered in its own right, as distinct from these other practices.

Influencer boxing is a business venture not linked to charity endeavours. Its main participants are high-net-worth social media influencers (SMIs) rather than traditional media personalities, celebrities, or athletes. Influencer boxing bouts are legitimate boxing contests, insofar as they adhere to the rules of boxing and the respective amateur or professional codes of practice. However, the events are not always sanctioned by the sport's governing bodies and the competitors are often read as faux boxing/boxers, on account of the quality of the bouts. As a sporting activity, influencer boxing occupies a quasi-liminal identity, understood as both the future of boxing and the beginning of the sport's demise. Influencer boxing is not a homogenous or monolithic entity. It is known by many names, including YouTuber boxing and crossover boxing. Throughout this chapter, I deliberately use the term influencer boxer in lieu of the others as it is a more expansive term capturing the range of activity that falls within this genre. Another way to think of it is that influencer boxing describes the sport/genre as a whole, whereas the other terms describe sections within it, much like one would recruit the term mixed martial arts to describe the activity, and the Ultimate Fighting Championship (UFC) to describe a component/brand of that genre of fighting.

Influencer boxing comprises a range of promotional outlets and vested parties producing standalone amateur and professional fight cards, or influencer bouts on the undercard, or as the co-main feature, of mainstream professional boxing cards. Of the many outlets and players within this world, two families sit atop the influencer boxing mountain. Olajide Olayinka Williams Olatunji (aka KSI) runs the Misfits Boxing promotional company and fights, alongside his brother Deji Olatunji on the DAZN platform in association with Wasserman Boxing. The brothers Jake and Logan Paul both compete as influencer boxers. Jake Paul runs Most Valuable Promotions, a company that represents traditional and influencer boxers, and whose fights are broadcast by major sports platforms, such as DAZN and Showtime. Across their various social media platforms (Twitter, YouTube, and Instagram), KSI and Jake Paul have 37.5M and 44.8M followers, respectively. The prominence of KSI and Paul in the online sphere and within the sport of boxing epitomises them as influencers in the truest sense of the word. At the time of writing, KSI had competed in and won four boxing competitions, but is only listed as having one official boxing bout (against Jake Paul's brother, Logan) via the official record keeping website of amateur and professional boxing, BoxRec. Jake Paul is listed as having competed in seven official bouts, winning six. Through their engagement with influencer boxing, KSI and Logan Paul have begun to claim legitimacy and be read as legitimate boxers (albeit to different degrees). Through the work of their promotional companies, which are clearly aligned with traditional boxers and/or traditional boxing outfits (promoters and broadcasters), and their activities within the ring, they clearly blur the boundaries between traditional and influencer boxing, and they enact legitimising practices that are redefining the sport(s).

Influencer Boxing: A Serious Circus

Traditional boxing is understood as a dangerous activity and serious work. The health risks associated with boxing are well known and the perceived and actual dangers associated with boxing, such as levels of attendant pain, injury, and death, are part of the reason the sport remains controversial (Perkins et al., 2014). Long before Dr Harrison Martland's 1928 landmark paper on pathologised brain damage in deceased boxers, those involved in the sport knew the tell-tale signs of a punch-drunk boxer Changa, Vietrogoski and Carmel, 2018). The phenomenon was so readily recognised by those connected to prize fighting that it represented 'a whole vernacular economy that shaped the culture of boxing' (Casper and O'Donnell, 2020, p. 4). Understandings of the syndrome extended beyond boxing communities and appeared in pop culture references, from Ernest Hemmingway's 1926 short essay, 'The Battler', and Rod Skelton's creation of a former 'punchy' boxer, Cauliflower McPugg in the 1940s and 1950s (Carter, 2012, p. 175), to Andy Capp cartoons in the 1960s (Wallace, 2018). How boxing functions, its value, and its impact are understood through a complex network of narrative resources that extend far beyond the confines of the gym. They bleed out of these spaces, as porous as the bodies that share them, into pop culture and public discourse. They form the cultural narratives through which boxing is understood, allowing writers such as Joyce Carol Oates to proclaim, with a degree of certainty, what boxing *is* and *is not*. For Oates, boxing is antithetical to play, 'one doesn't *play* boxing' because it is an activity consumed with an 'elemental ferocity', one that inspires 'savagery', 'the murderous infancy of the [human] race', and an event within which a boxer may lawfully kill their opponent (Oates, 1987, pp. 18–19).

In a critique of a KSI influencer boxing bout in August 2022, pundit Steve Bunce stated that the event was a 'carnival attraction', operating 'on the fringes of legal boxing' and was 'not sport' (Bunce, 2022). The event included a full card of influencer boxers, fighting at the sold-out O2 arena in London. Promoted by Wasserman Boxing, a bona fide boxing promotions company, it featured as a pay-per-view event on DAZN, a global sports entertainment platform with a heavy focus on elite professional boxing. For all intents and purposes, the event *was* authentic boxing. But for Bunce, too many aspects of the card undermined the event's legitimacy as a genuine boxing competition. For example, the headliner, KSI, fought two opponents in one night, lending itself to the type of boxing seen at British fairground attractions between the 1600s–1970s,[3] rather than contemporary professional boxing events. It is this that leads Bunce to write the event off as a carnival and fringe activity. Importantly for Bunce, there was a lack of seriousness about the KSI event, resulting in the contest being dangerous, stupid, and beyond acceptable standards.

> At the sold out O2 YouTube event, last Saturday, featuring KSI in two – we'll – comedy fights, one of his truly hapless and hopeless opponents had to lose ten kilos in two weeks. And was taught to fight so that he could – wait for it – get in the ring at a sold out O2, to fight KSI. He was banged out. He was clueless. That's not sport. We wouldn't allow that in an amateur gym. This is dangerous entertainment. But not dangerous because it is competitive, it's dangerous because it is – we'll – stupid. . . . Next week [the podcast] is all about real boxing, real champions.
>
> (Bunce, 2022)

For Bunce, the dangers of influencer boxing are real – people can get hurt – but the activity itself is not *real boxing*; it is a form of dangerous and grotesque play. For the purists, as a form of play, it cannot be considered a legitimate form of boxing because of the public narratives presented by Oates and others about what boxing *is*. As a form of play, the type of influencer boxing promoted by KSI is not taken seriously. These claims were exacerbated by Misfits Boxing when, on March 4, 2023, they staged the first boxing tag team match, a two-versus-two bout akin to the types of antics witnessed in professional wrestling. For KSI and his promotional outlet, influencer boxing is a mix of serious competition with sports entertainment.[4] The position put forth by KSI is not at odds with academic and popular readings of traditional boxing.

Since its inception as a legal activity, boxing moved out of the shadows and into the theatres and music halls to appeal to mass audiences and an emerging middle class (Horall, 2001). Boxing, for John Sugden, 'was one of the earliest developments of a sports entertainment industry' (Sugden, 1996, p. 188), and for Kath Woodward, boxing 'is increasingly entertainment' (Woodward, 2004, p. 14). Why then should the type of sports entertainment promoted by KSI be read as antithetical to boxing proper? In an article first published in December 1954, sportswriter A. J. Liebling muses on the demise of boxing on account of the introduction of televised boxing bouts, 'television threatens all boxers who are not already headliners' (Liebling, 2004, p. 165). For Liebling, the advent of televised bouts damaged the supply chain of boxing, the small clubs and boxing shows which served as a steady stream of income for young boxers, enabling them to ply their skills and learn their trade through weekly competitions. Televised bouts delivered a death blow to the small clubs, resulting in fewer boxing stars emerging. As a former boxer, Al Thoma states in the Liebling article that the outcome is a commodified form of low-quality entertainment served to an undiscerning mass audience who no longer cares for or recognises quality fighters and quality boxing bouts. Al Thoma's critique of televised boxing bouts shares similarities to Bunce's critique of the KSI promotion that the focus on producing an end product with mass appeal damages the sport by promoting individuals with star appeal but without any credible boxing background. It reframes the investment in the star and the product, rather than grassroots talent.

One of the sticking points in the distinction between the influencer boxing bouts promoted by KSI and traditional boxing is where the line is drawn between serious work and entertainment. For 'Roy', a boxer interviewed as part of Loïc Wacquant's seminal work, the distinction is simple. Boxing is a job. The ring performance is entertainment and the training is where the serious labour takes place (Wacquant, 1995b, p. 502). Through his studies of the sport, Loïc Wacquant demonstrated that boxing is understood as a form of physical work (Wacquant, 1995a). To be able to assume the identity of a boxer, one must commit to a 'ritual of mortification' (Wacquant, 2005, p. 145) and the 'daily work' of 'occupational exertion' (Wacquant, 1995a, p. 66). It is through the daily, routine work that boxers do with and upon their bodies that pugilistic excellence is acquired. These daily routines 'produce and reproduce the belief underlying [the] symbolic and material economy that constitutes the pugilistic world' (Wacquant, 1992, p. 222). Daily practice in the boxing gym constitutes an 'interminable journey of exploration' of the 'pugilist's craft' and the transformation of 'one's body into an impeccably tuned fighting machine' (Wacquant, 1995b, p. 511). Inherent in Wacquant's reading of the sport is an understanding that the acquisition of a boxing identity takes time, and it is an identity 'forged' within the 'prosaic obscurity of the training gym' (Wacquant, 2004, p. 237). The latter point is echoed by John Sugden, who acknowledges that whilst publicly the identity of the boxer is understood through their performance in the ring, that performance is 'built upon weeks of hard road work, gym training, fasting and related abstinences' (Sugden, 1996, p. 51). Similarly, for Kath Woodward, it is through the routine practice of boxing training that embodied selves are re-created, 'Boxers *are* their bodies and only become boxers through practice and physical engagement' (Woodward, 2008, p. 544). For Loïc Wacquant, the mundane conversations in the gym form the *hidden curriculum* that 'orally impregnate the boxers with the core values and categories of judgement of the pugilistic universe' (Wacquant, 1992, p. 321). But because these conversations do not remain the sole purview of boxers, nor do they remain confined to the boxing gym itself, they become part of the narrative fabric of boxing through which boxers and non-boxers are able to define and understand the sport. If one might expect a certain level of alignment between the physical and narrative practices of identity work – that is, that one would only have access to and be legitimately able to recruit shared narrative resources through engagement with complimentary physical practices – then influencer boxing functions as a potentially troubling anomaly. It enables certain individuals – those who have already amassed a high level of social and fiscal capital – to potentially fast-track the process of identifying as a boxer and thus accessing the social rewards associated with this identity.

In the example cited by Steve Bunce, where an influencer boxer had just two weeks to make the required fighting weight, there is a stark absence of the type of corporeal investment expected of a body performing the identity of a boxer. By combining Woodward's, Sugden's, and Wacquant's reading of the work required to assume a boxing identity, it is possible to argue that the body of the influencer boxer referenced by Steve Bunce has not invested the requisite time and energy into becoming a boxer. Their claims to a boxing identity are illegitimate; they are not *real* boxers. If this view is extended to the wider phenomenon of influencer boxing, where novice and debutant combatants lay claim to the identity of a boxer, it is understandable why the legitimacy of these claims is questioned. Whilst influencer boxers might not have made the necessary investment in the daily routine of training to be read as on an *interminable journey* towards becoming a boxer, they are happy to assume and perform the identity through engagement with some of the requisite physical practices and through the adoption of the shared narrative resources of boxing. What influencer boxing exposes is a low threshold of the amount of investment required to benefit from the social capital assigned to these practices and resources, and, therefore, the identity of a boxer.

Boxing Identities and the Celebrity Capital Life Cycle

A boxing identity is seductively captivating because of the narrative resources that define the sport. Through the fashioning of a successful boxing body, the sport offers 'disadvantaged, disenfranchised, and marginalised *men* the promise of agency and increased socio-economic capital and standing' (Crews and Lennox, 2020, p. 25). A boxing body enables the performance of a 'publicly recognised heroic and legitimate body' offering 'salvation from obscurity and an illegitimate past' (Ibid). In short, to be a boxer is to be *somebody*. To be a boxer is to matter. On face value, the cultural narratives of the sport seem at odds with the individual identities of influencer boxers. Influencer boxers already enjoy a form of internet stardom and celebrity capital on account of their position as social media influencers (SMIs). However, if influencer boxing is read through the celebrity capital life cycle framework (CCLCF) proposed by François Carrillat and Jasmina Ilicic, it becomes clear why the sport of boxing offers such a seductive draw to SMIs. Carrillat and Illicic outline the CCLCF as consisting of four stages: acquisition, consolidation, abrupt downfall/slow decline, and redemption/resurgence. The framework accounts for the fluctuations in the celebrity capital of an individual over their career. Based on Bourdieu's (1986) field theory, celebrity capital is defined as the acquired media visibility and recognisability of an individual. Celebrity capital can be converted into economic, political, and social capital for celebrities, and celebrity capital 'relaxes the assumption that celebrities belong to rigid categories (e.g., actors, athletes, business)'. SMIs may therefore find influencer boxing lucrative and appealing for the way in which it enables them to navigate the celebrity capital life cycle and build celebrity capital outside of the online space where it was first developed (Carrillat and Ilicic, 2019, p. 63).

Carrillat and Ilicic note that, 'Celebrities require recurrent media visibility to generate or maintain their celebrity capital, suggesting that renewal and repetition of media visibility is important to avoid fade and decline' (Carrillat and Ilicic, 2019, p. 63). Because, as Gillian Brooks et al., observe, SMIs are 'famous online for becoming famous online'(Brooks, Drenten and Piskorski, 2021, p. 58), in order to maintain celebrity capital they must remain relevant in a competitive online space, establishing ways to diversify their audience and income base by attracting 'widespread attention [and] converting well-knownness into a type of sociocultural currency' (Brooks, Drenten and Piskorski, 2021, p. 529). Under this framework, boxing offers lesser known SMIs (that is, those not known outside of the online spaces where they developed micro-celebrity status) the opportunity to acquire celebrity capital in a new sphere and in front of new audiences. Because influencer boxing is such a hot and contested topic, it generates significant amounts of attention, which is needed by influencers to cultivate celebrity capital (Carrillat and Ilicic, 2019, p. 64). To this end, the motivations for SMIs and non-SMIs to enter the boxing space share a certain alignment, both potentially engaging with boxing to matter. Whilst the definition of mattering may differ between the two groups, they share a motivational drive to turn physical effort into sociocultural and publicly recognisable capital. In the same way traditional boxing offers its participants the chance to transition from a nobody to a somebody, influencer boxing offers SMIs the chance to transition from a celetoid to a fully fledged celebrity.[5] SMIs recruit the physical and narrative practices of boxing as part of a celebrification process.[6] For Brooks et al., '[a]ccess, constructions of authenticity, and a consumable persona are characteristics of celebrification in the digital age' (Brooks, Drenten and Piskorski, 2021, p. 530). Boxing, as a form of sports entertainment focused on issues of credibility and authenticity, lends itself ideally to the process of celebrification. The narrative resources of boxing become fundamentally important to the crafting of an authentic and consumable persona and the acquisition of celebrity capital.

The consolidation stage of the CCLCF refers to celebrities at the height of their fame who leverage their symbolic and reputational capital to maintain recognisability and media visibility, with a view to turning celebrity capital into financial rewards. In their study of celebrification, Brooks et al. offer a conceptual model for the process. This mode consists of three practices: generative practices (where SMIs develop celebrity capital through their original endeavours online), collaborative practices (where activity across platforms and with other individuals and partners enhances their celebrity capital through enriching their relationships with their fans), and evaluative practices (where the celebrity capital of an SMI is legitimised through the valuation of worth they bring to the new markets they enter). In the work of Brooks et al., and Carrillat and Ilicic, focus is placed on how celebrity capital is leveraged to gain brand endorsements. However, within the realm of influencer boxing, the boundaries between who or what is the brand are blurred. Due to the reciprocal nature of the relationship, it is possible to argue that the SMIs, influencer boxing, and traditional boxing are all brands within their own right, and are all using one another to different degrees in forms of collaborative and evaluative practices to reach new audiences and establish legitimacy. If the CCLCF is extended beyond individuals to brands, it is possible to argue that the three aforementioned brands are actively engaged in the process of consolidation of status, visibility, and relevance through a desire to capitalise on the audience portability of SMIs. Influencer boxing draws upon traditional boxing to perform legitimating practices. Self-elected bodies, such as the Influencer Championship Boxing Championship (ICB Championship) and the Influencer Fight League (IFL), function as sanctioning bodies and award titles and belts to their competitors. These practices mirror those of the sanctioning bodies of traditional boxing and serve to authenticate not just specific SMIs, but the endeavour of influencer boxing generally. Similarly, traditional boxing sanctioning bodies, such as the World Boxing Council (WBC), have actively sought to endorse influencer boxing and benefit from the affiliation with the athletes and their practices. The WBC has awarded influencer boxers with two belts. The first was awarded to Jake Paul in recognition of his debut amateur fight against Deji. The second, the 'Diriyah Champion' belt, was awarded to Tommy Fury when he beat Jake Paul in February 2023 and was accompanied by an official WBC cruiserweight ranking for Fury. In 2022, the World Boxing Association (WBA) presented Paul with a championship belt in recognition of how he has changed the boxing business model. Influencer boxing and SMIs are further legitimised through the broadcasting relationship Paul has struck with Showtime and Top Rank, and KSI has developed with DAZN. In their totality, these practices demonstrate the need all parties have (SMIs, influencer boxing, and traditional boxing) to consolidate status and perform legitimising acts by authenticating the endeavours and the individuals.

Carrillat and Ilicic define the abrupt downfall or slow decline stage of the CCLCF as a period of decreased media visibility, acknowledging that very little research examines this stage of the cycle. They suggest that further research is required to investigate strategies to mitigate scandals and to identify when decline has begun. The relationship between SMIs, influencer boxing, and traditional boxing, specifically in regard to the Paul brothers, provides new insights into the role boxing performs for SMIs during this stage of the cycle and the extent to which the narratives and practices of boxing help mitigate scandal. In December 2021, Jake Paul sat with journalist Graham Bensinger for his show *In Depth with Graham Bensinger*. In the interview, Paul detailed how he turned away from producing content for YouTube (although not entirely) on account of several lawsuits he faced, which he argues all stemmed from reactions to content he had made for the platform. Boxing, for Paul, came at a time in his life when his celebrity capital was experiencing disruption. He faced scandal and a potential decline in his ability to generate economic capital from his digital content. Reflecting on his bout with former MMA fighter Ben Askren, Bensinger observed how six days before the fight, Paul was accused of sexual assault by TikTok star Justine Paradise. Paradise would be one of two women who accused Paul of sexual assault that year. Paradise alleged the attack took place at Paul's mansion and base for his social media label *Team 10*, a collective of SMIs funded by and working with, for, and under the direction of Paul. Other members of the Team 10 collective have made allegations that Paul bullied, harassed, and exploited them. The interview between Bensinger and Paul took place inside a boxing gym, with the two sitting under a spotlight and, behind them, boxing bags and speed bags hanging in silhouette.

Paul: When you see a star fall or start to be accused of something, all the haters come out of the woodwork.
Bensinger: And that's a tough one to come back from – I mean the headlines are plastered everywhere –
Paul: Yeah. It is a smear on my name for the rest of my life. . . . And before you know it, people from the event – 'oh, this sponsor is pulling out. This sponsor is pulling out. You know we might have to cancel the fight. Blaaa, blaa, blaa.' And I was just like, wow! I just worked – you know I made it out of this situation with my brother in Japan, where everything – lost all my money, dropped – all my sponsors dropped me – made it out of that, squeaky clean. Two years running. Just for one day to wake up and it felt like the cycle was repeating itself.

(Bensinger, 2021, 04:20 to 05:44)

The Bensinger video recruits the iconography of boxing for obvious reasons; the content is primarily about Paul as a boxer and was aired three days before his fifth professional contest. To that end, the staging of the video is in keeping with many pre-fight interviews conducted with professional boxers. But for Paul, the iconography of boxing performs an additional function. It subtly and subconsciously draws attention to the popular readings of boxing, born out of the narrative resources of the sport. Namely, that boxing is restorative and an antidote to juvenile delinquency, offering its participants a path to restoration. For Jake 'The Problem Child' Paul, it is understandable why these narrative promises and the aesthetics of boxing are appealing. For an individual on the brink of losing everything due to scandal, boxing offers a recognisable heroic identity for Paul to adopt to appease and calm his sponsors. Boxing, understood as a disciplined and disciplining activity, enables Paul to embody an identity under reform. The narrative resources of boxing enable Paul to rebuild his reputation, thus regaining control of celebrity capital and potential for future economic growth and gains.

The ability to rebuild from scandal, decline, or downfall is the ability to experience redemption or resurgence. According to Carrillat and Ilicic, the redemption/resurgence stage of the CCLCF is an under-researched area, requiring further work to understand comeback strategies for celebrities. Influencer boxing provides this opportunity, demonstrating how closely aligned the CCLCF is with the narrative resources of the sport. As outlined in Crews and Lennox, a major motivational drive for boxers is access to a redeemed or salvaged identity (Crews and Lennox, 2020). Indeed, narratives of redemption and salvation form the bedrock of the narrative resources of the sport. Paul's pursuit for redemption through boxing is evidenced through his interview with Graham Bensinger and remained present in his seventh professional contest in 2023. In the post-fight press conference following his loss to Tommy Fury, a reporter asked Jake about his motivations for starting boxing. Paul responded:

> Yeah, look. Boxing found me in a moment in my life where I needed discipline. I was going down this crazy path in Los Angeles, that you know, probably would have ended up with me dead or in jail. And seriously, boxing saved my life and I fell in love with the sport and that's why I have dedicated everything to it. I love this sport. I owe this sport a lot and that is why I will continue to make a massive impact inside and outside of the ring.
> (Top Rank Boxing, 2023, 38:19 to 38:52)

It is clear that Paul values the publicly recognised restorative properties of boxing and is comfortable recruiting the narrative resources of the sport to position his own story of redemption and salvation. For Paul, like many other boxers, it is the physical practices of the sport that provide him with the discipline to avoid a lifestyle that would result in early death or incarceration (Lennox, 2012). It might not be surprising to see the recruitment of this narrative resource at a stage in Paul's career where he has invested a degree of time (five years) into the sport, and had, following his bout with Tommy Fury, been legitimised as a *real* boxer by both his opponent and many boxing pundits. However, what is surprising is the recruitment of this narrative resource by Paul at the outset of his career.

Following his amateur debut and win over Deji in August 2018 – on the undercard of his brother's (Logan Paul) fight against Deji's brother (KSI) – during a post-fight interview, Paul explained the importance of his victory:

> I worked so hard for this. . . . This year, this year just in general, has been tough for me, man. Controversies, friendship fallouts, lawsuits, the list goes on. It hasn't been an easy year. And this fight for me was fighting against all those things. It wasn't just some boxing match. It was putting my heart on the line to show myself that I can conquer those things. That I can overcome adversity, no matter how hard situations are. I wanted to give up. And tonight, I'm a [sic] celebrate this win, but I'm also excited to announce that I'm launching a clothing line called RNBO. Rise and be original. That's my saying guys. You gotta rise every single day, fight like a champion and be original. Go to shop RNBO dot com right now. There's only five hundred shirts so go fast.
>
> (KSIvsLogan, 2018, 36:57 to 38:25)

Paul's post-fight interview performs two important roles. Cynically, Paul uses the narrative resources and physical practices of boxing to promote his personal brand, launching a new business venture in the immediate aftermath of his first amateur bout. He simultaneously engages with the redemption/resurgence and consolidation stages of the CCLCF. He chooses the platform of boxing and the visibility and recognisability afforded to him through his win to drive efforts to increase his celebrity capital. The example from Paul demonstrates how the stages of the CCLCF need not be understood as linear and progressive. Celebrities can engage in the stages simultaneously to optimise visibility and to embolden their own personal brand and their economic relationships with sponsors. The recruitment of the redemption and salvation narrative resources at such an early stage in Jake Paul's engagement with the sport (one fight in) offers an interesting and important challenge to scholarly assumptions about boxing. It demonstrates that whilst individual boxers might need to demonstrate their willingness to undertake an interminable journey of dedicated training and time spent in boxing gyms to be considered *real* boxers, that journey does not need to be sufficiently progressed to enable them to recruit and benefit from the sport's narrative resources. The threshold for access to the sport's narrative resources is low, making those narratives and their identity rewards available to entry-level participants. Further research would benefit from considering the extent to which non-participants can access and benefit from these narrative resources. If the relationship between the sport's narrative resources and physical practices is more fluid and casual than previously conceived, it opens up the potential to consider the transportability or transferability of narrative resources and the performance of identity work in the sport and in other areas of narrative inquiry.

Conclusion

Influencer boxing proves problematic for boxing purists on account of the threat it poses to the sport. In the closest thing to a description of purists, sportswriter, Katherine Dunn argues:

> [Boxing is] supposed to be a kind of Spartan Zen, fierce but silent except for the periodic bell and the smack of leather on flesh. The purists prefer that a boxer's identity be revealed and defined only by what happens inside the ring. But the curse of all the arts is that the most magnificent performance won't pay the rent if nobody's watching.
> (Dunn, 2009, p. 116)

For Dunn's purists, boxing is not flashy, it does not contain showmanship, and the life of the combatants outside of the ring matters not one jot. Boxing identities are forged and revealed between the ropes, in the ring. The activity is modest, noble, and a fierce and pure form of sporting competition. For these purists then, the distinctions between influencer boxing and traditional boxing should be clear. Whilst both provide a form of sports entertainment, traditional boxing is supported by a deep and rich network of grassroot talent crafted through years of investment in the habitual, repetitive, and rehearsed physical practices of the sport. Its combatants (Zen-like Spartans) are dedicated to the sport and take training and competition seriously, fully understanding the dangers posed by embodying the identity of a fighter. For purists, influencer boxing is a form of grotesque play supported by individuals who, through the privilege and fame acquired outside of boxing, are afforded the opportunity to perform the identity of a boxer and are rewarded handsomely for doing so. But because influencer boxing draws from a small talent pool of internet-famous micro-celebrities, it does not benefit the sport as a whole because it does not serve to develop grassroot talent and does not promise to offer credible sporting competitions. On this basis, it would be easy, as many have, to dismiss influencer boxing altogether. However, an outright dismissal does not stack up. Key players within traditional boxing, from broadcasters, journalists, pundits, and sanctioning bodies, have sought to legitimise SMIs' engagement with boxing and, in doing so, have helped legitimise influencer boxing. This legitimising process is self-serving to the business needs of the sport. For its long-term sustainability, the sport needs to attract new and younger audiences and has thus sought a business model capable of expansion into new markets. Only time will tell what the true impact of influencer boxing will be on traditional boxing. What is evident already is the impact influencer boxing has on understandings of narrative identity work as it pertains to the relationship between the recruitment of shared narrative resources and habitual, repeated, and rehearsed physical practices. The field of narrative inquiry does not quantify how much time and investment constitutes the 'extended process through which identities and selves are constructed and taken up as part of a person's personal or ontological narrative' (Smith and Sparkes, 2008, p. 19). Nevertheless, it might be surprising to see how quickly individuals assume and perform the identity of a boxer regardless of how far along they are on the *interminable journey* of becoming a boxer. Because access to certain social groups and personal identities bring forth access to certain shared narrative resources and, in the case of boxing, access to certain sociocultural rewards, further research is needed to better understand the relationship between narrative identity and physical practices. Because access to a greater pool of narrative resources gives individuals increased ways to live their lives, it is crucial to better understand the relationship between narrative identity formation and individual ontological journeys. It would be crucial for further research to focus on understanding how far along an individual journey a person can start benefiting from the identity rewards of new or different narrative resources.

Notes

1 This is based on a situation where a different individual would hold each of the following belts: WBA Heavyweight Super Champion, WBA Heavyweight World Champion, WBC Heavyweight Champion, IBF Heavyweight Champion, WBO Heavyweight Champion, and Ring Heavyweight Champion.
2 In January 2023, one of the leading sports streaming platforms, DAZN, joined forces with KSI's promotion company, Misfits Boxing, and announced a five-year deal to broadcast influencer boxing bouts. DAZN is a multi-sport platform, but it is best known for its commitment to broadcasting professional boxing and its partnership with leading boxing promotion companies, such as Matchroom and Wasserman Boxing.
3 See the National Fairground Archive. www.sheffield.ac.uk/nfca/collections/billywood.
4 See Mams Taylor in Ranson, J. (2023) 'Boxing purists ain't going to like this one': KSI's new boxing promotion Misfits announces the first-ever WWE style TAG-TEAM boxing match, with social media stars set to debut the idea next month', *Mail Online*, 2 February 2023.
5 A celetoid is someone who experiences a moment of fame but disappears from public consciousness quickly.
6 Brooks *et al.*, outline the concept of celebrification as derived from the work of Chris Rojek (2001) to argue that it is the production and reproduction of a celebrity identity.

Bibliography

Bensinger, G. (2021) *Jake Paul on sexual assault allegations: 'I think someone paid her'*, 15 December 2021. Available at: https://www.youtube.com/watch?v=j6G9d0EBpG8 (Accessed: 20 January 2022).
Boddy, K. (2008) *Boxing a cultural history*. London: Reakton Books.
Brooks, G., Drenten, J. and Piskorski, M.J. (2021) 'Influencer celebrification: how social media influencers acquire celebrity capital', *Journal of Advertising*, 50(5), pp. 528–547.

BT Sport Boxing. (2023) *'He's a flake. He's not a serious fighter!' Jake Paul blasts Tommy Fury for missing press conference*. 8 February 2023. Available at: https://www.youtube.com/watch?v=FMpaJQlO-f4&list=WL&index=1 (Accessed: 8 February 2023).

Bunce, S. (2022) *In conversation with Savannah Marshall 5 Live Boxing with Steve Bunce* [Podcast]. 29 August 2022. Available at: https://www.bbc.co.uk/programmes/p0cx2v2w (Accessed: 31 August 2022).

Carrillat, F. and Ilicic, J. (2019) 'The celebrity capital life cycle: a framework for future research directions on celebrity endorsement', *Journal of Advertising*, 48(1), pp. 61–71.

Carter, N. (2012) *Medicine, sport and the body: a historical perspective*. London: Bloomsbury Academic.

Casper, S.T. and O'Donnell, K. (2020) 'The punch-drunk boxer and the battered wife: gender and brain injury research', *Social Science & Medicine*, 245, 112688.

Changa, A.R., Vietrogoski, R.A. and Carmel, P.W. (2018) 'Grey Matter: Dr Harrison Martland and the history of punch drunk syndrome', *BRAIN: A Journal of Neurology*, 141(1), pp. 318–321.

Crews, S. and Lennox, S.P. (2020) *Boxing and performance: memetic hauntings*. Abingdon, Oxon: Routledge.

Dunn, K. (2009) *One ring circus: dispatches from the world of boxing*. Tucson, AZ: Schaffner Press.

Horall, A. (2001) *Popular culture in London c. 1890–1918: the transformation of entertainment*. Manchester: Manchester University Press.

KSIvsLogan. (2018) *Deji VS. Jake Paul – Full Fight #KSIvsLogan*. 31 August. Available at: https://www.youtube.com/watch?v=6R08SayU3bU&t=1952s (Accessed 8 February 2023).

Lennox, P.S. (2012) *Narratives of performance: an interdisciplinary qualitative ethnography investigating the storied lives of amateur and professional boxers*. PhD thesis. Exeter University. Available at: https://ore.exeter.ac.uk/repository/handle/10036/4060?show=full (Accessed: 20 January 2022).

Liebling, A.J. (2004) *The sweet science*. New York: North Point Press.

Oates, J.C. (1987) *On boxing*. New York: Harper Collins.

Perkins, P., Hahn, A., Lucas, R. and Keegan, R. (2014) 'The boxing conundrum: is there a place for a new variant of the sport?', *Journal of Research in Humanities and Social Sciences*, 2(9), pp. 9–25.

Smith, B. and Sparkes, A.C. (2008) 'Contrasting perspectives on narrating selves and identities: an invitation to dialogue', *Qualitative Research*, 8(1), pp. 5–35.

Sugden, J. (1996) *Boxing and society: an international analysis*. Manchester: Manchester University Press.

Top Rank Boxing. (2023) *Jake Paul vs Tommy Fury | POST-FIGHT PRESS CONFERENCE*. 26 February. Available at: https://www.youtube.com/watch?v=tkcqtdEO1xY&list=WL&index=1(Accessed: 1 March 2023).

Wallace, R. (2018) ' "She's Punch Drunk!!": humor, domestic violence, and the British Working Class in Andy Capp Cartoons, 1957–65', *The Journal of Popular Culture*, 51(1), pp. 129–151.

Wacquant, L.J.D. (1992) 'The social logic of boxing in Black Chicago: toward a sociology of pugilism', *Sociology of Sport Journal*, 9(3), pp. 221–254.

Wacquant, L.J.D. (1995a) 'Pugs at work: bodily capital and bodily labour among professional boxers', *Body & Society* 1(1), pp. 65–93.
Wacquant, L.J.D. (1995b) 'The pugilistic point of view: how boxers think and feel about their trade', *Theory and Society*, 24(4), pp. 489–535.
Wacquant, L.J.D. (2004) *Body & soul: notebooks of an apprentice Boxer*. New York: Oxford University Press.
Wacquant, L.J.D. (2005) 'Men at work', in Gattuso, J. (ed.) *Shadow boxers: sweat, sacrifice & the will to survive in American Boxing Gyms*. Milford, NJ: Stone Creek Publications, pp. 145–148.
Woodward, K. (2004) 'Rumbles in the jungle: boxing racialization and the performance of masculinity', *Leisure Studies*, 23(1), pp. 5–17.
Woodward, K. (2008) 'Hanging out and hanging about: insider/outsider research in the sport of boxing', *Ethnography*, 9(4), pp. 536–561.

Chapter 3

Ducking and Diving
Why Boxing Clubs Hit the Targets Other Sports Cannot Reach in Deprived Communities

David Barrett, Lee Edmondson, Robbie Millar, and P. Solomon Lennox

Boxing is regarded by many keen and casual observers to be more successful than most sports in terms of engaging participants from areas of multiple deprivation in challenging locations which have been 'abandoned' by clubs and governing bodies from other sports.[1] Data compiled by Sport England in 2017 reveal that 38% of all affiliated boxing clubs are located in the most deprived 20% of neighbourhoods in England. This contrasts with the pattern evident in the majority of sports, which favour more affluent parts of the country, and underlines the importance of boxing clubs to the delivery of opportunities for participation in physical activity in deprived areas. England Boxing categorise their affiliated clubs into three main groups:

- Clubs whose sole purpose is to train champion boxers who will win regional, national, and possibly international championships.
- Clubs who also want to train champions but will engage in some kind of community interventions in order to raise much needed money to help create the champions.
- Clubs whose main purpose is to use the sport of boxing to engage with people within the community that suffer from some sort of social exclusion, but they still engage in training competitive boxers.

This chapter focuses on clubs in the third category, specifically examining the skills, abilities, and experience of community boxing coaches. Through semi-structured interviews with 56 coaches from clubs across England, this chapter demonstrates the important role boxing clubs provide to hard-to-reach and marginalised people in areas of multiple deprivation. Whilst the findings support previous readings on the role and function of boxing clubs to local communities, this study offers new insights into the impact boxing clubs and boxing coaches have on individuals who do not identify as a boxer.

Barrett, Edmondson, and Miller worked with England boxing staff to co-design the semi-structured interviews. These interviews were utilised in focus groups at a two-day research event in November 2019. The event generated over 60 hours of recorded conversations that were transcribed verbatim. The transcriptions were then coded using Quirkos software which supported analysis of the content and allowed some quantification and statistical analysis. The coding enabled a systematic analysis of what was said, by whom, and to what extent. The coded content was examined using principles from Thematic Analysis, a common approach in health-related research that steps beyond academia into the policy or practice arenas (Braun and Clarke, 2014). Analysis of the transcripts identified four broad themes:

- Local Deprivation Rates and Participation
- Boxing Coaching and Leadership
- Culture and Ethos
- Funding and Impact

Local Deprivation Rates and Participation

Sport England's Club Count mapping exercise, conducted in the summer of 2017, used postcode data to locate affiliated clubs in over 80 sports. It permitted an analysis of distribution by deprivation, as clubs were mapped to ONS Super Output Area Level (LSOAs). As part of the exercise, clubs were assigned a value according to where they were located in relation to the 2015 Indices of Multiple Deprivation (Gill, 2015), which measure relative levels of development at a small area level using a range of economic and social indicators. LSOAs were grouped into quintiles (bands of 20%) according to their overall deprivation score, ranging from 1 (the most deprived) to 5 (the least deprived). In the majority of the most popular sports, there is a tendency for clubs to be located in less deprived areas. Overall, 48% of all clubs were located in the least deprived quintiles according the IMD 2015. This pattern holds true across the range of sports, although there are some notable variations. Tennis clubs are much more likely to be located in more affluent areas, with more than 64% in less deprived quintiles. Similarly, golf (61%), equestrian (56%), and cricket (54%) clubs tend to be located in areas which are less affected by multiple deprivation. There are few sports which run counter to this trend, though boxing is a notable exception, with almost 40% of affiliated clubs located in the most deprived parts of England. Indeed, a quarter of all boxing clubs are found in the most deprived 10% of neighbourhoods. Other sports with a location bias towards more deprived areas include swimming (46%) and, among the 'other' sports with fewer clubs overall, rugby league (29%), snooker (28%), basketball (25%), weightlifting (25%), and volleyball (22%). However, none of these sports has the same gravitational pull towards deprived neighbourhoods as boxing.

The results of Club Count prove that boxing clubs are more likely to be present in deprived areas when other sports are (increasingly) absent. Moreover, boxing clubs are more likely to be in deprived areas than any other sports. Boxing is one of the few sports maintaining a presence and, therefore, one of the few activities available. The unique advantage of the sport is being positioned in areas which are otherwise bereft of facilities, a trend which has accelerated in recent years as cuts to local government budgets have resulted in reduced investment in publicly owned sports halls, swimming pools, and outdoor pitches. The presence of boxing clubs in areas of multiple deprivation means they are better suited to serve marginalised communities and participants excluded from access to other sports.

The links between deprivation and participation in boxing are referenced in the academic literature on the sport, primarily through ethnographic studies of the sport in the UK and USA, as well as through qualitative studies in Norway, Ireland, and Australia. In describing the drive for American immigrants to participate in boxing in the middle of the nineteenth century, ethnographer John Sugden suggests there is a compensatory drive on the grounds of 'urban deprivation' and 'racial and ethnic discrimination' providing the 'motivational impulse to step into the ring' (Sugden, 1996, p. 23). Fighting as compensation for 'urban poverty, racial and ethnic discrimination and relative deprivation had been established as the common denominators of prize fighting and subsequently professional boxing' (p. 24). For Sugden, boxing serves as a vehicle to enable escape from urban deprivation, providing its participants with strategies of how to survive the ghetto (p. 56). However, for ethnographer Loïc Wacquant, the idea that boxing provides participants from highly deprived backgrounds a route out of the ghetto is one of the sport's great misconceptions (Wacquant, 1992, p. 222). The rather grandiose claims that boxing serves as a vehicle for escape form socioeconomic deprivation may not be the lived reality for most boxing clubs or participants. However, it is clear boxing and boxing clubs perform an essential role within communities of multiple deprivation.

An investigation by Perkins and Hahn (2019) of recruitment and retention rates in a boxing programme delivered by a Police Community Club in Canberra, Australia, demonstrated that the key to retention was the feeling of safety created by the club. In Northern Ireland, Ferguson, Hassan, and Kitchin (2018) adopted a case study approach to highlight how sport can be used to improve educational and employment outcomes for hard-to-reach young people. They focused on a boxing club in a severely deprived neighbourhood of Belfast which engaged young people from a Protestant background who had been excluded from education and employment opportunities. The research used mixed methods to assess whether the club achieved outcomes relating to the confidence/self-esteem of young participants, diversion from crime and anti-social behaviour, academic qualifications, and improved resources and capacity for young people locally. In a similar vein, Morton, O'Brien, and O'Reilly (2019) examined a boxing training and mentoring programme for participants with a history of drug use in an urban community in Dublin. Qualitative data collected by participants and practitioners involved in the programme showed that boxing gave the protagonists a robust and credible identity, which they associated with passion for the sport. Instead of being identified as 'drug addicts' by the local community, the participants became known as 'boxers'.

In this context, the boxing gym functions as an empowering environment within the local community that commands 'respect'. Each of these studies speak to Sugden's notion of the boxing gym operating as a temporary or permanent sanctuary from problems exacerbated by multiple deprivation (Sugden, 1996, p. 92). The notion of sanctuary is present in the study conducted by Jump and Smithson (2020), who found that a co-designed boxing workshop with 28 individuals with serious criminal convictions reduced reoffending rates. The participants of the Jump and Smithson study found boxing provided a space for defeat without the feelings of shame or stigmatisation associated with their experience of the criminal justice system. In each of the studies outlined here, boxing gyms have a positive impact on its members by offering stability, order, safety, and respect. In the boxing gyms in England, safety and respect are modelled and enforced through clarity of boundaries and standards of behaviour. For a coach from the Southern Counties, boxing is understood as 'a leveller', where all participants are given the opportunity to engage on 'the same playing field'. Certain levels of behaviour, such as bullying, are simply not tolerated.

The England boxing clubs included in this study spoke to the transformative potential of boxing on the individuals and communities they serve. For hard-to-reach individuals, the activity of boxing, and the social capital ascribed to the identity of a boxer, may make it easier for hard-to-reach individuals to engage, and/or for individuals engaged in criminal activity to desist from crime.

> Put it this way. If you wanted to join the Tennis Club, you wouldn't necessarily be allowed to walk away from a gang situation, but if you join a boxing club it is more likely to be respected and accepted.
> (Female Leader, London in Barrett, Edmondson and Miller, 2019)

Boxing clubs in England provide a place where individuals can enact lives and identities that are perhaps prohibited to them through other organisations, institutions, and systems of power.

Boxing clubs are well positioned to serve a participant market who might overwise have been abandoned. As a coach from the Southern Counties stated, there is clearly high demand for boxing in areas of high deprivation, 'In our community which is in the bottom 10% of deprivation, we have got 3 boxing clubs and no football at all' (Male Coach, Southern Counties in Barrett, Edmondson and Miller, 2019). Boxing clubs are typically led by people from the communities in which they are located, which is critical to their success. They are able to tap into goodwill locally because they have the respect of the community and, critically, can demonstrate a genuine determination to succeed. Clubs generate pride in the community by engaging with traditionally hard-to-reach and marginalised participants. While this may be undervalued by wider society in the opinion of most community coaches, they themselves understand the importance of the pride and recognition derived from success.

> If you are a kid who is a pain in the arse of the community and if you gain success in the boxing, it is a massive thing for the community because that one kid did all sorts of work for the community. . . . It is sort of the community recognises them as one of their own and if communities don't come to boxing gyms, they don't hear their names.
> (Male Coach, Yorkshire Region in Barrett, Edmondson and Miller, 2019)

Boxing clubs are ideally placed to act as the tip of the spear in terms of engaging with deprived and marginalised communities. They function as transformative spaces and have the potential to enact positive change on the individuals and communities they serve. A significant amount of the power and potential of boxing spaces resides the leadership teams of boxing clubs, specifically boxing coaches.

Boxing Coaching and Leadership

Coaches have the power to act as agents of change. They have significant influence over the operations of the club and the individual members. The bond between boxer and coach is an intense one, and, for some participants, it becomes one of the most important personal relationships in their lives. The intensity of this relationship may change over time as participants engage with or disengage from competitive boxing. The development of long-term friendships and networks through sport is a form of social capital which many protagonists cite as being both a cause and an effect of participation, and boxing is no exception. Further, the boxing community sees itself as unique, due in large part to the intense physical and confrontational nature of the sport, but also as a result of its position in the community. In fact, many of the characteristics which boxing clubs and coaches feel set them apart are common to other sports and settings. Nevertheless, the strength and depth of the relationships enjoyed by coaches and boxers (whether recreational or competitive) takes on additional meaning when placed in the context of the environment in which a club operates. For a Southern Counties coach, boxing has a certain 'kudos' in the local community, attracting participation because:

> to be able to say 'I go to a boxing club' holds a lot of weight. . . . Some of the kids who come in aren't even interested in boxing and don't want to

compete, but being able to say that they go to the club gives them a bit more of a reputation.

(Male coach, Southern Counties in Barrett, Edmondson and Miller, 2019)

Coaches become a fixture in the lives of boxers at their clubs by virtue of being reliable and therefore dependable. For many participants, the relationship with their coach is one of the few reliable and dependable things in their lives. Some boxers come to view their coach as a mentor; a role which most are happy to embrace. The strength of the bonds takes on additional significance for those whose lives outside the gym are particularly turbulent:

The relationship between the boxing coach and the kids is a thing that would encourage that sort of disclosure. And I don't mean disclosure necessarily in the negative sense of the word but just that sharing what's happening in their lives.

(Female Coach, London Region in Barrett, Edmondson and Miller, 2019)

Actually there's a real opportunity for them to add to what they can do. Even if you just have someone come down and just support someone with their homework just one day a week, you could completely transform what you do now because people already trust you, people are already engaging with you.

(Male Coach, London Region in Barrett, Edmondson and Miller, 2019)

Getting the buy-in from members of the local community, on account of the positive reputation boxing has through its image of heroic masculinity, enables coaches to work with individuals and community leaders to enact change. A coach from the London Region described the ability of his club's leadership team to interact with leaders of local gangs to help to peacefully resolve local issues and deescalate tensions. In this example, the intervention was possible because the coaching staff was respected by the local community on account of their record of boxing 'at the top level'. His achievements in the ring have purchase outside of boxing, carrying a recognised weight that affords him the opportunity to act as a confidant and mediator to resolve issues. According to a Western Counties coach, the bond established between boxer and coach is akin to a familial bond. This bond is a powerful antidote to the lure of gang culture.

The reality is when these kids realise 98% of boxing coaches have a true passion and a family thing, most clubs say 'welcome to the family' which is important as most could just join a gang because they've got nothing going on at home. If you do it right the bond is there forever.

(Male Coach, Western Counties in Barrett, Edmondson and Miller, 2019)

In the context of challenging inner-city neighbourhoods where violence between rival gangs is frequent, the idea that a sport which is aggressive and confrontational could help to relieve tensions would appear to be a paradox. Much of the training which takes place in community clubs is non-contact, however, and is designed to improve participants' fitness. Within the gym, technical work and sparring is strictly controlled and carried out under close supervision. This gap between the perception of the sport and the reality of training at a boxing club is hard for some to comprehend. As a leader in the London Region observes,

I had it last week with the social worker, who was trying to block the placement of a child on the grounds that 'he had a problem with aggression and boxing is terribly violent.' We all started laughing, and I think, where do these people live? but there are probably hundreds of thousands of people that have got a very fixed view of it.

(Female Leader, London Region in Barrett, Edmondson and Miller, 2019)

Boxing coaches place importance on the role of the sport and training as a vessel through which anger issues can be successfully managed and moderated. 'Those kids that have got that aggression, the minute you let it out, before it rots inside, it's going to take the aggression away' (Male Coach, London Region in Barrett, Edmondson and Miller, 2019). Indeed, it is evident that, for a percentage of participants, boxing training and competition is less important than having access to a space where they can socialise and relax. For those for whom training is important, previous studies (Lennox, 2012) have demonstrated how training alone can produce specific social cultural rewards.

If you look at how many people we get into the club, not many who come through the door will ever compete . . . boxing is more about what you get from the training itself.

(Western Counties in Barrett, Edmondson and Miller, 2019)

This study aligns with previous work that argues the sociocultural identity rewards that come with establishing a publicly recognised identity as a boxer are one of the most fundamental motivational drives for participants. However, the work by Barrett, Edmondson, and Miller offers potentially important new insights into the cultural value of boxing gyms. As articulated by a Southern Counties coach, for those participants who cannot, or do not, train in all aspects of boxing, such as those associated with victim support, the ability to access and belong to a community boxing club provides a safe and structured space. What is evident from the focus group is a strong sense of how boxing gyms function as spaces that widen individual social networks and, through the identity of *a boxer*, provide individuals with access to global connections.

> Anywhere you go in the world, if you meet somebody who has been involved in boxing, it's a bar room conversation straight away, because of the experience, knowing or understanding that nervous feeling that you get when you go into the ring. Anybody who's boxed, they know that terror and having to overcome it.
> (Male Coach, London Region in Barrett, Edmondson and Miller, 2019)

In the example provided from the London Region coach, competing as a boxer is key to developing the identity of a boxer and thus access to a shared global network of people with similar positive social experiences. Further research would benefit from focusing on the extent to which individuals associated with boxing but not highly active in the training or competing as boxers still benefit from these identity rewards. Or, whether they develop and benefit from other identity rewards that, without boxing, would not have been available to them.

Culture and Ethos

As a sport with a global presence, boxing enjoys a popularity which transcends nationalities and builds bridges between cultures. The sport has the advantage of being easily understood with simple but effective rules, and widespread acceptance as a valid form of competition (even if this is challenged from time to time and from place to place). As such, there is a familiarity which leads to a high degree of inclusivity.

First- or second-generation migrants from countries with a proud tradition in international boxing, such as Ireland, Italy, or Pakistan, can find a common bond with the local population, which hopes to break down barriers (Hayward, 2020). This proved to be the case in the study conducted by Tjønndal and Hovden (2021), who found that Muslim women's boxers in Norway were able to craft a boxing identity that enabled them to bridge divides between two social circles who initially disapproved of their engagement with boxing: white male boxers in the boxing club and male authority figures within their families. Through our qualitative study, we found that boxers from minority groups in England who identified with successful athletes from within their communities were more likely to participate in the sport. Diverse representation matters.

> We had a chap who became the first Pakistani fighter to win a national championship and that effect on the community was massive. Even though that was about 10 years ago we still have families coming in and parents bringing their kids because they see him as an inspiration.
> (Male coach, Midlands in Barrett, Edmondson and Miller., 2019)

Coaches demonstrated the inclusivity of their clubs by referring to boxing as a religion.

> Whatever you are, whatever you do, just bring it here, and train. We don't care in this gym. Right now, we're all-inclusive. We've got one religion here. It's just boxing.
> (Male Coach, London Region in Barrett, Edmondson and Miller, 2019)

This inclusivity is often under-emphasised and underappreciated by people who are not part of the boxing community. It takes on additional significance for participants from marginalised groups. A male coach from the Eastern Counties described how the friendliness of his gym, and the accepting nature of people who were struggling to fit into other sports, found boxing to be an antidote to social exclusion. As pseudo places of worship who are accepting of people that might otherwise be socially excluded, boxing gyms and boxing coaches in England hold a significant power over their charges. For a coach from the North West Counties, the threat of expulsion from a boxing club had a more meaningful impact on unruly youths than police threats or paternal attempts to correct disruptive behaviour. The strength and closeness of the relationships between boxing coaches and boxers (Lennox and Rodosthenous, 2016) provides coaches with a deep understanding of the social and domestic lives of their charges. This enables them to apply rules, boundaries, and pressure flexibly and in a tailored manner.

> We have a couple of members who do get a bit more leeway when they are pushing their behaviour a bit, but I know what's going on in their house so I have to give them a bit of leeway as they don't have anywhere else they can express themselves or vent.
> (Western Counties in Barrett, Edmondson and Miller, 2019)

The coaches in England echo the narrative resources of boxing, which portray these spaces as sites where men are allowed to be kind to one another (Dunn,

2009, p. 11) and where a very 'special carnal fraternity' is formed between individual boxers who train together (Wacquant, 2004, p. 68). These bonds are modelled through the actions of the coaches, but enacted by individual participants.

> I remember when I started boxing (and I was terrible!), I remember running into a British champion at the time and he would . . . the respect that he would give me . . . I remember him always saying 'just by stepping into the room you're doing what most people wouldn't do and that shows a huge amount of nerve, bravery'. I'm just a kid, but for a British champion to say that to me was amazing.
> (Male Coach, Mersey and North West Counties in Barrett, Edmondson and Miller, 2019)

Community boxing clubs are conspicuously equitable in the way that participants are treated by coaches. The emphasis is on the discipline and structure of training, rather than the status of the boxer, whether this relates to ethnicity, sexuality, or boxing ability.

> It takes away any prejudice and judgement, the thing that they value in the gym is their work ethic. We have all seen bully kids come in who think they are as hard as nails and they end up getting no attention. Then we get quiet kids who might have been bullied and they work hard, they focus, and they train, and they end up becoming the popular kid.
> (Male Coach, West Midlands in Barrett, Edmondson and Miller, 2019)

Further research would benefit from challenging the quasi-religious qualities assigned to boxing, its spaces, and its people. It is evident from this study that boxing spaces are equitable and inclusive for individuals willing to conform to the expected attitudes and behaviours of the spaces. These attitudes and behaviours are set and enforced by coaches and the club's leadership teams. In the examples provided in this study and those cited where individuals exhibit behaviours outside of expected norms (for example, bullies), they find continued engagement with community boxing clubs problematic or untenable unless they are willing to conform. However, not all behaviours or individuals are treated the same. Certain behaviours, such as criminal activity, might be better tolerated on account of the belief that boxing will ultimately *save* an individual from a life of crime. Evident is the need and willingness of coaches in England to flex approaches to suit the needs and dynamics of their clubs and the participants. Whilst clubs clearly have a fraternal and familial culture, there is also sufficient scope for individualism, which is presented as paramount to enacting positive change and retaining a strong and effective culture and ethos.

Funding and Impact

The delivery of community boxing programs, despite being driven by volunteers, requires continuous financial support. Traditional sources of income are under increasing pressure as a result of competition from other activities, and the financial hardships faced by participants and their supporters. In such strained circumstances, clubs must look elsewhere for funding with corporate sponsorship and grant funding common sources of secondary income. The justification for providing money may be to generate secondary impacts which reach beyond the confines of the boxing club.

Boxing clubs are accustomed to operating on a shoestring. With so many clubs located in deprived neighbourhoods, the ability to generate income from their own delivery of boxing activities is limited by the low incomes of their members. Coaches may therefore frequently overlook payment for individual sessions, choosing instead to retain the participant. In the long run, however, this cannot be sustained indefinitely.

> My point of view is that kids who live in our community are paying a massive price for their start in life, so the last thing that I want to do is to take another pound off it. What I don't want is for a kid to have to walk past our gym because they don't have £3. Boxing is the sport that takes kids in so I don't think many gyms would turn people down, but that is just how we have run for the last 20 years.
> (Male Coach, Southern Counties in Barrett, Edmondson and Miller, 2019)

When members struggle to find the money to pay their fees, clubs and coaches often find creative ways for them to contribute to the club. Payment in kind is a common way of recouping costs, albeit indirectly. In the absence of direct payment, there is always the danger that the service provided by a community club may be undervalued. Community clubs are increasingly diversifying their activities in response, charging fees at a higher level for sessions aimed at the fitness and lifestyle market, retaining surplus funds to subsidise core activities. However, this risks diluting the ethos of community boxing clubs, which tend to be run as not-for-profit entities. Given the choice, most clubs would elect to invest in coaching if funds were available.

Paradoxically, in these circumstances, a challenging or deprived location can be a deterrent for people with a greater ability to pay for the coaching that they receive. Competition in the fitness sector is fierce, with larger corporate operations such as David Lloyd and Virgin offering boxing fitness classes in modern purpose-built facilities. Boxing clubs, as well as being able to compete on price, have the advantage of presenting a publicly recognised, authentic boxing experience.

Investment by public agencies is a powerful vote of confidence in the ability of boxing clubs to make a difference to the lives of their members, and to the wider community at large. The commonly held view among coaches is that decisions about boxing clubs are made by people who do not understand what boxing clubs do, the challenges they face, or the issues they tackle. Funding is often sought by and provided to clubs to support the delivery of not only boxing-related activities, but also a broader range of diversionary interventions which aim to generate secondary impacts. These may include reduced crime and anti-social behaviour, improved educational outcomes, and increased training and employment opportunities. In this context, it is surprising that the Home Office has refused for several years to allow prisons and young offenders institutes to include boxing, or indeed any martial art, on its curriculum of activities available to prisoners and detainees (Meek, 2018). Similarly, organisations and agencies with responsibility for education have resisted calls to include boxing in the national curriculum for physical education although, contrary to popular belief, it has never been explicitly banned in schools (MicInerney, 2016).

It is less surprising, therefore, to note that some clubs have struggled to make the case for investment in the face of this apparent bureaucratic resistance to consider boxing as a valid and worthwhile activity for young people. Quantifying the impacts and benefits of boxing is the key to unlock the door to continued funding, but clubs must increasingly demonstrate that inward investment generates a social as well as a sporting return on investment. Traditionally, social impact measures have only focused on new participants, but the argument made by community club coaches is that some account should also be taken of those who are retained that might otherwise have dropped out. If social impacts are the desired outcome, there has to be a way to capture their scope and extent.

Conclusion

Throughout the interviews which inform this research, coaches were keen to stress that, in their opinion, 'boxing is different'. When pressed, some found it hard to articulate how and why boxing stood out from other sports in what it does for its participants. As other investigations of the social and community impacts of sport have found, there is no magic formula which can be applied to every club. There are some characteristics which stand out as being distinctive, however.

Boxing clubs are located in deprived neighbourhoods and serve the marginalised and excluded communities which Sport England has identified as the key target groups in increasing participation in sport and physical activity. For people on low incomes, cost remains one of the most significant barriers to participation in any sport, and boxing has two advantages in this regard. First, boxing is a low rent, low-cost sport, in part because it often takes place in locations which other sports have left behind. Clubs are adaptable enough to make use of almost any usable space and are therefore able to exploit opportunities which other clubs would be forced to refuse. Second, because boxing clubs are (uniquely) present in deprived neighbourhoods, the hidden costs of distance and time are taken out of the equation.

Boxing clubs therefore have a head start in reaching out to participants from the most deprived neighbourhoods, but this is no guarantee of success. It is also essential to generate a welcoming environment within the gym, and this is dependent on the input of the volunteers who sustain community boxing clubs. They recognise that, as representatives of their clubs, they must compensate (at least to some extent) for the often spartan surroundings in which they operate. This takes on additional importance when establishing and maintaining enduring relationships with participants who come from turbulent backgrounds where authority figures may be absent. Coaches frequently assume the role of mentor to young people who lack any other positive role model in their lives. In this context, participants feel supported, respected, and valued, cementing their engagement with the club and the sport. This may come at a personal cost to coaches, however, many of whom sacrifice their own time to go the extra mile.

Community boxing clubs do outstanding work in engaging with participants from groups which have traditionally been among the hardest to reach, including those from Black and minority ethnic groups, and from deprived neighbourhoods. Consequently, coaches and club officials are forced to confront some of the most challenging social issues, which have direct and indirect impacts on them and their participants. This places significant expectations on a volunteer workforce which wants to respond appropriately but lacks the formal training necessary to do so. Boxing remains more vulnerable than most sports to criticism, however, some of which questions its right to exist as a sport, let alone feature as a suitable activity for young people. These conversations inevitably focus on the risk of injury in the ring without acknowledging that this represents only a small minority of what community boxing clubs deliver. Irrespective of any concerns regarding how participation is tracked in clubs, coaches can justifiably point to their successes with vulnerable young people as justification for their continued intervention.

The challenge for community boxing clubs is to persuade third-party organisations that, for the majority of young people attending a gym, the attraction is not so much boxing *per sé* as being an active member of a club which accepts them. In these circumstances, the activities delivered by a club are less important than its continued existence, although the club must retain boxing as part of that identity. In promoting itself to organisations which might be willing to engage with the sport, boxing needs to demonstrate that while competitive boxing may be the 'hook' which pulls young people through the door, the value of what clubs do is in the breadth and depth of activities they provide. Boxing offers an important lesson to other sports in the way that young participants can train alongside and learn from successful adults. Community coaches believe that this tangible form of success within reach provides a significant spur to new boxers, which in their view could and should be replicated in other sports.

Note

1 See Meek, 2019; Lammy, 2017; Sampson, 2015.

Bibliography

Barrett, D., Edmondson, L. and Miller, R. (2019) 'England boxing leaders focus group'.

Braun, V. and Clarke, V. (2014) 'What can "thematic analysis" offer health and wellbeing researchers?', *International Journal of Qualitative Studies on Health and Wellbeing*, 9(1), p. 26152.

Dunn, K. (2009) *One ring circus: dispatches from the world of boxing*. Tucson, AZ: Schaffner Press, Inc.

Ferguson, K., Hassan, D. and Kitchin, P. (2018) 'Sport and underachievement among protestant youth in Northern Ireland: a boxing club case study', *International Journal of Sport Policy and Politics*, 10(3), pp. 579–596.

Gill, B. (2015) *The English indices of deprivation*. Available at: https://assets.publishing.service.gov.uk/government/uploads/system/uploads/attachment_data/file/465791/English_Indices_of_Deprivation_2015_-_Statistical_Release.pdf (Accessed: 5 May 2022).

Hayward, P. (2020) 'Hero status is not only about glitz and glamour – Tyson Fury has helped demystify the traveller community', *Daily Telegraph*, 20 February 2020.

Jump, D. and Smithson, H. (2020) 'Dropping your guard: the use of boxing as a means of forming desistance narratives amongst young people in the criminal justice system', *The International Journal of Sport and Society*, 11(2), pp. 55–69.

Lammy, D. (2017) *The Lammy review: an independent review into the treatment of, and outcomes for, black, Asian and minority ethnic individuals in the criminal justice system*. Available at: www.gov.uk/government/organisations/lammy-review (Accessed: 5 May 2022).

Lennox, P.S. (2012) *Narratives of performance: an interdisciplinary qualitative ethnography investigating the storied lives of amateur and professional boxers*. PhD thesis. University of Exeter.

Lennox, P.S. and Rodosthenous, G. (2016) 'The boxer – trainer, actor – director relationship: an exploration of creative freedom', *Sport in Society*, 19(2), pp. 147–158.

Meek, R. (2018) *A sporting chance: an independent review of sport in youth and adult prisons, ministry of justice*, August. Available at: https://assets.publishing.service.gov.uk/government/uploads/system/uploads/attachment_data/file/733184/a-sporting-chance-an-independent-review-sport-in-justice.pdf (Accessed: 5 May 2022).

McInerney, L. (2016) 'Despite popular belief, boxing has never actually been banned in schools', *Schools Week*, 15 November. Available at: https://schoolsweek.co.uk/despite-popular-belief-boxing-has-never-actually-been-banned-in-schools/ (Accessed: 5 May 2022).

Morton, S., O'Brien, K. and O'Reilly, L. (2019) 'Boxing and substance use rehabilitation: building skills and capacities in disadvantaged communities', *Community Development Journal*, 54(3), pp. 541–559.

Perkins, P. and Hahn, A. (2019) 'Factors underpinning at least three years of participant adherence to a community-focused modified boxing program', *Open Journal of Social Sciences*, 7, pp. 298–331.

Sampson, A. (2015) *An evaluation of the longer term outcomes of the pathways programme at fight for peace*. London: University of East London.

Sugden, J.P. (1996) *Boxing and society: an international analysis*. Manchester, UK: Manchester University Press.

Tjønndal, A. and Hovden, J. (2021) '"Will God condemn me because I love boxing?" Narratives of young female immigrant Muslim boxers in Norway', *European Journal of 'Studies*, 28(4), pp. 455–470.

Wacquant, L.J.D. (1992) 'The social logic of boxing in black Chicago: toward a sociology of pugilism', *Sociology of Sport Journal*, 9, pp. 221–254.

Wacquant, L.J.D. (2004) *Body & soul: notebooks of an apprentice boxer*. New York, NY: Oxford University Press.

Chapter 4

Narratives of Struggle

Boxing, Gender, and Community

Supriya Chaudhuri

Introduction

The sporting body presents itself as a site of inscription, bearing the marks of personal and social struggles in a field contested by gender, race, ethnicity, religion, and nation. While these contestations are common to all our experiences of society and citizenship, the field of organized sport – a space of leisure, even 'entertainment', attracting both cultural and financial capital – makes them visible in a form rigidly overdetermined by the distinctions of sex and gender on the one hand, and national affiliation on the other. Such visibility may vary, however, with differences of status, economic privilege, and power-relations in society. This study looks at a group of Muslim women boxers in an underprivileged neighbourhood of the South Asian city of Kolkata (formerly Calcutta). Its focus is not so much on individual boxers and their pursuit of sporting excellence, as in the traditional boxing story, but on the adoption of a sports practice by a marginalised group in adverse social and economic conditions. Crucial to my account is the idea of bodily *habitus* as inculcated through training, and the struggles of individuals who are required to contend with differing social and moral expectations, producing, and being produced by the structures of which they are consciously and unconsciously part.

For Pierre Bourdieu, the contemporary field of sporting practices is:

> the site of struggles in which what is at stake, *inter alia*, is the power to impose the legitimate definition of sporting practice and of the legitimate function of sporting activity – amateurism vs. professionalism, participant sport vs. spectator sport, distinctive (elite) sport vs. popular (mass) sport; and this field is itself part of the larger field of struggles over the definition of the *legitimate body* and *the legitimate use of the body*.
>
> (1993, p. 122)

Global sport has witnessed, over the past several decades, a growing unease about 'the definition of the legitimate body': whether human, other animal, cybernetic, or mechanical; whether enhanced by biotechnological interventions such as drugs, prostheses, and advanced equipment; and whether assignable to a specific sex or gender category. But we might also explore the connection between 'the legitimate use of the body' and the body's negotiation of social space, its formation of a *habitus* or disposition that governs its interactions with its environment and its chosen spheres of activity, and the extent to which habitus is learned, as opposed to being unconsciously acquired. For athletes, the process of learning sport-specific dispositions is as much of a struggle as the many other struggles that constitute part of the everyday social and contribute to the formation of a self in the world.

Habitus is a term central to Bourdieusian sociology, and it has proved extremely influential in analysing social dispositions, especially when they contribute to unequal or hierarchical structures in which we collectively acquiesce. I found it useful for understanding the lives and struggles of the group of Muslim women boxers in my study during my interaction with them at the Kidderpore School of Physical Culture in Kolkata, speaking with trainees and coaches there, and drawing upon a prior documentary and visual archive. My experience in working with these sources led me to interpret habitus, not in the standard Bourdieusian sense of an unconsciously acquired disposition, but as partly inculcated through environment and upbringing, and partly learned through training and discipline. This view is also offered by the anthropologist Saba Mahmood in her exemplary account of Muslim women's piety movements in Cairo. Mahmood returns here to Aristotle in order to contest what she sees as Bourdieu's socioeconomic determinism, his focus on 'the unconscious power of habitus through which objective social conditions become naturalized and reproduced', and his 'lack of attention to the pedagogical process by which a habitus is learned' (Mahmood, 2005). For Mahmood, habitus in the older Aristotelian tradition of moral cultivation implies 'a quality that is acquired through human industry, assiduous practice, and discipline'. It is an embodied practice that becomes instinctive, but this does not cancel the individual's agency or her participation in the process of learning through which habitus is acquired (Mahmood, 2005, p. 136). In a socioeconomic space regulated, especially for women, by extremely conservative norms of behaviour and piety, this emphasis upon the subject's agency in the inculcation of bodily practice allows us to understand the everyday struggles of the social, a field whose violence we take for granted.

Early uses of the term habitus connect it not only to mental habits inculcated through training, but also to bodily practices. In a lecture delivered on May 17, 1934, at the Société de Psychologie in Paris, the sociologist Marcel Mauss used the phrase 'techniques of the body' to speak of a social habitus rooted not so much in behaviour, but in physical, that is, bodily disposition. The lecture, which was later published in the Society's *Journal de psychologie normal et patholigique*, is significant in that it offers an early example of the modern use of the term habitus, to be found again in Norbert Elias's *The*

Civilizing Process (1939), but authoritatively claimed much later by Pierre Bourdieu in an afterword to Erwin Panofsky (Bourdieu, 2005). As Mauss himself pointed out, the concept of habitus can be traced back to Aristotle's notion of *hexis*, meaning a moral disposition so inculcated through practice that it permanently orients and determines our actions and responses. The term is used by Max Weber and Maurice Merleau-Ponty, but it was Bourdieu who made habitus a crucial element in his generalised economy of practices, inasmuch as it 'designates a double relationship, comprising socialisation and a permanently lasting manner of entering into relation with the social world' (Bourdieu, 2020, p. 122). Thus elaborated, the concept of habitus, together with 'field', has become a key concept of modern sociology, but its link with the original Maussian context, that of the 'techniques of the body', is not always stressed.

Mauss's essay may be taken as an early and tentative attempt to classify the range of bodily practices that society inculcates in human individuals and proceeds to treat as natural. He emphasises that it is not just imitation, but education or training that produces bodily habitus: it is not the result of 'the metaphysical *habitudes*, that mysterious memory', but habits, that vary not so much with individuals, but 'with societies, educations, proprieties and fashions, prestiges' (Mauss, 1973, p. 73). He saw in them 'the techniques and work of collective and individual practical reason' rather than 'the soul and its repetitive faculties', and focused on the body, since it is 'man's first and most natural instrument, or more accurately, not to speak of instruments, man's first and most natural technical object'(Mauss, 1973, p. 75). Beginning his examination, he notes that techniques of the body manifest a 'sexual division'; that is, that they are first of all gendered. The implication is that this happens through socialisation, but a piece of unreflecting sexism follows:

> A man normally closes his fist with the thumb outside, a woman with her thumb inside; perhaps because she has not been taught to do it, but I am sure that if she were taught, it would prove difficult. Her punching, her delivery of a punch, are weak. And everyone knows that a woman's throwing, of a stone for example, is not just weak, but always different from that of a man: in a vertical instead of a horizontal plane. Perhaps this is a case of two instructions. For there is a society of men and a society of women. However, I believe that there are also perhaps biological and psychological things involved as well.
>
> (Mauss, 1973, pp. 76–77)

It is unclear whether Mauss is here confusing what he considers a biological propensity with the bodily habitus produced by different kinds of training ('two instructions'). Setting aside the question of physical strength, which involves other factors, I know from long experience that *both* boys and girls must be taught to make a fist with the thumb outside. Additionally, many men cannot throw 'horizontally', since this too is a technique that children learn, though more boys than girls are taught it. Women (and men) who learn to box incorporate, as Bourdieu's collaborator Loïc Wacquant terms it, the pugilistic habitus: what fighters take for a natural capacity is in effect 'this peculiar nature resulting from the protracted process of inculcation of the pugilistic habitus, a process that often begins in early childhood' (2004, p. 98). This, Wacquant says,

> erases the scholastic distinction between the intentional and the habitual, the rational and the emotional, the corporeal and the mental, [and] pertains to an embodied practical reason that, being lodged in the depths of the socialized organism, escapes the logic of individual choice.
> (Wacquant, 2003, p. 99)

At the same time, the pugilistic habitus, in its prolonged inculcation, must contend with, and in its chosen context, override, other habitudes produced by social, religious, and domestic conditioning, thus making social space not a passively experienced set of determinants, but a site of active struggle, structuration, and reconstitution by agents who, as Bourdieu puts it, 'distort the space in their neighbourhood' (2004, p. 33). I would like to carry this perception forward into a study of a South Asian neighbourhood and its chosen sports practice, boxing.

India's Boxing Story

Boxing in India is mainly an amateur sport, though professional boxing has made some headway in the past decade. It involves little of the glamour, monetary rewards, and brutal, agonistic spectacles that define boxing in the West. Though there are references in the Sanskrit epics to *muṣṭiyuddha* ('fighting with the fists') practiced in indigenous gymnasia (*akhāḍās*), boxing never acquired the rich traditions of *mallayuddha* (wrestling) in India, and its origins remain colonial. There are records of boxing matches organised by the British in the colonial capital, Calcutta (Kolkata), from the late nineteenth century, with Indian boxers making occasional appearances. The American Jack McAuliffe started India's first boxing club in Calcutta around 1898. From the early twentieth century, tournaments incorporating weight categories, padded rings, regulation gloves, and London rules were held in both Calcutta and Bombay (Mumbai), often with Army or Navy support. Enthusiasts like Captain James Knox and Albert E. Fleming promoted the sport in schools and among the Anglo-Indian and Armenian communities. A major impetus was the arrival in Calcutta of the England-educated Bengali Paresh Lal Roy, who had won the featherweight title at Aldershot, boxed for Cambridge, and won the Brigade Squadron Championships as a member of the Royal Flying Corps during the first World War. In 1930, Roy founded the Bengal Amateur

Boxing Federation (BABF); boxing flourished under his tutelage and that of his protégé Santosh Dey (Dasgupta, 2004). Post-Independence, Prithviswar (Kalu) Mishra, secretary of both the BABF and the newly formed Indian Amateur Boxing Federation (IABF) for over 20 years, was instrumental in sending Indian boxing teams (mainly boxers from Bengal) to the London (1948) and Helsinki (1952) Olympics. In the next 50 years, however, while the sport took off in other states, like Punjab and Haryana, Bengal boxing declined, and Kolkata, a chaotic, overcrowded, and increasingly impoverished city marked by the traumas of Partition, labour migration, industrial recession, and the flight of capital, lost its reputation for producing national-level boxers. Its only notable success came in 2002, when Mohammad Ali Qamar won the light-flyweight gold medal at the Manchester Commonwealth Games (Dasgupta, 2012, pp. 56–61).

Despite a setback in 2014 when the IABF was suspended by the International Amateur Boxing Association and de-recognized by the Sports Ministry to be replaced by the Boxing Federation of India, Indian boxing has grown exponentially over the past two decades. Beginning from conditions of neglect and adversity when most boxers came from extremely deprived backgrounds, boxing gained state and private support with Asian and Commonwealth Games medals for Dingko Singh and Mohammad Ali Qamar, followed by Olympic medals for Vijender Singh, M.C. Mary Kom, and Lovlina Borgohain. Indian women's boxing owes most to the legendary Mary Kom of the northeastern state of Manipur, winner of six gold medals from 2002 to 2018 at the AIBA Women's World Championships. Over the years, four other Indians, including the exceptional Laishram Sarita Devi, have won gold medals at these championships in their respective weight categories. Most recently, a Muslim woman boxer from Hyderabad, Nikhat Zareen, overcame religious and social prohibitions to win flyweight gold medals at both the Istanbul world championships and the Birmingham Commonwealth Games (2022). But the struggle of the Muslim women boxers of Kolkata has not gained for them even a fraction of the support given to Zareen, now an officer with the Bank of India, sponsored by Adidas, and part of the Target Olympic Podium scheme of the Sports Authority of India.

The Muslim Women Boxers of Kolkata

For these young women, an example closer to home was Mohammad Ali Qamar, who grew up like them in one of Kolkata's most impoverished areas, the docklands of Khidirpur (Kidderpore), and learned to box at the Kidderpore School of Physical Culture under the watchful eyes of coach Mehrajuddin Ahmed, better known as Cheena-bhai. Qamar remains the club's biggest success, an inspiration to the young boxers who congregate there from the same urban catchment area, the severely deprived neighbourhoods of Ekbalpur, Metiabruz, Khidirpur, Mominpur, Garden Reach, or Watgunge, adjacent to the River Hooghly. Demographically the area is predominantly Muslim, a historical legacy from 1856, when the exiled ruler of Awadh, Nawab Wajid Ali Shah, settled in Metiabruz with his retinue. Over time, the aristocratic families migrated to more central locations, and these dockland areas became densely clustered urban slums, housing dockworkers, garment-makers, tradespeople, petty criminals, gambling dens, and minor gang lords. Following the Partition of India in 1947, Kolkata's Muslim population (20 percent of the total) was increasingly ghettoised as the community became concentrated in specific neighbourhoods, and they experienced conditions of social exclusion even in a nominally secular urban setting. Muslims in India, according to the 2011 Census, have the lowest literacy rates of any religious group; are poorly represented in mainstream education, state, or private sector jobs; and suffer inequality and discrimination in access to health and other services, despite some gestures towards inclusion and upliftment made by successive state governments in Bengal.[1]

The Khidirpur-Ekbalpur-Metiabruz area draws large numbers of migrant labourers from the nearby states of Bihar and Uttar Pradesh; the languages of this urban pocket are Hindi and Urdu, rather than Bengali. Women receive little education and are expected to marry early, look after the household, and earn by working in the embroidery or garment-making industries on a piece-rate basis. Their social mobility is restricted, with a renewed insistence within the Muslim community on wearing the *hijab* or the more enveloping *burqa*, though older women often follow the more traditional Bengali Muslim practice of covering the head with the end of the sari. Families are crowded sometimes seven or eight to a room, with little space for cooking, eating, study, prayer, or sleep. The narrow lanes between the houses afford room for only one person to pass, and much of the day's business, washing clothes or utensils, fetching water, buying vegetables, and going to work or to school, is conducted under the eyes of neighbours. Muslim women's lives are thus summed up in the historic *Sachar Committee Report* of 2006:

> Women, sometimes of their own volition, sometimes because of community pressure, adopt visible markers of community identity on their person and in their behaviour. Their lives, morality, and movement in public spaces are under constant scrutiny and control. A gender-based fear of the "public", experienced to some degree by all women, is magnified manifold in the case of Muslim women. The lines between "safe" and "unsafe" spaces become rigid. The community and its women withdraw into the safety of familiar orthodoxies, reluctant to participate in the project of modernity, which threatens to blur community boundaries. It was said that for large number of Muslim women in India today, the only "safe" space (both in terms of physical protection and in terms of protection of identity) is within the boundaries of home and community. Everything beyond the walls of

the ghetto is seen as unsafe and hostile – markets, roads, lanes and public transport, schools and hospitals, police stations and government offices.
(Cabinet Secretariat, Government of India, 2006, p. 13)

What is being described here is a range of bodily practices that are naturalised and incorporated into the everyday social interactions of ordinary Muslim women in India, especially those who inhabit the severely restricted space of the urban ghetto. The objective conditions of society, especially those engendered by class, location, and 'the economic bases of the social formation in question', are inscribed in the bodies and dispositions of social actors as their habitus (Bourdieu, 1977, p. 83). At the same time, we cannot underestimate the potential (if not habitual) agency of both individual and community in the struggle for social space, especially in conditions of privation and suffering. For lives lived on the brink, a risk may be worth taking.

The Kidderpore School of Physical Culture (KSOPC) was founded in 1950. It has a tin-roofed clubhouse, with a rudimentary gymnasium and outdoor boxing ring, in Nawab Ali Park, down Ekbalpur Lane, just off the arterial Diamond Harbour Road. The park has football and cricket grounds surrounded by concrete stands and offers an oasis of open space in a crowded neighbourhood. In the 1990s, young girls from the neighbourhood, watching their brothers train with coach Mehrajuddin, began to press for admission to the boxing club. The BABF president Asit Banerjee, who was coaching girls from Bengal and Manipur at the South Calcutta Physical Culture Association (SCPCA) in Deshpran Sasmal Park (Kalighat), argued for the inclusion of women's boxing in the IABF agenda at its 1998 general meeting in Pune. Under his leadership, the BABF began to focus on women's boxing, encouraging young girls from these marginalised, urban areas to break out of traditional practices of seclusion and early marriage, and empower themselves through sport. One of Banerjee's first protégées was Razia Shabnam, who cut short her career in the ring to qualify as an international referee and judge, and went on to coach young women trainees at the Kalighat club. Razia works with a secular non-profit welfare organisation, *New Light*, which runs a hostel for children of sex workers in Kalighat. Over nearly 20 years, Razia has been one of the driving forces in women's boxing, a hugely inspiring coach instilling passion, rigour, and grit in her pupils with her fierce advocacy of women's ability to excel. Several of her pupils have gone on to achieve medals at state and national levels, notably the sisters Ajmira and Kashmira Khatun, featured with their mentor Razia in Alka Raghuram's documentary, *Burqa Boxers* (2016).

I met Mehrajuddin, Razia Shabnam, and Zainab Fatima on my visits to the KSOPC, while some 50-odd children, 15 to 20 of them girls, clad in regulation boxing shorts and singlets (with the girls adding vests, leggings, or trackpants), assembled within the fenced club precincts to stretch, warm up, skip rope, and go for mandatory runs around the grounds, led by their seniors. Post-pandemic, practice has resumed for the club's 187 trainees, including around 20 girls. A notice on the door of the gym indicates separate hours for 'ladies' to use the machines (which Razia and Zainab did while I was there), but everyone trains together in the yard, girls sparring with boys in regulation gear, though the parents, watching the children practice from the adjacent concrete stands, are more conservatively dressed, the men in skullcaps and the women in burqas. The younger girls, Shazia, Aman Farah, Nazma, and their friends, were eager to engage, proud of their achievements at the under-10 or under-12 levels, and confident of progress: "I want to be a boxer!" said Aman to me before running off.

In conversation, Mehrajuddin and Razia both spoke of significant changes in attitudes, both within their community and in society generally, towards women's boxing. When Razia started boxing, she was a genuine pioneer, braving social disapproval, though with her parents' support, and there were only one or two women at the Khidirpur club. This has changed radically, and not just because of the international success of Indian women boxers: there is much greater acceptance by the community. Zainab Fatima, one of three sisters featured in Anusha Nandakumar's (2019) documentary, *Boxing Ladies*, is now a coach at the Khidirpur club. I watched her taking trainees through warm-ups and sparring. 'You know this is a very conservative Muslim neighbourhood', she said, 'but our small group of girls, right from the under-10s, will never miss training: their parents bring them' (Zainab Fatima, Interview at KSOPC, May 16, p. 202). In 20 years, women's boxing has gained genuine role models and aspirational goals. But despite the collective investments of the past two decades, and medals won at state and national levels, there have been no spectacular international successes for the Muslim girls of Ekbalpur-Khidirpur in Kolkata, no individual stories of boxing excellence to match those of Mary, Sarita, or Nikhat. Rather, what we have here is a dogged persistence by an impoverished and marginalised community, in pursuit of a sport that has brought little by way of monetary reward or public laurels, but has meant, especially for girls and women, a process of learning the painful, conscious acquiring of a way of life – a bodily habitus – that can radically alter them as agents in social space. Zainab explained:

> Girls take up boxing for two reasons: either to gain rewards like trophies and jobs, or to become stronger, to cope with the dangers and risks of women's everyday lives. I think it is the second motive that is important. Of course, being a boxer will not save you from assault or violence on the streets, no one thinks that. But it can change your mentality, you can look life in the face, learn how to focus, to conserve and use your strength, to stand up for yourself.
> (Zainab Fatima, Interview at KSOPC, September 7, 2022b)

Mehrajuddin emphasised that, in the absence of state or private sponsorship, club fees are still nominal, and the gym equipment was procured largely through his own efforts (Mehrajuddin Ahmed, Interviews at KSOPC, May-September 2022). There is no infrastructural state support, and no residential programmes for boxers unless they are picked up at the national level. The lack of jobs is a major concern. Razia Shabnam spoke frankly of her disappointment that after years of hard training and handfuls of medals, women boxers are not recruited by the police, armed forces, public sector industries, or railways, unlike other successful Indian athletes. New opportunities have emerged through the burgeoning fitness industry (Zainab's sister Sughra is a trainer with CultFit), while professional boxing, as club veteran, ex-hockey player Claude Noronha explained, drew KSOPC's male boxers. Mujtaba Kamal's outstanding career was cut short by injury; his nephew Faizan Anwar, also a KSOPC product, is ranked among India's top pro boxers (Sen, 2021). In two decades, the community has seen some economic and educational progress. The children are all in school and look healthy, the parents appear solvent, and the atmosphere in the club is bright and lively. I asked Razia Shabnam about the Muslim community's attitude towards women's boxing, to which she responded:

> For me, there is no difference between Muslim and Hindu communities. There are only two communities: one of men and one of women. What does religion matter when women are held back? Women boxers have to struggle like all women everywhere.
> (Razia Shabnam, Interview at KSOPC, May 16, 2022)

While Muslims in India are a particularly endangered community today, with the rise of Hindu majoritarian politics and a deliberate stoking of communal hatred, Razia did not speak of boxing as a defence against assault or social violence. For her, the discipline, labour, and patience involved in the acquisition of the pugilistic habitus are transformational in themselves, despite the absence of public rewards.

Politics, Community, and Nation

In a pioneering article on Khidirpur's Muslim women boxers, Payoshni Mitra argued that sportspersons from minority communities in India are under compulsion to assert their loyalty to the nation (Mitra, 2009). India's Partition along religious lines in 1947 saw the birth of two nations, 'secular' India and Islamic Pakistan (followed by the liberation of Bangladesh, formerly East Pakistan, in 1971). Although India's Muslim population, 14.2% of the total even after Partition, is the third largest in the world, affirming the Constitutional promise of a secular democratic polity, being Muslim in India is double-edged. Muslims also face the threat of being branded as Islamist by the Hindu majority.

Religious or ethnic marginalisation might act as strong motivators to identify with the nation through sport Mitra, 2009, p. 1845). In 2007–2008, when Mitra was doing her fieldwork, India was dangerously polarised by the killings of Muslims during the Gujarat riots of 2002 after alleged arson on a train carrying Hindu devotees at Godhra railway station. Divisive and communal forces are even stronger today, with the ruling Hindu majoritarian Bharatiya Janata Party (BJP) bringing in legislation that might, in the future, require every Indian to prove her citizenship rights.[2] Protests against the Citizenship Amendment Act of 2019 were followed by the destruction of Muslim lives and property in the East Delhi Hindu-Muslim riots of early 2020. Incidents of anti-Muslim violence have steadily increased, though not in Bengal, with its significant Muslim population and populist, anti-BJP state government.

As a citizen, the sportsperson cannot escape the representational character of political selfhood – not just through inclusion in the national imaginary, but as potential agent and actor (Farred, 2012). Politics and sport are inseparable for the Muslim athlete whose triumphs and defeats become a test of nationalism. Nikhat Zareen was officially felicitated after her Commonwealth Games gold medal, but the cricketer Mohammed Shami (and even his captain who supported him) received thousands of hate messages after India lost to Pakistan in the T20 World Cup in 2021. Even the Sikh cricketer Arshdeep Singh, representing a different religious minority, was mercilessly trolled as a Khalistani separatist after dropping a catch in a recently concluded Asia Cup match against Pakistan. Consequently, political agency often remains implicit, silent, and unavowed. India's most celebrated women boxers, M.C. Mary Kom and Laishram Sarita Devi, come from the North-Eastern state of Manipur, home to a long-drawn-out armed insurgency. Mary belongs to the indigenous Tibeto-Burman Kom Rem hill tribe; her father-in-law, a pastor, was shot dead in 2006 by unknown representatives of the 'Manipur Komrem Revolutionary Front'. But while Manipur's women activists have shown extraordinary courage in protesting military repression, state-sponsored killings, and the oppressive and unconstitutional Armed Forces Special Powers Act, Mary Kom, six-times world champion and founder of a boxing academy in her home state, has never openly taken a political stand, not even to condemn the everyday racism experienced by North-Eastern people (Chaudhuri, 2012). Duncan McDuie-Ra views her iconicity as 'instrumental' for the Indian state, describing her as the symbolic 'other' of the Manipuri activist Irom Sharmila, whose protest hunger-strike lasted 16 years, from 2000 to 2016 (McDuie-Ra, 2015). Natasa Thoudam points to subversive gaps and silences in Kom's co-written autobiography, *Unbreakable*, though the film version casts Bollywood's international star Priyanka Chopra as Mary Kom, 'effacing' her distinctive North-Eastern features in an act of mainstream appropriation.[3] By contrast, the journeys of Mary, Sarita, and Chhoto Loura are more sensitively and faithfully traced in Ameesha Joshi and Anna Sarkissian's 90-minute documentary, *With this Ring* (2016).

Thus, while economic deprivation and political, religious, ethnic, or gender marginalisation might act as powerful motivations in a sporting career, the sportsperson herself is placed in the 'overburdened conjuncture of sport and national self-understanding', as Grant Farred observed of the Black French male footballer, Lilian Thuram (2012, p. 1041). The Muslim women boxers of Khidirpur, lacking state recognition or reward, and denied elevation into the 'national imaginary', carry the burden of subaltern silence. Yet in their everyday struggle for self-affirmation, space, and visibility, they are also representative of their community and their gender. They are unavowed – or disavowed – political actors in a threatened public sphere.

The Work of Representation

Over the past 15 years, a distinctive body of cultural work has accumulated around the women boxers of Ekbalpur-Khidirpur. Given the relative obscurity of the community and its lack of exceptional national or international stars, this audiovisual and textual archive constitutes itself as a cultural surplus. Called into being by a phenomenon that challenges religious and social stereotypes, it presents obstacles to interpretation for the 'viewer from outside'. In its representational density and excess, this body of work is today inseparable from the phenomenon itself, distorting the space in its neighbourhood. It is a powerful, even inspiring archive, though it has failed to supply the cultural capital normally accruing from international exposure and aesthetic mediatisation.

In 2006, the Canadian photographer David Trattles heard about the women boxers of Khidirpur on a radio show and came to Kolkata to record their lives.[4] His exhibition, 'The Boxing Ladies', at the Seagull Arts and Media Resource Centre, Kolkata, in January 2008, featured around 60 black-and-white photographs of the girls, at work in the ring and with their families at home. The under-exposed, slightly raw quality of the photographs, focusing on the endless motion of the boxers in training and their exhaustion after a bout, produced an intense impression of physical and mental absorption. Even as still images, the photographs built up a narrative around the different spaces the girls inhabited: at home, hurrying down the street, or training in the ring. Trattles's camera does not reproduce the body images of these women athletes for consumption; he honours their everyday struggles by respecting their privacy. Intense, absorbed, the women inhabit the restricted freedom of the boxing ring as though it were a metaphor for the external constraints with which they must contend.

Soon after, Payoshni Mitra, then my doctoral student, now CEO of the Global Observatory for Gender Equality and Sport in Lausanne, made a documentary film called *The Bold and the Beautiful* (13 minutes) about Khidirpur's women boxers (Mitra, Unpublished, 2008). The film began, ironically, with Joyce Carol Oates's classic statement, 'Boxing is for men, and is about men, and is men. A celebration of the lost religion of masculinity, all the more trenchant for being lost' (1987, p. 72). Mitra's study of the community as challenging stereotypes of nationalism and gender was published two years later. Her film explores the physical spaces inhabited by these young women, following the twins Shakila and Sanno Baby, both national-level boxers, down the narrow lanes from their home to the boxing club. It recorded their physical confidence, their unselfconscious pleasure in new freedoms of the body that crossed gender boundaries as they fought 'like boys', wearing tracksuits and trainers, the drills, exhaustion, and satisfaction of pushing their bodies to the limit. Mitra interviewed the sisters Ainal, Zainab, Bushra, and Sughra Fatima, residents of Watgunge, training at the KSOPC, and spoke with Razia Shabnam, while Shakila and Sanno's mother, the widowed Banno Begum, appears in the film. Almost without exception, the parents – Razia's father Rahat Hussain, a former wrestler; the Fatima sisters' father Mohammad Kais, who used to box; and their mother Ruksana Begum, who had dreamt of playing basketball – were, despite initial hesitation and objections from more conservative relatives, supportive of their daughters. Boxing connoted freedom and strength for girls facing poverty, oppression, and the dangers of life lived on the margins (Mitra, 2009, p. 1846). The choice of boxing, rather than football or cricket, suggests a willing adoption of the pugilistic habitus of the kind that, according to Wacquant, begins in the ghetto street (2004, p. 98). On camera, they display the fruits of this hard-won bodily inculcation; the pain and absorption of hard practice in the ring or with the punching bag, the physical confidence of negotiating the alleys and byways of their neighbourhood. These bodily expressions are far removed from the commoditised images of the female (or male) athletic body in modern sports media.

Trattles's title was taken over for Anusha Nandakumar's short film, *Boxing Ladies* (2019), about three of the Fatima sisters, Zainab, Bushra, and Sughra (Ainal had married and quit the sport). The documentary, which won a national award and was shown in international competition, was Nandakumar's course submission in 2010 at the Satyajit Ray Film and Television Institute, Kolkata. Using her predecessors' gritty, understated style, it offers a close, in-depth analysis of the Fatima sisters' lives, showing their daily chores; the poverty that forces them to drop out of school because of unpaid fees; the rebelliousness that drives the youngest, Sughra, to cut off her beautiful long hair (Zainab, when I met her, still had hers); and the inadequate nutrition about which their mother expresses anguish. Nandakumar stresses the sisters' commitment to the boxing life and its requirements of dress, practice, discipline, and even a contained aggression that they proudly display on the street, but she also reveals the lack of real opportunities in their environment. Bushra works in a telephone booth; Zainab helps with the cooking and the piece-rate tailoring through which their mother supports a family of nine, including six girls. Boxing has transformed them; they look at ease in their bodies as they return from practice, joking over their shared mobile phone, but there is no assurance of their future within or outside the sporting life.

Similar themes, with other names and faces – Ajmira and Kashmira Khatun, Simi Parveen, Karamjit Kaur – appear in a photo essay from 2015 (in competition in Lugano, 2016) by the Madrid-based Italian photographer and videographer Alice Sassu, used for a *Washington Post* article by Nicole Crowder Crowder (2015). One of Sassu's subjects, Ajmira Khatun, plays a major role in California-based Indian-American filmmaker Alka Raghuram's feature-length, award-winning documentary, *Burqa Boxers* (2016). Sassu had shown the sisters Ajmira and Kashmira commuting to the Khidirpur club from the tiny suburb of Ghutiari Sharif, resting place of a Muslim saint, Pir Ghazi Mubarak Ali. Raghuram picks up Ajmira's story from where Sassu had left it, placing it beside representative histories of two other girls trained by Razia Shabnam: Taslima Khatun, resident of the New Light hostel in Kalighat, and Parveen Sajda. The film focuses on the SCPCA and its president, Asit Banerjee, rather than the Khidirpur club (though Ajmira trains at the KSOPC). Unlike its predecessors, the film is full of light and air, using a more open style of storytelling in dispersed locations, including the Sports Authority of India campus, with three narratives placed side by side. Taslima is brought to the New Light hostel by her mother to save her from the sex trade; Ajmira's love for boxing manages to survive her father's disapproval, her brother's beatings, and family poverty; Parveen's state title is no help to her in securing a job with the police, and she ultimately marries and quits the sport. In a remarkable scene, Razia asks the girls: 'What do you fear?' One girl writes down her answer: 'People'. Razia, herself married with two boys, is a fierce advocate of the boxing life, urging that only discipline and training will enable women to face challenges, endure, and excel.

Still, empowerment is an ambivalent term in Raghuram's exploration of Muslim women's lives, as in Sarah Banet-Weiser's analysis of popular feminism and popular misogyny in the West (2018). Boxing enables self-development for Muslim women but no permanent release from poverty, patriarchy, and social disadvantage. Raghuram's title, *Burqa Boxers*, and the opening shot of Razia Shabnam praying, appear nods to convention. Establishing a context of Muslim piety, they misrepresent a secular Indian urban setting where women athletes do not wear burqas to training (Razia dismissed the notion as obsolete). Only Parveen, soon to be married, is shown wearing a burqa in the film. This visual stereotype would better have suited Ariel Nasr's remarkable documentary, *The Boxing Girls of Kabul* (2011), which shows Afghan women boxers turning up in burqa and hijab to train (in tracksuits) for the 2012 London Olympics (*The Boxing Girls of Kabul*, 2011). Their defiance of social restrictions evokes both admiration and regret today, after the Taliban takeover of Afghanistan in 2021 and the prohibition, not just of sport, but basic education to girls and women.

The success of *Burqa Boxers* has led to an unexpected spin-off; plans are afoot for a new fiction film called *In the Ring*, to be directed by Raghuram – a thriller featuring a woman boxer where, so the producer Sreyashii Sengupta informed me, Razia Shabnam will play a role. This might invest the lives of Khidirpur's most deprived residents with the hyperbolic glamour of the popular film industry, but we must still ask what work this cultural archive – which includes innumerable articles, features, and other films that I have not discussed – is doing. How effective is it in capturing the community's narratives of struggle and women's negotiations with social space, structured habits, and the possibility of change? Is mediatisation an adequate catalyst for economic and infrastructural development?

Conclusion: Habitus and Space

Arguably, this exceptional visual and textual archive relies upon cultural assumptions associated with the labels 'Muslim', 'woman', and 'boxer' (and even, perhaps, 'Kolkata') on a par with Dr Johnson's celebrated, misogynistic comment about women preachers: 'It is not done well; but you are surprised to find it done at all' (Boswell, 1906, p. 287). Johnson's dismissal of Quaker women preachers denies substance to their vocation: we too would be wrong to approach the self-affirmation of a community and group as a cultural curiosity. Razia Shabnam's rejection of standard assumptions about 'traditional' Muslim society, supposedly intent on secluding its women and holding them back, is a reminder that the social realities she negotiated in her own life were far more complex. We need to be more attentive to what these women are doing as actors in social space.

The objective structures in place within any community, the Bordieusian habitus, functions as 'a matrix of perceptions, appreciations, and action [and] makes possible the achievement of infinitely diversified tasks' (Bourdieu, 1977, p. 83). It is also a form of violence. As they grow up, girls are subjected to everyday behavioural injunctions and petty controls relating to physical deportment and posture, how food should be prepared and consumed, and how and when one should speak, thus inculcating durable, gender-differentiated bodily dispositions that they will reproduce in society. At the same time, within these crowded, impoverished neighbourhoods in Khidirpur-Ekbalpur-Watgunge, daily life is itself a struggle, laying bare the inadequacy of learned dispositions in closing the gap between aspiration and survival. Proximity in physical space functions as 'an organizational template for social space, identifying where and how capital is distributed, power is displayed and practiced, inequalities are reinforced, and oppositions are retained or eliminated'(Rashid, 2021, p. 47). In conditions of extreme hardship, women's work, both in domestic spaces and through the use of such space for monetary earnings through tailoring or embroidery, is absolutely vital, so that their agency as actors in and mediators of physical space is a visible element of these social structures. The identity of Muslim women and their conformity to religious norms must continually negotiate the social space available to them, the risks and violence of their environment, and their capacity for resistance.[5]

Boxing, a sport that draws both young boys and girls from these neighbourhoods, is not an accidental choice. It promises an alternative habitus, based upon long hours of bodily training and practice, a building up of physical and mental strength, and the expenditure of the self in a contact sport that is both exhausting and satisfying. While boxers may indeed hope, like other athletes in a poor nation like India, for jobs and rewards, the ring is itself a space of self-affirmation. As Saba Mahmood puts it,

> one result of Bourdieu's neglect of the manner and process by which a person comes to acquire a habitus is that we lose a sense of how specific conceptions of the self (there may be different ones that inhabit the space of a single culture) require different kinds of bodily capacities.
>
> (2005, p. 139)

Young women who box are impelled – like many other agents of social transformation – by a different conception of the self from the one that has been inculcated by their socioeconomic circumstances, yet it is *also*, in a sense, generated by the violence, vulnerability, exploitation, and need they experience every day, and which produces a considerable measure of community and family support for their aspirations. Like prayer for the Muslim women of Cairo, boxing for these girls and women allows them to put in the long hours of training and discipline that they realise is necessary for the inculcation of a new habitus, the pugilistic habitus that is not so much an instrument of emancipation as something that resides in the body, as a way of being. Boxing is not a symbolic act, not a social tool of 'empowerment'. It is a means, for this community and its members, particularly its women, for a construction of selfhood.

Notes

1 See Biswas, M.Z.H. (2015) 'Socio economic conditions of Muslims of West Bengal: an enquiry into their social exclusion', *International Journal of Humanities & Social Science Studies*, 2(2), pp. 2349–6711; and Hussain, N., Abbas, M.Z. and Owais, S. (2012) 'Muslims in West Bengal: trend of population growth and educational status', *Islam and Muslim Societies: A Social Science Journal*, 5(1), pp. 39–56.
2 Plans for a National Register of Citizens, revived along with the Citizenship Amendment Act, 2019, indicated that proof of citizenship would become more difficult, especially for Muslims. The Act led to widespread agitations, during which the civil rights activist Harsh Mander argued that Muslims were in fact truer 'Indians', saying: 'The Muslim brothers and sisters and children who are present here are Indian by choice. The rest of us are Indians by chance. We had no choice. We had only this country. You [Muslims] had a choice and your ancestors chose this country'. See 'Constitution, love, ahimsa: Harsh Mander's speech', *The Wire*, 5 March 2020.

Available at: https://thewire.in/rights/harsh-mander-jamia-speech-supreme-court-full-translation (Accessed: 5 September 2022).
3 See Kom, M.C.M. and Serto, D. (2013) *Unbreakable: an autobiography*. Delhi: Harper Collins, and Thoudam, N. (2022) 'Mary Kom's collaborative autobiography: negotiating authorship', *Journal of Comparative Literature and Aesthetics*, 45(3), pp. 70–80. For criticism of the decision to cast Priyanka Chopra as Kom, see: www.outlookindia.com/website/story/priyanka-chopra-the-role-of-mary-kom-should-have-gone-to-someone-from-the-northeast/409747.
4 David Trattles's photographs of the women boxers of Khidirpur were exhibited in Toronto in May 2006, toured India in 2007, and were shown as 'The Boxing Ladies' at the Seagull Arts and Media Resource Centre, Kolkata, in 2008. See www.davidtrattles.com/exhibitions/index.html
5 See Chaudhuri, S. (2022) 'Marked unsafe: women, violence, and the state of risk', in Ellman, P.L., Basak, J. and Schlesinger-Kipp, G. (eds.) *Psychoanalytic and sociocultural perspectives on women in India: violence, safety and survival*. London: Routledge, pp. 29–30.

Bibliography

Ahmed, M. (2002) *Interviews at KSOPC*, May-September 2022.
Banet-Weiser, S. (2018) *Empowered: popular feminism and popular misogyny*. Durham: Duke University Press.
Biswas, M.Z.H. (2015) 'Socio economic conditions of muslims of West Bengal: an enquiry into their social exclusion', *International Journal of Humanities & Social Science Studies*, 2(2), pp. 2349–6711.
Boswell, J. (1906) *The life of Samuel Johnson LL.D.* vol. 1. London: J.M. Dent.
Bourdieu, P. (1977) *Outline of a theory of practice*. Translated from the French by R. Nice. Cambridge: Cambridge University Press.
Bourdieu, P. (1993) *Sociology in question*. Translated from the French by R. Nice. London: Sage.
Bourdieu, P. (2004) *Science of science and reflexivity*. Translated from the French by R. Nice. Chicago: University of Chicago Press.
Bourdieu, P. (2005) 'Postface to Erwin Panofsky', *Gothic architecture and scholasticism*, in Holsinger, B. and Petit, L. (eds.) *The premodern condition: medievalism and the making of theory*. Chicago: University of Chicago Press, pp. 221–242.
Bourdieu, P. (2020) *Habitus and field. General sociology. vol. 2: Lectures at the Collège de France, 1982–1983*. Translated from the French by P. Collier. London: Polity Press.
The Boxing Girls of Kabul (2011) Directed by A. Nasr. [Documentary film]. *The Boxing Girls of Kabul*. New York City, NY: iN DEMAND.
Burqa Boxers (2016) Directed by A. Raghuram. [Documentary film]. *Burqa Boxers*. Junoon Pictures.
Cabinet Secretariat Government of India (2006) *Sachar committee report: social, economic and educational status of the Muslim community in India (2006) a report*. Available at: www.minorityaffairs.gov.in/WriteReadData/RTF1984/7830578798.pdf (Accessed: 20 June 2022).
Chaudhuri, S. (2012) 'In the ring: gender, spectatorship, and the body', *International Journal of the History of Sport*, 29(12), pp. 1759–1773.

Chaudhuri, S. (2022) 'Marked unsafe: women, violence, and the state of risk', in Ellman, P., Basak, J. and Schlesinger-Kipp, G. (eds.) *Psychoanalytic and socio-cultural perspectives on women in India: violence, safety and survival.* London: Routledge, pp. 20–31.

Crowder, N. (2015) 'Eye of the tiger: girls boxing for self-defense, empowerment in Kolkata, India', *Washington Post*, 19 May 2015. Available at: www.washingtonpost.com/news/in-sight/wp/2015/05/19/eye-of-the-tiger-girls-boxing-for-self-defense-empowerment-in-kolkata-india/ (Accessed: 20 June 2022).

Dasgupta, S. (2004) '"An inheritance from the British": the Indian boxing story', *International Journal of the History of Sport*, 21(3–4), pp. 433–451.

Dasgupta, S. (2012) *Bhiwani junction: the untold story of boxing in India.* Delhi: Harper Collins.

Farred, G. (2012) '"Keeping silent": the problem of citizenship for Lilian Thuram', *Ethnic and Racial Studies*, 35(6), pp. 1040–1058.

Fatima, Z. (2022a) *Interview at KSOPC*, 16 May 2022.

Fatima, Z. (2022b) *Interview at KSOPC*, 7 September 2022.

Hussain, N., Abbas, M.Z. and Owais, S. (2012) 'Muslims in West Bengal: trend of population growth and educational status', *Islam and Muslim Societies: A Social Science Journal*, 5(1), pp. 39–56.

Kom, M.C.M. and Serto, D. (2013) *Unbreakable: an autobiography.* Delhi: Harper Collins.

Mahmood, S. (2005) *Politics of piety: the Islamic revival and the feminist subject.* Princeton: Princeton University Press.

Mauss, M. (1973) 'Techniques of the body', *Economy and Society*, 2(1), pp. 70–85.

McDuie-Ra, D. (2015) '"Is India racist?": murder, migration and Mary Kom', *South Asia: Journal of South Asian Studies*, 38(2), pp. 304–319.

Mitra, P. (2008) *The bold and the beautiful',* documentary film, 13 mins., included in *'ungendering sport: towards a revaluation of the female athlete in India.* Unpublished PhD dissertation. Jadavpur University, Kolkata, India.

Mitra, P. (2009) 'Challenging stereotypes: the case of Muslim female boxers in Bengal', *International Journal of the History of Sport*, 26(12), pp. 1840–1851.

Nandakumar, A. (2019) *The boxing ladies*, 25 May. Available at: www.youtube.com/watch?v=HaSmfznzjEI (Accessed: 10 June 2022).

Oates, C.J. (1987) *On boxing.* New York, NY: Harper.

Rashid, M. (2021) *Physical space and spatiality in Muslim societies: notes on the social production of cities.* Ann Arbor: University of Michigan Press.

Sassu, A. (2015) *Photo-essay.* Available at: www.alicesassuphotography.com/a-fighting-spirit/ (Accessed: 20 June 2022).

Sen, E. (2021) 'Faizan Anwar, new kid in the boxing ring', *The Telegraph*, 21 September. Available at: www.telegraphindia.com/sports/faizan-anwar-new-kid-in-the-boxing-ring/cid/1831572 (Accessed: 7 September 2022).

Shabnam, R. (2022) *Interview at KSOPC*, 16 May.

Thoudam, N. (2022) 'Mary Kom's collaborative autobiography: negotiating authorship', *Journal of Comparative Literature and Aesthetics*, 45(3), pp. 70–80.

Trattles, D. (2004) *The boxing ladies.* Available at: www.davidtrattles.com/exhibitions/index.html (Accessed: 20 June 2022).

Wacquant, L.J.D. (2004) *Body and soul. Notebooks of an apprentice boxer.* New York, NY: Oxford University Press.

Chapter 5

Practicing Otherwise
Feminist Boxing Challenges Mainstream Narratives of Combat Sports

Elisa Virgili

Introduction

This chapter investigates the construction of genders in (or rather through) boxing. It investigates the construction of masculinities and femininities in a discipline traditionally considered masculine and still, albeit with major changes in recent years, practiced more by men. I focus on two specific community boxing gyms in Italy. These gyms engage with issues of gender construction in the sport by rethinking how boxing is practiced and experienced. The chapter examines how community gyms, such as the two case studies, function as sites where the rules of the sport can be changed. Through a focus on boxing bodies socialised as feminine, the chapter asks how community gyms and the bodies that inhabit them practice the deconstruction of hegemonic masculinity. The chapter argues that an understanding of the work within community feminist gyms helps destabilise and counter notions that boxing gyms are, or should be, the last bastion of masculinity. Through the adoption of the term *somateque*, I demonstrate how sport can be changed by the diversity of bodies who inhabit the sites where the sport is practiced and experienced. The plurality is important, for it is not through a single body that change occurs but through the collective. A feminist approach to rethinking the noble art from the ground up is criticality important; after all, nobility and feminism have not historically got along.

The experience of the Feminist Community Gym Le Sberle is told through the lens of my personal experience,[1] and the re-reading of academic and journalistic interviews through which the group has told its story over time. Therefore, I tried to report the very narrative that the group wants to give of itself through social media or stories within city or national political assemblies, but also in its own fanzine. On the other hand, the experience of the TeCiacco Gym in Naples was collected through an interview with one of its founders and through various exchanges that took place within a national coordination of community gyms – exchanges that included training and collective discussions.[2]

Training as a boxer has allowed me to use the body to better understand what it means to be a boxer and to embody the role of a woman boxer within the

DOI: 10.4324/9781003312635-7

different gyms I have attended over the years. As an ethnographic researcher I am affected by my subjectivity (my class and cultural background) as well as my body (my gender, sex, and race). My positionality conditions my research. On the one hand, my subjectivity and my body impact my perceptions and they contribute to how the reality unfolds and reveals itself as I observe and participate. Of course, there are different strategies offered by different disciplines to minimize this problem. The methodology used is, as mentioned, ethnographic or auto-ethnographic research, participatory research in which direct observation and face-to-face interaction are the main tools of analysis and in which the gymnasium is analysed as a theatre where the positions of actors and actresses occupying it are never random.

As a female white person, I have a different position from the Black girls who are part of the gym, but also from the few boys who attend it, and from non-binary people. I was able to not only see things from a different perspective (Woodword, 2004, pp. 60–64), but to also bring something different to the spaces I have walked through. However, my privilege sometimes did not allow me to see other dynamics or underestimate them. Ultimately, one is dealing with a sport where the body in its relationship with the other(s) plays a key role. The modification of body and its coming to terms with fear and pain are at the basis of this reflection, as depicted by Preciado, this is a body essay, a somato-political fiction, a theory of the self, or a self-theory. What comes into play or what I am interested in recounting, however, is not so much my perceptions or emotions as my own; what will be discussed here is, as previously mentioned, a personal perspective, also taking into account how this crosses political spaces and is part of a social field.

According to most feminists, personal histories are lenses through which one can read theoretical positions placing the body at the crossroads between a biological datum and a storehouse of cultural data and social dynamics. Feminist epistemology refers to embodied knowledge formed by bodies and experiences where the boundaries between the subject and the object of knowledge are blurred.

Incorporating Boxing

This research is conducted from the subjective and embodiment experiences (Channon and Jenning, 2014) of those who practice sports. This kind of phenomenological interpretation as applied to combat sports, for example, by Paradis, show how boxing practices are also incorporated from the perspective of gender in the way they take on movements that are considered typically masculine, in the way they change their body posture, and, finally, in the way they change the body itself to become more *masculine*.

There is quite a large body of literature, especially in sociology, that examines the construction of genders through sport, mostly based on how gendered postures are repeated and represented (Allen-Collinson, 2011, p. 291).

However, it may be reductive to think of acting in a strictly theatrical and representational sense. Perhaps it might be more useful to look at how genders are incorporated into the gymnasium from the phenomenological theory of acts (Al-Saji, 2000, p. 56). It is about understanding what social agents constitute reality through language, gestures, and symbolic signs. On whom constructs what, within phenomenology itself, the debate is still open: how much do I decide and define the reality around me and how much does the context define me as a subject (as an embodied subject)? Is it a chronologically linear process with a beginning and an end, or is it a constant development? Gender is constructed through repetition and the bodily practices in the boxing gym help construct gender, but can also contest hegemonic gender norms.

I'll start from Simone de Beauvoir's famous statement that 'women are not born but become', which somehow precisely reinterprets the doctrine of constitutive acts of the phenomenological tradition.

> In this sense, gender is not a stable identity or a locus of agentivity from which various acts descend; on the contrary, it is configured as an identity constituted weakly over time and instituted through the stylized repetition of the same acts and words. Moreover, gender is instituted through the stylization of the body and this, consequently, must be understood as the common-mode through which proxemics, movements and actualizations of various kinds constitute the illusion of a self-endowed with an enduring gender.
> (Butler, 2015, p. 120)

In other words, one cannot rely forever on being male or female and cling to their identity representations in their various declinations. To drop this quote into our context: I cannot expect and reproduce a standard model of femininity or masculinity in the repetition of the bodily acts of a sport, particularly a combat sport connoted by the construction of a typology of hegemonic masculinity. I cannot think that my being a woman (particularly in the gym, but also outside) is the same now as it was when I first trained, that my body and my gestures have not changed in relation to the bodies I have sweated with over the years, that, in turn, have changed as well (Channon and Phipps, 2017, pp. 32–35).

Gender, then, according to this interpretation, is continually given and constructed in the repetition of acts (be they linguistic or bodily), but it is not so much an outward-facing act as it is, so to speak, about taking up postures in the deepest sense of the term. It is in fact something that the body assumes, something that blurs the boundary between outside and inside, between social construction and biological datum, and between sex and gender. Gender is, then, not limited to an external act or a social norm to be respected, but is something we incorporate or have incorporated. It is not political but bio-political. Preciado (2015) helps us understand this concept even better. The subject, which is a body, is a living geopolitical archive, a 'somatheque' in which the experiences the subject has are deposited. In this particular case, it is the experiences of training, fighting, locker rooms, and attempts to radically change the norms that govern all of this.

Boxing bodies change, and particularly female bodies take on characteristics that are usually attributed to males: the shoulders and chest become larger, the arms muscular, and the body loses those soft lines one expects a woman to have. And all this is constantly observed and criticised by a sociocultural context based on heteronormativity. Especially when this is grafted onto already nonconforming, non-binary, trans, or non-white bodies. These bodies do not stay in the gym but inhabit the outside world and different social contexts where they bring their new characteristics. These new features are in themselves a challenge to the norms. However, they also perform their changed gender there. The body changes in the movements at the gym, having learned and incorporated jab/hook/mount. Furthermore, part of those movements determines the way we move outside the gym as well, even in redefining a feminine way of moving that, through different devices such as family, school, and friends, we have been taught since childhood. In this sense, the body is an archive, a somatheque, where different norms, teachings, and movements that define genders have been sedimented and, in turn, are defined by those who incorporate them, leaving a space open for negotiation on norms (Mennesson, June 2016).

The experience of the boxing gyms that are recounted in the following seek to show how this happens on and through the bodies of female boxers, not only as individuals training but as a sports-political group.

The Feminist Community Gym Le Sberle

To tell the story and experience of this gym and its users, I will start with an image: the gym's logo. The image depicts the effigy of the Virgin Mary, specifically the statue that sits atop Milan Cathedral, a symbol of the city. The Virgin Mary depicted on the logo, however, wears a sports bra and boxing gloves, and behind her waves the antifascist badge, not red and black but fuchsia and black. This image indicates several characteristics of Le Sberle's group and just as many tensions. The symbol is that of the city in which they are rooted, but it is also a symbol far from the city centre, far from the suburbs in which they train. It is a Catholic symbol that reminds us of the church's interference in the city and the bodies of the women who inhabit it, but it also reminds us of one of the struggles to be carried on: that for our own bodies, also through the community sport. The flag is the antifascist one, which, however, does not suffice per se; it is necessary to remember the feminist context.

The Transfeminist Community Gyms

Le Sberle is a community gym. Some of the boxers who train at Le Sberle and Te Ciacco in fact come from that background and continue to attend collective workouts organized by the community gym city network. Reflections on these gyms more generally thus derive in part from my own attendance at these gyms and in part from interviews with the female boxers who have attended and do attend them.

Assuming that there is no univocal definition due to the lack of strict codifications, an attempt will be made in brief to give a description of what community gyms are in Italy. This is only functional to understanding how they can be a different terrain for reasoning about gender categories than other types of gyms and how specifically the two experiences recounted here develop within this context (Piazza, 2012).

Community gyms are spaces that usually dwell within social centres at the national level, a project embedded in a certain subculture and political substratum that attempts to rethink sports. They develop within antifascist, self-managed and 'Occupy' movements, reflecting not only on the function of sports and what they should be and represent, but, transversally, also on the relationship between body and society that is characterised by mutual influence (Pedrini, 2020). Starting from an anti-capitalist reflection, community gyms usually offer free or almost free workouts, on the one hand to be accessible to anyone and on the other hand to untie sports from a commercial logic to rethink them as a social and political moment (Milan, 2019).

Le Sberle (literally, 'The Slaps') was born as a group in September 2018, during a three-day feminist camp at Ri-make, the occupied school where its attendees still train. Four girls who were training as boxers in other community gyms in Milan decided to launch a feminist community boxing workshop, without knowing exactly what this meant. It is clear how, in this context, the construction of gender and its deconstruction takes place in a different and radical way, in the sense of rethinking from the roots of the categories (Milan and Stefania Milan, 2020). It was, on the contrary, a form of reasoning by negatives: having experienced community boxing in other, by definition anti-sexist, contexts, they began to develop the idea that it was not enough to remove sexist behaviours and words from training and locker rooms but it was also necessary to start over – to radically transform the spaces where they train in the most literal and political sense of transforming at the root.

As Akim Oualhaci points out – albeit in a very different context both in terms of discipline (Thai boxing) and geographical position (the research is set among banlieues in Paris) – in community gyms, with regard to combat sports, there is a tension between the valorisation of community masculinity that we might define 'militant' in the classical sense, and respectable masculinity. This tension is open to and in dialogue with the principles of anti-sexism, which seeks to deconstruct the stereotypical characteristics of masculinity and a certain antifascist machismo, but also those of the boxer himself and the gymnasium as preparation for street confrontation. In the popular Italian gyms I have observed and trained in, the deconstruction of this figure of the boxer-militant is an issue. This figure is challenged during training in the following ways: preferring technique over strength and talking about respect for the sparring partner and attention to differences in bodies and experience. In parallel, this figure is also questioned in assemblies through reflection on turns to speak and the space to be left for people who do not usually speak. These are small, everyday practices that deconstruct *machism* in the gym as well as political *leaderism*, figures that often match in popular gyms. More generally, the questioning of power devices leads, if only by logical inference, to the questioning of masculinity.

There is a difference in terms of generational characteristics whereby younger people, who have come into more contact with contemporary feminist movements, have a different predisposition to questioning masculinity. Conversely, those who train or have a central role in the life of the gym, which passes through, for example, seniority of presence within the same gym, also play a significant role in legitimising these practices. However, it seems that it is mainly in the relationship that each person establishes with another subject that hegemonic masculinity is really challenged ('relationship' understood as the very bodily and practical one of the exercises and the discussions that take place outside and inside the gym).

The context in which this takes place is that of public space, also understood as a space of social and political conflicts, largely occupied by male subjectivities and an equally occupied sports space. Here, the very presence of women in 'male' spaces/sports disrupts and troubles the hegemonic practices that take place within them. How masculinity and, by virtue, all genders are constructed and performed in those spaces is altered by the presence of female-presenting bodies. However, their presence alone does not lead to an egalitarian atmosphere and set of practices. Female-presenting bodies still need to negotiate rigid perceptions of gender norms and their bodies are conditioned through the practices that have helped establish notions of militant and respectable masculinities within the Italian context. Within feminist boxing gyms, participants seek to question gender in a more holistic and radical manner, not by simply removing sexist behaviour and practising anti-sexism, but by developing tools to break loops and perform boxing (and therefore gender) differently. The very presence of women in traditionally 'male' spaces and sports disrupts and troubles the hegemonic practices that take place within them through the presence of their bodies, discussions, and adaptation of practices. This can take place in a more or less confrontational manner. This is not meant to claim that women in gyms have a pedagogical function, or even that it is only one of conflict. Rather, it is to understand how female boxers and, more specifically, female masculinity, can disrupt the machinery of heteronormative genders (Matthews, 2015).

Bodies and Spaces

In order to start over from the roots, then, it is necessary to plant these roots in new soil first. The Sberle's Gym location choice was not casual. Physically, it is a former school with a gymnasium inside it and this was logistically advantageous. Over the years, then, tools, bags, and gloves were added to be available to all. Arranging the space was first and foremost an exercise in self-management, but also an opportunity to rethink the spatial organisation of a gym (Sassatelli, 2000), starting from the locker room that was designed to be mixed. Such an attempt has already been carried out by several other community gyms: locker rooms in community gyms are often absent, partly for practical reasons. An initial division between genders is thus eliminated, and the absence of the locker room also alters that transition between gender roles outside the gym and those assumed during training. However, in a place where the majority of bodies are female, trans, or non-binary, this creates a dimension where most subjectivities feel safer, non-judged, and non-sexualised. Of course, the attempt of other community gyms remains valid but, once again, it is a matter of reversing the perspective starting with the bodies occupying that space. A mixed locker room where most people are straight, cis males still turns out to be a place that is at least challenging for all other subjectivities, even if anti-sexist practices and reflections are carried out in that same place. Additional small attention to the care of the body – of all bodies – make the locker room more welcoming, like a shelf with tampons available to all and personal hygiene products. Ultimately, arranging the space has also meant researching, learning, and incorporating new skills usually thought to be typically male-oriented and socially part of informal male upbringings, such as using a drill to assemble punching bag brackets and other manual labour.

The roots were planted so deeply in that place also, and especially, for another reason: other feminist collectives had passed and were established there, and this guaranteed a favourable foundation the community gymnasium, values in common with the other activities in the space, and opportunities to share practices and knowledge. So, the first event was the community feminist boxing workshop, which was well attended both by people completely new to the discipline and boxers from other community gyms who answered the call to rethink boxing practices together from a feminist perspective. Thus, a need felt by many was being somehow addressed. From that moment on, the group continued with weekly and bi-weekly training sessions. But what does it mean to rethink boxing from a feminist perspective (Guthrie, 1997, p. 22)? In practice, the group tries to organise the workouts in a horizontal and self-managed manner. More experienced boxers lead most of the training, but all are invited to propose exercises and especially, while attending the gym and gaining more skills, users are invited to share them and take care of part of the training. Those who do not feel like contributing in this way can take care of other aspects, like cleaning the space or preparing dinner after the workout.

During the sessions, users must constantly try to remember that each person can train as far as they can/want to. If anyone experiences excessive fatigue or is afraid to do an exercise, no one will be pushed to do it (Young,

1980). Rather, the invitation is to listen to one's body to understand its limitations and possibilities. This is perhaps one of the main elements of deconstructing boxing as built on masculine value parameters, as mentioned earlier (Mennesson, 2016). To aim not at endurance at all costs but at listening to one's own body is, on the one hand, deconstructing the kind of hegemonic masculinity inherent in boxing values and, on the other, promoting one of the foundational practices of feminism (Virgili, 2017). A further step is to do it in the relationship with others: to know how to listen to one's own body in relation to the feedback that the partner gives us during an exercise or during sparring and, vice versa, to know how to interpret the signs that the other person gives us in order to modulate the exercise as well as create a space of freedom where all feel able to make suggestions on how to improve the exercise and ask to moderate force or speed. An attempt is made not to eliminate biological differences between bodies, but to enhance them. This is also a reversal of perspective: mixed training does not mean that I must train like male boxers, but that together we can organise a different kind of training to enhance different sports parameters ranging from strength, technique, and strategy. Consequently, we can understand how different bodies can make more use of one parameter or another (Spencer, 2011). In the specifics of training, talking about a feminist approach means having attention to bodies, starting with the muscular component that is different, the physical fitness, the sports experience, and the psychological security that one has been able to achieve with their body.

The goal is to practice an accessible sport where the diversity and the difference of the other must be at the service of the group, and the training is based on the exchange and continuous comparison that can lead to the well-being and the feeling of security of each individual component. Of course, this process is not without its critical issues, like the relationship between the individual person and the group, the difficulty of improving athletically while remaining an accessible group, and the difficulty of being able to mediate between the competition component (even with oneself) of the sport and inclusiveness. A further difficulty lies in a fundamental characteristic of boxing: aggression. Although this is considered a socially masculine characteristic, it is also present in the type of boxing we are describing here.

Trying to be men, or making oneself bear the 'markers of masculinity', shapes the experience of males and influences their attitudes and behaviours, whether they adhere to a hegemonic ideal of masculinity or construct themselves in reaction to it. Given the role that homosociality and competition play in dominant masculinity, some places are traditionally considered 'more masculine' than others – among them, certainly the sports context. Boxing gyms are, in general, a masculine environment permeated by values – respect, courage, competition, and physical strength – claimed within the gym as related to a specific gender affiliation (Woodword, 2004). There are few women boxers in the gym, and even fewer who make it to the fight. The male presence characterising gyms is considered natural to all its members; in contrast, the female presence, as exceptional, must be argued and legitimised, particularly in commercial gyms. The female body in a boxing gym continues to be perceived as a foreign body, acceptable only to the extent that it is defeminised, if it has unremarkable feminine traits and 'beats like a man'. The vulnerability of bodies, in a context of hegemonic masculinity, is not considered.

We can understand how the construction of the feminine gender takes place through changes and contradictions in boxing since we are talking about entering a typically masculine sphere and by contrast the characteristics of genders appear to us more clearly. But what I would like to do here is to see how two gyms constructed primarily by women and non-binary subjectivities also modifies the other pole and the way one can think combats sports. I would then begin to see how this is constructed: masculinity is not necessarily tied to a body biologically identified as masculine; it is not a simple effect of the male body, any more than femininity is of the biologically feminine body.

Even for a woman, being masculine does not necessarily mean being the same as men; it does not mean imitating men. Here, Halberstam (1998) comes to our aid with their *Female Masculinities* text. Through its pages, a long history of female masculinity is told, intersected with a history not only of gender, but also of sexual orientation.

Normalised society seems to identify what masculinity is quite clearly. Indeed, it consolidates those more normal versions of masculinity subjectivities built on the subordination of possible alternative versions of masculinity itself – meaning that one way of being male (usually straight, white, and winning) prevail over others (Hickey, 2008). 'Society reduces any form of female masculinity to a deviation and a deviation from the norm constituted by dominant masculinity so that the latter – the masculinity of males – can present itself as authentic' (Halberstam, 1998, p. 10). Masculinity becomes legible precisely when it abandons the body of middle-class white males and when it abandons its most taken-for-granted position – so taken for granted that it is no longer conceived as a social construction, but as a natural normality.

The presence of women within gyms, through varying degrees of 'imitating masculinities', is functional to this mechanism to reveal what the dominant masculinity is, but if this occurs within the context of community boxing, it is not yet another mechanism for legitimising hegemonic masculinity but, instead, a device for highlighting and deconstructing it (Lauriola et al., 2004).

> It may be, as some influential voices claim, that somehow masculinity or masculinities are not the exclusive property of biologically male subjects – it is absolutely true that many biologically female subjects claim masculinity as their property. However, in terms of cultural and political power, it still makes some difference when masculinity occurs in biological males.
> (Connell and Messerschmidt, 2005)

This statement shows both that it is the correspondence between masculinity and males that sustains the social legitimacy of hegemonic masculinity itself, and how questioning of these very subjects is extremely effective.

What function, starting from a different perspective, namely the one of a gymnasium composed of primarily non-masculine bodies, can change a space and discipline that has long been based on masculinity? How do the two groups recounted in this text manage not only to practice a different kind of boxing in their gyms but to change an imaginary and constituted practice? We will see how these two gyms intersect with other more typically masculine collectives by trying to mix their practices, how they try to make their idea of boxing visible in public spaces, and how a workout becomes a political practice and gender deconstruction (Rana, 2017).

The predominance of female, trans, or non-binary bodies also influences the bodies of cis males at the time when the male subjectivities that train in this group have a dissident approach towards hegemonic masculinity, to the point that they claim it in other contexts they would not have felt comfortable practicing the sport because of homosocial environments where a certain expectation of masculinity is present. This different type of boxing practice is cultivated within the gymnasium, but also needs to go out into the streets to confront the outside world. Above all, however, it has to show the outside world different imagery of boxing and, at the same time, recover public space (such as parks) that are often unwelcoming to women who practice sports. Indeed, there have been several outdoor training sessions by this group, both in city parks and on political anniversaries, such as March 8 or April 25 (the day celebrating the liberation from the fascist regime in 1945). On the latter two occasions, the purpose was twofold: to be visible in public space but also to reiterate that this way of practicing sports is a way of doing politics and thinking. It is also a means of showing resistance to the disciplining that would like women's bodies to be weak, functional for reproduction, and relegated to the domestic space.

The former school site of the gymnasium, however, was vacated in July 2022. The Le Sberle group is still active and training in the park next to the former school, precisely because of the talk about visibility and public space that was made in the previous paragraph. However, this situation raises another issue: that of vulnerability (Crews and Lennox, 2020).

It is first about the vulnerability of individual bodies in the discipline of boxing: the possibility of hitting, being hit, feeling physical pain. This was at the centre of the group's discussions, particularly with respect to the mode of sparring and its intensity. This discussion is further complicated in relation to gender. The vulnerability of bodies seems not to be considered in gyms where most of those who spar are cis males. Thus, one of the changes that the feminist approach to the discipline of boxing can bring is precisely the consideration of bodies and subjects as vulnerable. The perception of vulnerability during outdoor training appeared even more evident, due to being exposed to cold, rain, and darkness. And it appeared not only as vulnerability of individuals, but as vulnerability of a political collective that is no longer in its safe space. Without a space, one is vulnerable precisely as a community: it is difficult to maintain the frequency of training, to organise discussions, or to feel comfortable in a space (Butler, 2015, pp. 91–93).

The Te Ciacco Experience in Naples

During their journey at Le Sberle, particularly during a solidarity initiative for sex workers promoted in the spring of 2020, they had the opportunity to get to know the Te Ciacco group of the Palestra Popolare Vincenzo Leone in Naples. I personally participated in the organisation of this campaign and the meetings between the two gyms. The group responded in a different way to a need that the two groups have in common: dealing with hegemonic masculinities. In fact, the Te Ciacco group also originated from some boxers who used to train in the Palestra Popolare as a mixed group, but felt the need to reflect differently on both the discipline of boxing and their own bodies (McCaughey, 1998).

The response they gave is different from the one from Le Sberle because they created a self-defence group encompassing different disciplines, from boxing to stick fighting to dance, and also pursued the principles of true feminist self-defence (Hollander, 2015, p. 200). Again, here the training is not structured by a trainer, but is rather conducted from time to time by a different person who offers the training. The physical workout is always followed by a small session where they discuss how they felt during the workout, the feelings they felt about their own bodies and in relation to others, the points to be improved, and the feel-good situations. This is also a feature in common with the Le Sberle group. The major differences between the two community gyms are the choice of discipline (self-defence instead of boxing) and the creation of a women-only group in the latter case (not in the biological sense). Concerning the discipline, Le Sberle has always emphasised that they do not practice self-defence, but boxing. This is because one of the most frequent questions asked of them as a feminist group is whether they practiced self-defence, as if it were almost impossible to think of boxing in this perspective that is not for defence (De Welde, 2003, p. 25).

What there is in feminist boxing is a certain awareness of their own potential, which is less expressed compared to men. In sports education, girls are rarely directed towards combat sports, and it becomes even more difficult when they grow up to express the characteristics required for this type of sport. In the gym, you can understand the effect a punch has on your body, understand how to deal with it, and understand the effects of physical pain. You can also understand what it means to punch another body. It is about becoming aware of one's own physicality – a habit that female bodies are usually less accustomed to (Guthrie, 1997, pp. 26–28). Most of the (mostly ethnographic) research investigating the relationship between gender and combat sports has focused on self-defence and how it is an avenue of resistance of the body and subject to the heteronormative system. A resistance that is based on a mechanism of both physical and psychological empowerment.

One of the most common and trivial questions people ask when a woman declares that she practices boxing is: so, if someone attacked you on the street. would you know how to defend yourself? On closer inspection, however, this question is not so trivial if you go a little deeper and look at it from the perspective of gender embodiment and about how the body confidence gained in training is a feeling that the body and the subject carry outside the gym into the streets. What McCaugheghey called 'physical feminism' is a process that deconstructs an assumed natural weakness of the female body (and subject). However, such a unilateral path is not sufficient. Certainly, the workouts are primarily work on the body, on one's own subjectivity, as well as endurance. With boxing, one learns not to defend oneself from aggression, but one begins to have a perception of oneself as a subject who does not always need by defended by someone else. Through boxing, you understand how strong you can be and what your body can do, even if this does not necessarily mean being able to defend yourself against an attack. It is about thinking of yourself as a strong subject/body in your own right, beyond having to defend yourself. Te Ciacco's self-defence, on the other hand, began precisely with the intention of being able to defend oneself, even in the street and not as a sporting discipline *tout court*.

The second relevant difference is that of the choice to not have a mixed group. The choice of Le Sberle was what some French collectives call *Mixitè Choisie*, being open to all but in the awareness of starting with bodies that are usually excluded. Several studies argue that mixed training, and thus the possibility of 'swapping' with people of the opposite gender, is already a step towards subverting gender norms. The experiences that have been recounted in this chapter, on the other hand, show how it is necessary to go a step further than mixed training; in fact, it is necessary to accompany this with political discourse on the deconstruction of norms, otherwise the risk is that of feeding other norms and stereotypes, for example by validating the stereotype that the only women who can box are the masculine ones or the only women who can access the men's gym space are the ones who are as good as males.

Moreover, it is the same methodological assumptions of this research that fuels this result. If, in fact, the analysis is based on male/female categories anchored to biological sex and not on an analysis of how different masculinities and femininities are performed, and, above all, it is taken for granted that there is a binary approach and correspondence between biological data and gender, the result can only be a re-proposition of gender norms, albeit with some variation. The girls in Naples chose, instead, to try a space that they felt was safer for all and a confrontation between more similar bodies facing the same difficulties. This does not mean remaining a closed group, but instead trying to get to know each other to face external difficulties together. Unfortunately, the specific experience of this group ended due to several difficulties of the gymnasium, but many of them have opened up more and more to the outside world by bringing boxing and stick fighting training sessions to the squares of their neighbourhoods to involve as many people as possible and, already with their presence of female bodies practicing combat sports in the squares, they contribute to changing the image of this sport.

Conclusions

In professional women's boxing matches we often see female boxers somehow mimic the male modes of boxing: the tension before the bout, the challenge, an arrogance that may not have so much to do with competitive play. Those images pose the question: do we really want to get to that ring in those ways? What is the price to be paid? Obviously, the prices to be paid would be many, foremost among them being that the link between sports and neoliberalism imposes on us. However, in this article, this path was not taken explicitly, even though it was discussed to some extent. In fact, the perspective of this article is primarily one of gender, and the questions asked are about whether to conform to a sports canon that is also a male canon. The two experiences that have been recounted have tried to answer this question through their attempts, but it is no coincidence that these attempts have been made within the context of popular sports where many other parameters of sport are being sought to be questioned, including that of being embedded in a neoliberal context that very often delineates the characteristics of the sport itself and, perhaps, of the genders that participate in it.

Through the account of the Community Feminist Gym Le Sberle and TeCiacco in Naples, we saw how the attempt to not be assimilated into the ways of a sport built on masculine canons as if they were universal and neutral is a radical one. We saw how these female boxers started from mixed contexts but felt the need to start from the ground up by founding new gyms where they could rethink boxing for their bodies. They have tried to rethink spaces, ways of training, ways of relating. While it is true that many of the characteristics that make sports masculine and feminine are socially constructed characteristics, it is also true that this social construction is inscribed in our bodies, and it is through these that we can change the canons of boxing and not try to force our bodies within existing ones.

Notes

1 I have been training with this group for three and a half years. My participation could partly be described as autoethnographic research. However, as my participation in the group preceded the research, I tried to base the analysis on interviews, collective discussions, and published material, as I will explain in more detail later.
2 The latter of which also took place online.

Bibliography

Allen-Collinson, J. (2011) 'Feminist phenomenology and the woman in the running body', *Sport, Ethics & Philosophy*, 5(3), pp. 287–302.

Al-Saji, A. (2000) 'The site of affect in Husserl's phenomenology: sensations and the constitution of the lived body', *Philosophy Today*, 44, pp. 51–59.

Amodeo, A.L., Antuoni, S., Claysset, M. and Esposito, C. (2020) 'Traditional male role norms and sexual prejudice in sport organizations: a focus on Italian sport directors and coaches', *Social Sciences*, 9(12), p. 218.

Brecklin, L.R. (2009) 'Evaluation outcomes of self-defence training for women: a review', *Aggression and Violent Behaviour*, 13(1), pp. 60–76.

Butler, J. (1989) *Gender trouble: feminism and the subversion of identity*. London: Routledge.

Butler, J. (2015) *Notes toward a performative theory of assembly*. London: Routledge.

Channon, A. and Jennings, G. (2014) 'Exploring embodiment through martial arts and combat sports: a review of empirical research', *Sport in Society*, 17(6), pp. 773–789.

Channon, A. and Matthews, C.R. (eds.) (2015) *Global perspectives on women in combat sports. Women warriors around the world*. London: Palgrave Macmillan.

Channon, A. and Phipps, C. (2017) 'Pink gloves still give black eyes: exploring "alternative" femininity in women's combat sports', *Martial Arts Studies*, 3, pp. 24–37.

Crews, S. and Lennox, P.S. (2020) *Boxing and performance*. London: Routledge.

De Welde, K. (2003) 'Getting physical: subverting gender through self-defense', *Journal of Contemporary Ethnography*, 32(3), pp. 247–278.

Guthrie, S.R. (1995) 'Liberating the amazon: feminism and the martial arts', *Women & Therapy*, 16(2–3), pp. 107–119.

Guthrie, S.R. (1997) 'Defending the self: martial arts and women's self-esteem', *Women in Sport & Physical Activity Journal*, 6(1), pp. 1–28.

Halberstam, J. (1998) *Female masculinity*. Durham: Duke University Press.

Haraway, D. (2008) 'Situated knowledges: the science question in feminism and the privilege of partial perspective author', *Feminist Studies*, 14(3), pp. 575–599.

Hickey, C. (2008) 'Physical education, sport and hyper-masculinity in schools', *Sport, Education and Society*, 13(2), pp. 147–161.

Hollander, J.A. (2015) 'Outlaw emotions: gender, emotion and transformation in women's self-defence training', in Channon, A. and Matthews, C.R. (eds.) *Global perspectives on women in combat sports: women warriors around the world*. Basingstoke: Palgrave Macmillan, pp. 187–203.

Jennings, L.A. (2014) *She's a knockout! A history of women's fighting sports*. Lanham: Rowman & Littlefield.

Lauriola, M., Zelli, A., Calcaterra, C., Cherubini, D. and Spinelli, D. (2004) 'Sport gender stereotypes in Italy', *International Journal of Sport Psychology*, 35(3), pp. 189–206.

Matthews, C.R. (2015) 'The Tyranny of the male preserve', *Gender & Society*, 30(2), pp. 312–333.

McCaughey, M. (1998) 'The fighting spirit: women's self-defence training and the discourse of sexed embodiment', *Gender & Society*, 12(3), pp. 277–300.

Mennesson, C. (2016) '"Hard" women and "soft" women: the social construction of identities among female boxers', *International Review for the Sociology of Sport*, 35(1), pp. 21–33.

Milan, C. (2019) 'Rebelling against time: recreational activism as political practice among the Italian precarious youth', *American Behavioral Scientist*, 63(11), pp. 1519–1538.

Milan, C. and Milan, S. (2020) 'Fighting gentrification from the boxing ring: how community gyms reclaim the right to the city', *Social Movement Studies*, 20(6), pp. 722–739.

Pedrini, L. (2020) *La boxe popolare*. Roma: Novalogos.

Piazza, G. (2012) 'Il movimento delle occupazioni di squat e centri sociali in Europa: una introduzione', *Partecipazione e conflitto*, 1, pp. 5–18.

Preciado, P. (2015) *Testo tossico. Sesso, droghe e biopolitiche nell'era farmacopornografica*. Roma: Fandango.

Rana, J. (2017) 'Ladies-only! Empowerment and comfort in gender-segregated kickboxing in the Netherlands', in Ratna, A. and Samie, S.F. (eds.) *Race, gender and sport: the politics of ethnic 'other' girls and women*. London: Routledge, pp. 148–167.

Sassatelli, R. (2000) *Anatomia della palestra: cultura commerciale e disciplina del corpo*. Milano: Il Mulino.

Spencer, D. (2011) *Homosociality, (homo)eroticism, and dueling practice in ultimate fighting and embodiment*. London: Routledge.

Virgili, E. (2017) 'Queering the box(e)', *Whatever. A Transdisiplinary Journal of Queer Theories and Studies*, 1, pp. 199–203.

Woodward, K. (2014) 'Legacies of 2012: putting women's boxing into discourse', *Contemporary Social Science*, 9(2), pp. 242–252.

Woodword, K. (2004) *Questioning identity: gender, class and nation*. London: Routledge.

Young, I.M. (1980) 'Throwing like a girl: a phenomenology of feminine body comportment motility and spatiality', *Human Studies*, 3(2), pp. 137–156.

Chapter 6

Reflections on the Empowerment of Women in Boxing from Athletes and Coaches in Norway Female Box

Anne Tjønndal

Introduction

Boxing is widely recognised as a male-dominated and gender-inequitable sport at all levels around the world (Lewandowski, 2022; Tjønndal, 2017; Woodward, 2006). Men's dominance in boxing is perhaps not surprising due to the valorisation of the knockout finish in boxing competitions in films and pop culture. Arguably, knocking someone out is an achievement associated with men, masculinity, and aggressiveness, rather than femininity and women. In Olympic boxing, international competitions for women were not arranged until 1994.[1] The first European Championship and World Championship was held in 2001. Women's involvement in boxing is increasing, especially since the inclusion of women's boxing in the 2012 Summer Olympics in London, UK (Smith, 2014). However, despite gaining acceptance in the Olympic Games, the number of spots open to women boxers are still substantially lower than their male counterparts. This was the case in London in 2012, Rio in 2016, and Tokyo in 2020.

My personal boxing experience is mainly situated in Norway, a country celebrated as a 'champion of gender equality'. I was a boxer long before I became a sport sociologist. My boxing journey began at the age of 16, and it was pure chance that I happened to find myself in a boxing gym as a teenager. At that time my mother had just been diagnosed with cancer and her illness defined much of my everyday life. I desperately needed to find a space that gave me a break from dealing with my mother's illness, and one day I saw an advert in the local newspaper for beginner boxing classes. The advert specified that boxing was great for 'for girls and boys', so I went to a class.

I never expected to fall in love with boxing, but what I felt at my first training session can only be described as love at first sight. Sadly, my mother died just five months after I started boxing. However, I truly believe that boxing helped me to cope with the grief of losing her at such a young age. My love of boxing led to a 15-year career as a boxer. I've been a national champion, a national pound-for-pound champion, boxed for the national team, and won medals at European tournaments. I was never a great boxer, but nevertheless

DOI: 10.4324/9781003312635-8

exceeded my own expectations of what I could achieve in the ring. As my love of boxing continued, I began educating myself as a referee and a coach. Over the last 20 years I have held multiple board memberships in local, regional, and national boxing organisations and have coached boys, girls, adults, children, and athletes of all skills. My experiences as a woman in boxing form the basis of this chapter and for my research on women's boxing in general. Even in Norway, a nation celebrated as a 'champion of gender equality', women are underrepresented in participation and leadership in boxing (Tjønndal and Hovden, 2016).

The aim of this chapter is to share some of my reflections on how boxing organisations could empower women in boxing as athletes, coaches, leaders, and volunteers. Specifically, in this chapter I examine and reflect on my experiences as a boxer, leader, and coach, and combine these with a meta-analysis of the knowledge I have accumulated about women's boxing through a decade of dedicated research. The result of this is a presentation of four key reflections on empowering women in boxing, all of which are illustrated using qualitative research data from a variety of previous research projects on women's boxing.

In the following section I briefly describe the context of my boxing experiences and most of my research: the development of women's boxing in Norway and the Norway Female Box project. Following this, I present some key topics and trends in current research on women's boxing globally. The third section of the chapter presents some methodological reflections on my endeavour to engage in this semi-autoethnographic and semi-meta-analysis of previous research. Finally, the second half of the chapter presents four reflections on empowering women in boxing, based on experiences from running the Norway Female Box projects and ten years of research on women's boxing.

Context: The Development of Women's Boxing in Norway and the Norway Female Box Project

While boxing has been a part of Norwegian sport for more than 100 years, women's boxing is a relatively new phenomenon, dating back to the 1980s (Goksøyr, 2008; Tjønndal, 2016). Women's boxing has grown rapidly in a rather short space of time, both in Norway and Scandinavia as a whole. Before 1988, women's boxing competitions were prohibited in Norway (Skoglöv, 2002). Since then, women's boxing has evolved substantially, from total exclusion to the International Boxing Association's (IBA) acceptance of women's amateur boxing (1994), the first World and European Championships (2001), and inclusion in the 2012 Summer Olympics. In this brief period, women's boxing has experienced considerable growth with regard to acceptance, participation, and gender equality. Thus, Norway, along with the rest of Scandinavia, seems to have been one step ahead in working towards equality and equal opportunities for female boxers. Norway has even produced one of the greatest women professional boxers of all time: Cecilia 'The First Lady' Brækhus.

As of 2022, approximately 24% of the members of the Norwegian Boxing Association are women. However, only 9% of registered boxing coaches are women (Hovden and Tjønndal, 2019). The project Norway Female Box was initiated in 2017 as a national project organised and funded by the Norwegian Boxing Association. The project was created by two women, myself and my coaching partner, Vera Schnabel. Our aim with the creation of Norway Female Box is twofold. First, the project aims to support female athletes by providing them with more opportunities to develop their boxing skills together with other women boxers and women coaches. This is important because many female boxers train in local clubs where most of the members are boys and men. In other words, they experience being in the minority in their daily sporting environments. Although training with men can be good practice, it does not simulate a realistic boxing situation in the same way as sparring with other women. The long-term goal is therefore to develop more female Norwegian boxers who can compete at an internationally high level. Second, Norway Female Box aims to recruit, empower, and support female boxing coaches, referees, volunteers, and leaders. The main activities in the project centre around training camps, participation in international tournaments, and social and educational activities. Typically, the project hosts national women-only training camps 3–4 times a year in different parts of Norway, supports participation in international tournaments, and hosts 1–2 educational activities.

The Norway Female Box project has its own logo. The story behind its development exemplifies the bottom-up nature of this women-centred approach to empowering women in boxing. To determine a logo, we held a competition in which girls and women from all Norwegian boxing clubs were encouraged to submit their own designs. The athletes then voted for their favourite proposal at one of the Norway Female Box training camps. Thus, the logo (shown here) was designed by an athlete and chosen by the athletes themselves.

The aim to support, develop, and recruit women coaches is implemented in several ways in Norway Female Box. Firstly, all the activities (training camps, competition trips, educational courses) are planned and organised by local women coaches in cooperation with the two head coaches (Anne and Vera). Thus, the coaches gain experience in planning, leading, and coordinating boxing activities and are able to practise and assume a head coach role in groups of 40–70 athletes; a role that most female coaches rarely experience in their local clubs. In addition, women coaches gain experience in coaching athletes in competitions and in practising team roles like cutman (responsible for preventing and treating physical damage to a fighter during the breaks between rounds) and coach. Norway Female Box also provides financial

Figure 6.1 Norway Female Box

support for women coaches who want to go abroad and gain their international coaching degrees with the International Boxing Association (IBA) and by hosting all-women coaching and referee courses. One of the main objectives is to make female coaches feel more capable of dealing with the various situations that can arise in competition settings, where injuries and knockouts can occur in a split second.

As of 2022, the Norway Female Box project has hosted collaborations with boxing clubs in Sweden, Belgium, England, and Ireland. Typically, between 50–60 women athletes (aged 10–50+) attend our national training camps. The project is currently partly funded through the Norwegian Boxing Association and has received 4 million NOK from DNB Sparebankstiftelsen to continue the project until 2026.

Current Research on Women's Boxing Around the World

Within the sociology of sport, most scholarly attention has been given to men's boxing, including famous works such as John Sugden's *Boxing and Society: An International Analysis* (1996) and Loïc Wacquant's studies of professional boxing in America (1995, 2001), as well as more recent sociological work (Matthews, 2019, 2021). In many boxing studies, both sociological and in other sport science fields, there is also a substantial sex-data gap (Wright, 2020; Matthews, 2020), which means that the genders of the boxers included in the sample are not discussed, mentioned, or analysed in a meaningful way (Zazryn, Finch and McCrory, 2003; Tjønndal, 2022). However, the marginalisation of women in boxing research is changing. Besides the early work of Jennifer Hargreaves (1994, 1997), women's boxing has gained increased attention from sport scholars around the globe since the early 2000s. The research on women's boxing is thematically and theoretically broad, but lacks cohesion and joint systematic efforts. For instance, there are multiple works on the history of women's boxing internationally (Smith, 2014; Gammel, 2012) and in various national contexts, such as Mexico (Van Bavel, 2022), the US (Gems and Pfister, 2014; Pfister and Gems, 2017), the Global South (Schneider, 2021), Norway (Tjønndal, 2016), South Korea (Kim, Kwon and Lee, 2015), and more.

Thematically, research on women's boxing has tackled issues such as the inclusion of women's boxing in the Olympic Games (Linder, 2012; Tjønndal, 2017), identity construction among female boxers, and female boxers' competition uniforms (Mennesson, 2000), to mention but a few. Research on women's boxing has also started to take intersectionality into consideration, with studies of different groups of women in boxing. For instance, there are a few studies of Muslim women's experiences of participation in boxing in different socio-geographical contexts (Mitra, 2009; Kipnis and Caudwell, 2015; Tjønndal and Jorid Hovden, 2021).

There is now a growing body of literature on women's terms and conditions as participants in the male-dominated sport of boxing, as athletes, coaches, volunteers, referees, and officials. Several studies have demonstrated how women boxers face gendered barriers and resistance to their sporting aspirations (Lafferty and MacKay, 2004; Tjønndal, 2019; Jennings and Velázquez, 2015). For instance, Cove and Young (2007) find that boxing coaches are hesitant to invest time and training in female boxers due to their current or expected family obligations. Some studies have examined similar barriers for women entering other roles in the sport of boxing. In our studies of women boxing coaches (Hovden and Tjønndal, 2021), we find that they often struggle to be accepted as 'real' coaches by male coaches and male and female athletes. In another study, McCree (2015) highlights the gendered barriers that female boxing officials face in Trinidad and Tobago. Similarly, Fitzgerald, Stride, and Drury (2022) highlight that women volunteers in boxing often have to prove themselves as capable in order to gain the respect of their peers in the community. Based on the current body of research, there is still a long way to go before gender equity in boxing is a reality for the women involved in the sport.

Methods: The Empirical Basis of the Chapter

The empirical basis for this chapter is a meta-analysis of ten years of previous research on women's boxing in Norway. Since 2014, boxing has been a substantial part of my academic work through multiple research projects.

Table 6.1 Empirical Basis of the Chapter

Tjønndal (2020)	78 social media posts by Norwegian boxing clubs and coaches during the 2020 COVID-19 pandemic
Tjønndal and Hovden (2021)	Six interviews with two immigrant Muslim women boxers in Norway
Tjønndal et al. (2022)	Systematic literature review (PRISMA) of protective headgear and injuries in Olympic boxing
Tjønndal (2019)	Interviews with three female boxing coaches and seven female boxers
Tjønndal (2017)	Document analysis of 81 texts on the inclusion of women's boxing in the Olympics, published between 2009–2016
Tjønndal (2016)	Document analysis of boxing magazines and the historical archives of the Norwegian Boxing Association
Hovden and Tjønndal (2021)	Interviews with five women boxing coaches, combined with an analysis of coaches' daily journals
Tjønndal (2014)	Quantitative survey of 87 Norwegian boxing coaches, combined with interviews with eight boxing coaches (three women and five men)
Hovden and Tjønndal (2019)	Interviews with six boxers (three male and three female)

In this chapter I connect and cross-analyse key findings from this research to provide some overarching reflections on the empowerment of women in boxing. I use findings from research projects focusing on both athletes and coaches to illustrate how boxing organisations can help to empower women in a variety of roles in their sport. Collectively, the research projects that form the basis of this chapter consist of qualitative interviews with 19 Norwegian boxers (both male and female), interviews with 16 boxing coaches (both male and female), a survey of 87 Norwegian boxing coaches, a document analysis of the historical archives of The Norwegian Boxing Association, and a social media analysis of Norwegian boxing clubs during the COVID-19 pandemic. This is summarised in Table 6.1, which follows.

In the meta-analysis of the findings and data from these previous research projects, along with my own work with Norway Female Box, I adopted a thematic approach. This yielded four lessons on the empowerment of women in boxing: 1) the need for women-centred approaches in boxing, 2) the importance of women role models, 3) gender quotas for coaches, and 4) men as change agents.

Researchers' Positionality and Reflections on Combining Qualitative Data from Multiple Research Projects

Knowledge of the field of study is regarded as a methodological strength in most qualitative approaches (Thagaard, 2018). For instance, Wadel (1991) argues that one does not engage in meaningful dialogue with research participants with the status of 'researcher'. Therefore, Wadel encourages researchers to seek local statuses in their research projects and meetings with the field of study. When it comes to boxing, I already have a local status in the field with 20 years of experience with boxing, as a boxer, volunteer, coach, referee, and leader. As an athlete, I have been a national champion and medallist in multiple European tournaments. Today, I am a coach at the local and national level, vice president of the Norwegian Boxing Association, and a member of the Coaches Committee in the International Boxing Association (IBA). I have national and international coach education and experience with coaching children, youth, and adults, both men and women. My understanding is that my knowledge of boxing has always given me an advantage when recruiting key participants in my research on women's boxing, as well as in establishing mutual trust with participants (Aase and Fossåskaret, 2007).

Methodological challenges related to doing qualitative research in a field that one is very familiar with are often connected to ensuring an analytical distance when analysing the material. However, it may be equally difficult for a researcher who is an 'outsider' in the field to understand what is happening in it. In many of the research projects that form the basis of this chapter, I have collaborated with researchers with no boxing background whatsoever. This has enhanced the rigour and quality of the analyses. Furthermore, this chapter makes use of the knowledge gained through these previous studies of women's boxing, along with my own experiences, skills, and accomplishments in the sport. In other words, part of the methodological approach is somewhat messy in that it is based on a type of autoethnographic approach combined with meta-analysis of findings from ten years of conducting different research projects. While these projects have different aims and scopes, they all address the overarching research topic of women's boxing. For instance, the project behind the publication of Tjønndal and Hovden (2021) aimed to examine the religious and gendered identities of female immigrant Muslim boxers in Norway. We investigated the power relations, dominant ideologies, and prejudices underpinning the life stories of these women boxers. Another example is Tjønndal et al. (2022), a systematic literature review to study gender, head injuries, and the use of headguards in boxing following the ban on headguards in men's elite boxing competitions.

Combining qualitative and quantitative data in a cross-sectional analysis as I have done in this chapter means engaging in a meta-analysis approach. This approach has its own strengths and weaknesses. One of the methodological weaknesses is related to comparison in terms of attempting to compare data and findings that are simply not comparable. This entails engaging in an analysis that produces connections between studies that are unreliable. Another methodological weakness relates to the risk of interpreting the data out of context; something that is an issue with qualitative data and non-generalisable quantitative data. However, when I have chosen to connect the findings from these different research projects in this chapter it is because I believe that the benefits of this approach outweigh the methodological weaknesses. The methodological strengths of this approach first and foremost relate to the opportunity to connect findings from smaller projects and reflect on the lessons learned in my work to promote women's empowerment in boxing. The data behind the research projects mentioned in this chapter contains a variety of samples and contexts with a view to producing knowledge that can be adopted in practice and further women's boxing in Norway and other countries around the world.

Reflections on Empowering Women in Boxing: Experiences from Norway Female Box and Ten Years of Research on Women's Boxing

In this chapter, I reflect on four lessons that I have learned about empowering women in boxing. These reflections are based on my experiences of creating and running the Norway Female Box project as a head coach. The four lessons are also informed by a decade of conducting research on women's boxing and 20 years of first-hand experience as a boxer, coach, referee, and leader in national and international boxing organisations. The four reflections highlighted in this chapter are: (1) the need for women-centred approaches in boxing, (2) the importance of women role models, (3) gender quotas for coaches on national teams, and (4) men as change agents in boxing. To illustrate each of the lessons learned through research and time spent in boxing gyms, I have included quotes from women coaches and boxers from various previous research projects. My aim is not to analyse these quotes, because that has already been done in earlier publications. Rather, they are meant to illustrate each lesson on empowering women in boxing.

The Need for Women-centred Approaches in Boxing

> Boxing is such a masculine sport, Norway Female Box is needed in order to recruit more women . . . here we have a safe space.
> (Female boxing coach, first published in Hovden and Tjønndal, 2021)

> I was in a clinch with the male head coach. He did not understand the significance of having separate practices for girls and women or of having a women's group in the club. So, after a while I was no longer allowed to organise such practices. But when I left, most of the female athletes also dropped out. They obviously had a need for these women-only practices.
> (Female boxing coach, first published in Hovden and Tjønndal, 2021)

Sports organisations have a long history of utilising women-centred approaches as gender political tools for the empowerment of women as athletes, coaches, leaders, and referees (Elling, Hovden and Knoppers, 2019). Such approaches are often considered to be a double-edged sword by sport scholars because there is always a risk that women-centred approaches in sport may reinforce gendered stereotypes, such as women are not as capable as men (Hovden, 2016). For instance, if a sports organisation advertises women-only coaching courses or women-only refereeing courses, it may signal that women need more education and support to reach the same skill level as their male counterparts. That is, of course, not true. Hence, women-centred approaches that consist of regular leadership training for specific roles in sport will often fail to impact the women who participate, especially if this is presented as something that women leaders are 'forced' to undergo (Rosvold and Anne Tjønndal, 2021). From my experience with creating and running a women-centred boxing programme for athletes, referees, and coaches, succeeding with such approaches requires constant attention to how activities are planned, framed, executed, and evaluated. Simply bringing women together for joint boxing activities is not sufficient. For the women coaches included in the programme, there is a need to design activities that will develop specific coaching skills and competencies that they do not have access to in their local gyms. This could include things such as *cutman* training or being given the responsibilities of a head coach for a competition or training camp.

Some women boxers might be the only women in their local boxing gym, or one of very few women in a highly male-dominated environment. For women boxers, women-centred approaches provide spaces for pugilistic pedagogy by sparring with other women. This is essential for success as a boxer, as all women boxers will at some stage face another woman in the ring. This may sound simple, but the opportunity to engage in combat sparring with multiple other women boxers cannot be underestimated. Some women, both athletes and coaches, also experience abusive behaviour from men in their boxing communities. For these women, any women-centred approach may help to avoid dropout from the sport. When it comes to girls and younger athletes, being part of a women-only environment with both adult female fighters and women boxing coaches may encourage them to pursue further engagement in boxing as adults. This is closely connected to my second reflection: the importance of women role models.

The Importance of Women Role Models

> The male coaches always try to protect and take care of me. They always tell me things like 'Don't hit too hard' when I fight, while female coaches they know that girls aren't made of glass! Because they have experienced what it's like to be a female boxer, they know that women's boxing is just a tough as men's boxing.
> (Female boxer, first published in Tjønndal, 2019a)

> Yes! I can also be a boxing coach. It becomes, in fact, a real possibility.
> (Female boxing coach, first published in Hovden and Tjønndal, 2021)

For young female boxers, a woman coach can be a source of motivation and inspiration. The embodiment of what it means to be a woman and a boxer will often form the basis for a bond of trust between athlete and coach. This may be especially important as boxers go through puberty and experience the pains of managing menstrual cycles with weigh-ins, strict training regimes, and competition schedules. My point here is not that gender is 'everything' in a coach-athlete relationship, but that the embodiment of experiencing the world of boxing through a female body impacts the relationship between athlete and coach in a meaningful way.

Norway Female Box has always been open to all women in boxing, regardless of sporting ambition or skill. Central to the programme has been that its activities are suggested, planned, and organised by the girls and women taking part and are run by women leaders, coaches, and referees. This means that women role models come in many forms in Norway Female Box. Firstly, young girls who have just started boxing may be inspired by adult boxers who have already achieved great skill and impressive results in the ring. Athletes may be inspired to transition to a role as a coach or referee after their boxing career has ended. For female boxers, seeing women who are bold enough to take on positions as head coaches and assume authority in the coaching role, show empowerment and strength, and in this way make themselves visible and respected, also to their male counterparts, is important for the recruitment of women as coaches in boxing.

Gender Quotas for Coaches on National Teams

> In tournaments and competitions, you rarely see any fighters have women in the corner. At the national championship, I was the only boxer with a woman as my main coach in the corner. Sometimes there are women coaches in the corner, but they are just assisting the main coach, giving the boxer water, cleaning the mouth guard, those kinds of things, they don't actually do any coaching. When I fight, people always notice that my main coach is a woman.
> (Female boxer, first published in Tjønndal, 2019a)

There are very few women head coaches in boxing. Almost always, the head coach is a man, and it is very common for the entire coaching team accompanying the national teams (both men and women) to be men. Even when it comes to young women's teams, the coaches are often men. I have always found this to be problematic, especially as male coaches have been shown to be the most frequent perpetrators of sexual assault towards girls and women athletes in sport (Johannson and Lundqvist, 2017; Parent et al., 2015).

If there are many competent women boxing coaches around the world, why are there so few women boxing coaches on national teams? Even on youth teams for girls? There is no clear-cut answer to this, although it could be connected to gendered recruitment processes in coaching and sports management (Skille *et al.*, 2021; Augestad *et al.*, 2021). Recruitment processes in coaching tend to favour men, and when gender equity in sports coaching is not on the policy, agenda policymakers seem to lack both the commitment and the will to target gendered imbalances. Thus, women in prestigious and powerful sports coaching positions represent the exception that signals that the opposite is the case.

Nearly all the coaching at the top level is carried out by men, whereas in local children's and youth sports, the coaches are often women. This was the case in Norwegian boxing in the 1990s and still holds true in 2022. Therefore, there is no reason to expect more women in head coach positions in boxing or working with the Norwegian national teams without formal regulations in place to further gender equity. Historically, gender quotas have been highly effective in furthering women in sports leadership in Norway, and the current system of introducing gender quotas to coaching squads for national teams is an efficient way of ensuring that more women are given the opportunity to advance their careers as boxing coaches.

Men as Change Agents in Boxing

> The head coach of our gym, he always looks at the skills of a person, not their gender. He's always been an advocate for women's boxing and whenever I am upset or feel unfairly treated in the boxing community because I am a woman, he comforts me and says: 'we just have to let the dinosaurs die' (referring to older male leaders).
> (Female boxing coach)

> It is important for the social environment in the gym that there are both male and female coaches and boxers. It creates a completely different cohesion, you can relax more, and it is not so tough.
> (Female boxer, first published in Hovden and Tjønndal, 2019)

The fourth lesson relates to the role of men as change agents in promoting gender equity and the empowerment of women in boxing. Men constitute the majority in almost all leadership roles, decision-making boards, and committees in boxing, both in Norway and around the globe. This means that men will also play a key role in the advancement of gender equity and democracy in boxing in the future. Any strategy to create change will therefore require more men to become involved in the drive to increase gender diversity in the governance and practice of boxing locally, nationally, and internationally. Alliances of women with men are a necessity both today and in the future in order to secure the empowerment of women in boxing. I would never have been able to build the Norway Female Box's national girls' and women's boxing programme as it is today without the help of many men. Men can act as change agents in boxing by supporting women boxers in their gyms, allowing women to become coaches, and by using their skills and knowledge in situations in which their competences are unfairly questioned.

Final Thoughts

Research from multiple countries around the world demonstrates the ongoing marginalisation of women in boxing. There are structural inequalities, such as the low number of athlete spots for women boxers compared to male boxers in the Olympic Games, or the lack of women elected to boards and top management positions in national and international boxing organisations. There are also cultural inequalities and institutionalised gender-based discrimination, in that coaches are reluctant to invest time in developing female boxers (Cove and Young, 2007) and in the way that women athletes, volunteers, and coaches struggle to be respected and feel a constant pressure to 'prove themselves' in boxing communities around the world (Fitzgerald, Stride and Drury, 2022; Hovden and Tjønndal, 2021; Kim, Kwon and Lee, 2015).

This chapter includes some of my reflections on the empowerment of women in boxing based on my experiences of creating and running the Norway Female Box project for five years and ten years of experience in conducting research on women's boxing. As the first intervention related to women's situations in Norwegian boxing, Norway Female Box seems to have been an important intervention for empowering women boxers and coaches in different parts of the country. In this sense, Norway Female Box could be considered a success, at least from the viewpoint of the Norwegian Boxing Association. However, the future of Norway Female Box as a national women-only initiative will depend on how it is integrated into the Norwegian Boxing Association as part of its general activities – that is, in strategic plans and coach education programmes. Such an integration is needed to transform Norway Female Box from an initiative that is dependent on a few individual women trailblazers to an institutional practice in the boxing world.

Feminist studies of sports organisations show that women-centred approaches (or women-only interventions), such as Norway Female Box, are not always sustainable in the long run. When such initiatives end, the situation often returns to the status quo and even to setbacks (Elling, Hovden and Knoppers, 2019; Hovden, 2016). The same might happen for women in Norwegian boxing should Norway Female Box be terminated. Therefore, women-centred approaches are not the only path to achieving gender inclusive environments in boxing, at least not in the long run. A central argument in this chapter is that a double strategy of formal regulations, such as the introduction of gender quotas for coaches on national teams and women-centred approaches with preferential treatment, are needed to recruit and empower women as athletes, coaches, referees, volunteers, and leaders in boxing.

Note

1 It should be noted that there was a demonstration of women's boxing at the Olympic Games in St. Louis in 1904.

Bibliography

Aase, H.T. and Fossåskaret, E. (2007) *Skapte virkeligheter – om produksjon og tolkning av kvalitative data*. Oslo: Universitetsforlaget.

Augestad, P., Hemmestad, L., Gils, B. and Thoresen, T. (2021) 'Omsorg som barriere, som kompetanse og som prestasjonsressurs', in Tjønndal, A. (ed.) *Idrett, kjønn og ledelse: festskrift til Jorid Hovden*. Bergen: Fagbokforlaget, pp. 76–94.

Cove, L. and Young, M. (2007) 'Coaching and athletic career investments: using organisational theories to explore women's boxing', *Annals of Leisure Research*, 10(3–4), pp. 257–271.

Elling, A., Hovden, J. and Knoppers, A. (2019) *Gender diversity in European sport governance*. London: Routledge.

Fitzgerald, H., Stride, A. and Drury, S. (2022) 'Throwing your hat in the ring: women volunteers in boxing', *Sport in Society*, 25(10), pp. 1831–1846.

Gammel, I. (2012) 'Lacing up the gloves: women boxing and modernity', *Cultural and Social History*, 9(3), pp. 369–390.

Gems, G. and Pfister, G. (2014) 'Women boxers: actresses to athletes – the role of Vaudeville in early women's boxing in the USA', *The International Journal of the History of Sport*, 31(15), pp. 1909–1924.

Goksøyr, M. (2008) *Historien om norsk idrett*. Oslo: Abstrakt forlag.

Hargreaves, J. (1994) *Sporting females: critical issues in the history and sociology of women's sport*. London: Routledge.

Hargreaves, J. (1997) 'Women's boxing and related activities: introducing images and meanings', *Body & Society*, 3(4), pp. 33–49.

Hovden, J. (2016) 'The "fast track" as a future strategy for achieving gender equality and democracy in sport organizations', in Vanden, A.Y., Cook, E. and Parry, J. (eds.) *Ethics and governance in sport: the future of sport imagined*. London: Routledge, pp. 35–43.

Hovden, J. and Tjønndal, A. (2019) 'The gendering of coaching from an athlete perspective: the case of Norwegian boxing', *International Review for the Sociology of Sport*, 54(2), pp. 239–255.

Hovden, J. and Tjønndal, A. (2021) '"If there were more women coaches around, I think things would be different": women boxing coaches' struggles to challenge and change a male dominated sport environment', in Norman, L. (ed.) *Improving gender equity in sport coaching*. New York: Routledge, pp. 234–253.

Jennings, G. and Velázquez, C.B. (2015) 'Gender inequality in olympic boxing: exploring structuration through online resistance against weight category restrictions', in Channon, A. and Matthews, R.C. (eds.) *Global perspectives on women in combat sports: women warriors around the world*. London: Palgrave Macmillan, pp. 89–104.

Johannson, S. and Lundqvist, C. (2017) 'Sexual harassment and abuse in coach-athlete relationships in Sweden', *European Journal for Sport and Society*, 14(2), pp. 117–137.

Kim, Y.J. Kwon, S. and Lee, J.W. (2015) 'Resisting the hegemonic gender order? The accounts of female boxers in South Korea', in Channon, A. and Matthews, R.C. (eds.) *Global perspectives on women in combat sports: women warriors around the world*. London: Palgrave Macmillan, pp. 204–218.

Kipnis, H. and Caudwell, J. (2015) 'The boxers of Kabul: women, boxing and Islam', in Channon, A. and Matthews, R.C. (eds.) *Global perspectives on women in combat sports: women warriors around the world*. London: Palgrave Macmillan, pp. 41–56.

Lafferty, Y. and MacKay, J. (2004) ' "Suffragettes in satin shorts?" Gender and competitive boxing', *Qualitative Sociology*, 27(3), pp. 249–276.

Lewandowski, D.J. (2022) *On boxing – critical interventions in the bittersweet science*. London: Routledge.

Linder, K. (2012) 'Women's boxing at the 2012 Olympics: gender trouble?', *Feminist Media Studies*, 12(3), pp. 464–467.

Matthews, R.C. (2019) 'Learning through boxing: the case of a male boxer', in Barker-Ruchti, N. (ed.) *Athlete learning in elite sport: a cultural framework*. London: Routledge.

Matthews, R.C. (2021) ' "The fog soon clears": bodily negotiations, embodied understandings, competent body action and "brain injuries" in boxing', *International Review for the Sociology of Sport*, 56(5), pp. 719–738.

Matthews, R.C. and Jordan, M. (2020) 'Drugs and supplements in amateur boxing: pugilistic amateurism and ideologies of performance', *Qualitative Research in Sport, Exercise and Health*, 12(5), pp. 631–646.

McCree, R. (2015) 'The fight outside the ring: female boxing officials in Trinidad and Tobago', in Channon, A. and Matthews, R.C. (eds.) *Global perspectives on women in combat sports: women warriors around the world*. London: Palgrave Macmillan, pp. 104–118.

Mennesson, C. (2000) ' "Hard" women and "soft" women: the social construction of identities among female boxers', *International Review for the Sociology of Sport*, 35(1), pp. 21–33.

Mitra, P. (2009) 'Challenging stereotypes: the case of Muslim female boxers in Bengal', *The International Journal of the History of Sport*, 26(12), pp. 1840–1851.

Parent, S., Lavoie, F., Thibodeau, M., Hébert, M. and Blais, M. (2015) 'Sexual violence experienced in the sport context by a representative sample of Quebec adolescents', *Journal of Interpersonal Violence*, 31(16), pp. 2666–2686.

Pfister, G. and Gems, G. (2017) 'The shady past of female boxers – what case studies in the USA reveal', *Sport in Society*, 20(8), pp. 998–1012.

Rosvold, M. and Tjønndal, A. (2021) 'Jeg skjønner ikke hvorfor vi må på egne kvinnekurs: Kvinnelige toppdommeres erfaringer med likestillingstiltak i håndball', in Tjønndal, A. (ed.) *Idrett, kjønn og ledelse: festskrift til Jorid Hovden*. Bergen: Fagbokforlaget, pp. 113–132.

Schneider, P. (2021) 'Sparring with patriarchy: the rise of female boxers in the Global South', *Journal of Gender Studies*, 30(8), pp. 887–900.

Skille, Å.E., Fahlén, J., Stenling, C. and Strittmarter, A. (2021) 'Dørvakter til særforbundsstyrer: Valgkomitérepresentanters syn på seleksjonskriterier og kjønnsbalanse', in Tjønndal, A. (ed.) *Idrett, kjønn og ledelse: festskrift til Jorid Hovden*. Bergen: Fagbokforlaget, pp. 306–322.

Skoglöv, A. (2002) 'Boxning skapad av män, för män och kvinnor', *Svensk Idrottsforskning*, 1, pp. 14–19.

Smith, M. (2014) *A history of women's boxing*. Lanham, MD: Rowman & Littlefield Publishers.
Sugden, J. (1996) *Boxing and society: an international analysis*. Manchester: Manchester University Press.
Thagaard, T. (2018) *Systematikk og innlevelse – en innføring i kvalitativ metode*. Bergen: Fagbokforlaget.
Tjønndal, A. (2014) *Ledelse og kjønn i bokseringen – En kvalitativ og kvantitativ studie av Ledelsesadferd og betydninger av kjønn blant norske boksetrenere*. Unpublished Master's thesis. Norwegian University of Science and Technology.
Tjønndal, A. (2016) 'Pugilistic pioneers – the history of women's boxing in Norway', *Sport History Review*, 47(1), pp. 3–25.
Tjønndal, A. (2017) '"I don't think they realise how good we are": innovation, inclusion and exclusion in women's Olympic boxing', *International Review for the Sociology of Sport*, 54(2), pp. 131–130.
Tjønndal, A. (2019a) '"Girls are not made of glass!": barriers experienced by women in Norwegian Olympic boxing', *Sociology of Sport Journal*, 36(1), pp. 87–96.
Tjønndal, A. (2020) '#Quarantineworkout: the use of digital tools and online training among boxers and boxing coaches during the COVID-19 pandemic', *Frontiers in Sports and Active Living*, 20(2), pp. 1–11.
Tjønndal, A., Haudenhuyse, R., de Geus, B. and Buyse, L. (2022) 'Concussions, cuts and cracked bones – a literature review on protective headguards and head injury prevention in Olympic boxing', *European Journal of Sport Science*, 22(3), pp. 447–459.
Tjønndal, A. and Hovden, J. (2016) 'Kjønn som sparringspartner. En kvalitativ undersøkelse av ledelse og betydninger av kjønn blant norske boksetrenere', *Tidsskrift for kjønnsforskning*, 39(3–4), pp. 186–202.
Tjønndal, A. and Hovden, J. (2021) '"Will God condemn me because I love boxing?" Narratives of young female immigrant Muslim boxers in Norway," *European Journal of Women's Studies*, 28(4), pp. 455–470.
Van Bavel, M. (2022) 'The commission knocked out cold: Laura Serrano and the end of the Mexico city prohibition of women's boxing in the 1990s', *Gender & History*, 0(0), pp. 1–18.
Wacquant, L.J.D. (1995) 'The pugilistic point of view: how boxers think and feel about their trade', *Theory and Society*, 24(4), pp. 489–535.
Wacquant, L.J.D. (2001) 'Whores, slaves and stallions: languages of exploitation and accommodation among boxers', *Body & Society*, 7(2–3), pp. 181–194.
Wadel, C. (1991) *Feltarbeid i egen kultur: en innføring i kvalitativt orientert samfunnsforskning*. Seek.
Woodward, K. (2006) *Boxing, masculinity and identity: the 'I' of the tiger*. Abingdon: Routledge.
Wright, J.E. (2020) 'Fast-track fisticuffs? An ethnographic exploration of time and white-collar boxing', *International Review for the Sociology of Sport*, 55(4), pp. 437–452.
Zazryn, T., Finch, C. and McCrory, P. (2003) 'A 16 year study of injuries to professional boxers in the state of Victoria, Australia', *British Journal of Sports Medicine*, 37(4), pp. 321–324.

Part 2

(De)constructing Self, to Be Somebody

Image 2 Boxers Shabnam Razia and Zainab Fatima at Kidderpore School of Physical Culture, Kolkata, India, 2022

Chapter 7

Trans Boxing
A Boxing Club, an Art Project

Nolan Hanson and Zac Easterling

> *Trans Boxing is one of those magical places where you just fit. There's no need to assimilate, to adjust, to be someone you're not. The coaches see you as a person, as an athlete, and as a member of an incredibly supportive community. I keep coming back for the people, for the validation as a boxer in the way I want to present, and of course for the incredible coaching.*
> – Al Gregory (2022)

> *Trans Boxing helped me get in touch with the most true version of myself. Having a community focused on the same thing all for different reasons is empowering. The coaches take their craft very seriously and it's inspiring as well as invigorating to learn from them. Boxing has truly helped me with my focus in all aspects of life.*
> – Bex Zank (2022)

Trans Boxing is an ongoing and co-authored art project in the form of a boxing club. In its first iteration, the project consisted solely of a weekly donation-based group boxing class that took place at a since-closed storefront gym in Bed-Stuy, Brooklyn. The growth of participation in the project has meant having to use a diverse range of locations to facilitate training, including educational institutions (Portland State University, San Francisco Art Institute, The James Baldwin School), community centres (The Door in Manhattan, Brooklyn Community Pride Center, Brooklyn Center for Anti-Violence Education), parks (Herbert Von King in Brooklyn, MacArthur Park in Los Angeles, McCarren Park in Brooklyn, Prospect Park in Brooklyn), art galleries (Cube Space Gallery in Berkeley, Wave Pool Gallery in Cincinnati, Amanita in Manhattan), boxing gyms (Overthrow Boxing Club in New York, Devilfish Athletics in Brooklyn, Gleason's Gym in Brooklyn), and Zoom. The platform of Trans Boxing has also been used to support various sub-projects, including collaborative publications, site-specific residency projects, performance workshops, and for-credit high school and college courses. Presently, between Trans Boxing's four coaches (Nolan Hanson, Zac Easterling, Kerry Thomas, and Miles Enriquez-Morales), the project hosts multiple weekly training sessions in New York City and Los Angeles.

DOI: 10.4324/9781003312635-10

Through theoretical and practical interventions into the rigidly gendered system of athletics, Trans Boxing reimagines the function of art and sports in society and provides a framework to explore concepts of identity, community, and embodiment. While consistently maintaining its functionality as a boxing club that provides accessible and inclusive boxing training for trans and gender-variant people, Trans Boxing developed into a community-building mechanism and relational platform that challenged more conventional approaches to art-making and boxing, such as painting, sculpture, dance, and so on.

Methodology

We take this opportunity to explicate the first sentence, 'Trans Boxing is an ongoing co-authored art project in the form of a boxing club'. The constellation of concepts – trans, boxing, art, project, and co-authorship – is brought together through the organizing logic of funk which is exemplified in this chapter by the work of Adrian Piper and L.H. Stallings. This text offers a reading of Trans Boxing which articulates how it understands itself in relation to other human endeavours. Specifically, it articulates how Trans Boxing is art. This chapter also makes clear on what grounds, and what type of art. In this capacity, the chapter also makes plain Trans Boxing's co-mingled critique of both mainstream boxing and art.

The insistence on Trans Boxing as art is more complicated than the question, 'Is boxing art'? We believe plainly that boxing is an art form, and assert that Trans Boxing uses the form of boxing to create a socially engaged work of art. Within the conventional studio-gallery system of art, a work of art implies a singular author producing objects within their chosen medium (for instance, a painter uses the form of painting to produce art objects). Socially engaged art is broadly defined as art that is collaborative, often participatory, and involves people as the medium or material of the work. The work is often not object-based and insists upon public engagement.

While certain components of Trans Boxing have been more proximal to 'traditional' art contexts than others, the project exists in spaces mostly outside of the studio-gallery system – it is not dependent on that system to produce, exhibit, and disseminate the work. Additionally, because the work is primarily experiential, the nature of the project resists commodification within the commercial art market. Before the 'social turn' (Bishop, 2006) in contemporary art in the 1990s, artists and art collectives had begun to use socially engaged approaches to challenge the conventional studio/gallery system and redefine the role of art in society. Artists and art collectives Adrian Piper, Allan Kaprow, Joseph Beuys, ACT UP, and Group Material created works that prioritised collective knowledge production, engaged with non-art world audiences and contexts, and encouraged co-authorship and collaboration. Critic Nicolas Bourriaud expands upon these concepts in his canonical 1998 text *Relational Aesthetics*, in which he defines the contemporary work of art as a 'social interstice' whereby experiences and life possibilities are made possible. 'Art', he writes, 'is a site that produces certain modes of sociability (human relations, social exchange, power dynamics) and subjectivity' (Bourriaud, 2002, pp. 14–16). These approaches to artistic practice offered alternative values and approaches, and enacted a powerful institutional critique of the mainstream commercial art world. These features present themselves in Trans Boxing and are active in its performed critique of art generally and the specific mass culture and administrative forces which make its intervention necessary.

To make clear the mode in which Trans Boxing is art, we consider it alongside philosopher and conceptual artist Adrian Piper's work 'Funk Lessons'.[1] In this work, Piper teaches predominantly white participants how to dance to funk music after giving some background in the flow of musical traditions which have given rise to funk, like soul, jazz, ragtime, and so on. These lessons eventually become a sort of party which is recorded and presented as the object, 'Funk Lessons'. Through 'Funk Lessons', Piper rejects the racial essentialism that would hold that funk, or any other manifestation of African American culture, was exclusively the possession of its original community. Funk and boxing are for everyone willing, a truth that Piper and Trans Boxing realize. For example, in 'Notes on Funk I', the first of four reflections on the various 'Funk Lessons' performed from 1982–84, Piper notes funk's origins in the cultural idioms of the African diaspora in the US, and how it is that the white participants have lacked access to the opportunities to learn important life skills that can be found in that tradition. 'Funk Lessons' is an effort to teach its participants a practice of survival that they lacked. This belief in the equality of access to areas of human knowledge and activity informs both our and Piper's pedagogy. Dancing to funk and boxing both need to be taught because we believe they are important skills and everyone who wants to learn them should have the opportunity. In this way, both Trans Boxing and Funk Lessons are art aimed at inclusivity. Piper is extremely intentional about her work and its perception. Her intention to teach some of funk's life-affirming skills (rhythm and how to move as a continuous mass) is an effort, not to teach white people how to perform blackness, per se, but to create a horizontality of being that would allow for participants to 'Get down and party together' (Piper, 1984, p. 130).

There are some significant differences between the projects. First, Trans Boxing's ongoing and ephemeral status rejects being made complete, and thus a consumable object. Second, Trans Boxing does not belong to an individual. In 'Funk Lessons', Piper provided a structure that included participatory elements, but the participants did not shape the structure. Trans Boxing, on the other hand, while initiated and overseen by a singular artist (Nolan Hanson), includes co-authored components which inform the ongoing conversation that is Trans Boxing. The other way to say this is that 'Funk

Lessons' is an artwork while Trans Boxing is an art project. Its nature is open and incomplete, meaning that it escapes capture and cannot be gripped and made possession by any person or institution. Because of this, Trans Boxing is for the fighters in a way that Funk Lessons could not be for its dancers. There is no work that can become someone's, only a project which is already ours, in common.

In early socially engaged art projects, participants and collaborators were often erased or instrumentalised as merely means to an end. This was a result of the studio-gallery system which creates an incentive (to the point of necessity) for art practices and projects to become works conflated with solo artists. These conditions are largely required if an artist is to be made legible and thus profitable/sustainable within the studio-gallery world. For this reason, we are wary of over-involvement with such institutions. The types of artistic practices Trans Boxing engages in vary, and several notable sub-projects which were produced between 2018 and 2021 exhibit the diversity of Trans Boxing's practices. 'Remote Pictures' was a collaborative installation that was exhibited at the Cube Space Gallery – a public art[2] gallery located on the ground level of a parking garage in Berkeley, California – in August 2021. For this project, Nolan and Ada Jane McNulty collaborated with Trans Boxing fighters to create a series of portraits that were printed on 5'x3' vinyl banners. The installation included sculptural materials which signified common materials found in boxing gyms; the banners were hung from the ceiling using stainless steel coil chains and were secured to cinder blocks at the base using resistance bands.

In 2020, through a residency with More Art – an NYC-based non-profit that supports public art – Nolan and their collaborator Hill Donnell initiated The James Baldwin School Boxing Club, a for-credit hybrid PE and art class for NYC public high school students at the James Baldwin School in the Chelsea neighbourhood of Manhattan. The course included remote and in-person participation and, in addition to boxing training, the class supported several visiting artists who led workshops, gave presentations, and collaborated with students on various interdisciplinary projects.

Trans Boxing has created several collaborative publications and interview projects, including *The Trans Boxing Zine* (2021) which includes interviews, essays, poetry, and photography by Trans Boxing members. *Talking About Trans Boxing*, a group interview between Trans Boxing participants and a group of undergraduate art students at Portland State University, was featured in the Winter 2021 issue of the *Social Forms of Art Journal*. In *The Whole Thing Done Changed*, Nolan transcribed a conversation he had with his boxing trainer Carl Westbrooks as they drove around Bed-Stuy, Brooklyn, the neighbourhood where Carl grew up.

How To Explain Belief was a two-part event that included a public lecture followed by a boxing workshop held at the Diego Rivera Gallery at the San Francisco Art Institute in February 2019. In the lecture, Nolan presented about

Trans Boxing and examined the project's relationship to theories of discipline, ritual, and belief that artist Gordon Hall explores in their lecture 'Extremely Precise Objects of Ambiguous Use' (Hall, 2019). During an artist residency at Wave Pool, an arts centre located in the Camp Washington Neighbourhood of Cincinnati, Ohio, Nolan explored the local history and existing boxing culture in the neighbourhood. Through their research, they found The Queen City Boxing Club, a gym founded by boxing coach and founder of Cincinnati's Black United Front, Jackie Shropshire, located in the West End neighbourhood. Nolan trained at the gym for two weeks and connected with the current head trainer and former USBA Super Middleweight champion Frank Rhodes. Inside the gym, located in the basement of a community recreation centre, were over 200 framed photographs and various ephemera of significant events in the gym's history. Nolan took photographs of photographs and created posters that were exhibited in the Wave Pool Gallery alongside posters that featured people from the New Bed-Stuy Boxing Center and Trans Boxing. The opening featured a performance by local musician Freedom Nicole Moore and a public outdoor screening of Frank Rhodes' 1995 USBA Super Middleweight title fight. Of the exhibition's title, *An Effort to Defend*, Nolan wrote, 'I've started to think of the title as an explanation of how I want my art practice to function in society; as a sort of defensive strategy' (Hanson, 2021).

In all these works, Trans Boxing is committed to the boxing tradition, and the rich history it offers us, and to collaborative work. Each example involves varying degrees of co-authorship and exhibits collaboration as a key component of Trans Boxing. Held together, these works reflect the project's overall commitment to education and art in the same vein as Piper, but at least in equal measure shows a commitment to the tradition of boxing. The intention of all this work is to produce more boxing in the world. In this way, Trans Boxing is similar to the Premier Boxing Champions (PBC)[3] or World Boxing Council (WBC).[4] The key difference between our project and the enterprises of the WBC or PBC is towards what purpose boxing is produced. It goes without saying that the PBC, a promotional company, makes boxing as a product for profit (something similar can be argued for the WBC sanctioning body), but Trans Boxing, with the idealism typical of artists, makes boxing for the love of boxing, art, and being. In this way, Trans Boxing exists as a critique of both mainstream art and mainstream boxing, because despite their seeming separation, the same ideological forces which determine the value of any one work of art also uphold gender segregation within boxing.

Trans Boxing is only possible through people coming together to form a community. Nolan planted a seed and continues to be the main gardener of Trans Boxing, but the germination of plants and boxing clubs takes the combined effort of an environment. Simply planting the seed is not enough. Nolan's realisation of the meaning behind this metaphor is what led them to the methodology which has always been a part of Trans Boxing's collaboration with others to nurture the club. Of course, every event of boxing is inescapably a co-authored production, there are always at least two fighters, but also, more practically, Trans Boxing exists as it does today, in terms of reach, polish, and longevity, thanks to the efforts of its collaborators and co-authors, including its participants/fighters. Despite the prevailing stereotypes of the solitary fighter, each training session, sparring match, and fight is a relational exchange, a co-authorship, and a conversation. This truth of fighting, its co-authorship, is echoed in the testimony of 18-year-old Trans Boxing fighter Teo Nalani:

> I go to Trans Boxing because I always wanted to be a boxer but always was intimidated to go. I had a hard time fighting for my identity growing up, so though I was fighting, I never felt like I won any of the fights. Coach taught me so much, about how to fight and about how to hold yourself. I look up to him so much, as a māhū and as a leader. Even on bad or scary days, when I go there I always leave feeling stronger. Trans boxing is one of my favorite homes. I want to keep fighting forever.
>
> (Nalani, 2022)

Jules Duze, a native New Yorker who joined Trans Boxing in 2021, feels similarly, saying,

> Trans Boxing provides a space for gender-nonconforming, trans folks, to feel safe, to know that they will not be judged, not be characterized, not be classified based on other people's expectations or ideas of our experience . . . I get so much from Trans Boxing. Alongside consistency and structure, and I am gifted with teammates who support me both in and outside the ring.
>
> (Duze, 2022)

For many trans athletes, the sport's gender-binary model, alongside hostile environments, unsupportive coaching, and discriminatory policies, have meant they felt they had to sacrifice serious participation in athletics. Trans Boxing member Sab Garduño writes:

> As an athlete, part of coming out meant saying goodbye to my sport: my lifelong dreams, an important part of my life. Trans Boxing for me represented an opportunity to continue my growth as an athlete, a man, and a person. More importantly, Trans Boxing was the first place where I learned how to exist and take up space as a person safely, surrounded by a driven, caring, community.
>
> (Garduño, 2022)

Anne Lieberman, a competitive Muay Thai fighter, expressed experiencing a similar loss when they came out:

> I have been involved in combat sports – specifically Muay Thai – for the past 13 years. I've competed and coached at high levels, won three

national championships, and dedicated so much of my life to a sport that I still love. But I had to walk away from a lot of that when I came out, and when I found Trans Boxing, I found a space that I didn't think could exist for me as an athlete – somewhere that felt affirming, where the training was serious, but I could simply exist as trans nonbinary person and an athlete at the same time.

(Lieberman, 2022)

The common sense one could gather is that for participants, there is a necessity to reject the myth of gender which polices self-expression. It's no coincidence, then, that they feel liberated in the role of the boxer. To be a boxer is to be that before anything else. It becomes the context that one's other characteristics (for example gender expression) are evaluated within. There is no intrinsic value placed upon these characteristics beyond the ability to perform in the ring. In the testimony of these fighters, we find a non-gendered utopianism – a world where their transness is not a cause for special, and definitely not discriminatory, treatment. Trans fighters, like many trans people more broadly, want their transness to be a non-factor; they want to be simply a fighter, or a person. This realisation invites an opportunity to re-evaluate what 'trans" means to Trans Boxing.

Trans Boxing understands 'trans' in this sense of co-authorship, as a movement beyond the discrete individualised body. The project is trans-individual. The horizon or boundary between beings becomes transversal in as much as they lose absolute meaning. The type of 'trans' which drives the word transience, more so than transition, becomes manifest in Trans Boxing by virtue of its co-authorship. Attention to this aspect of Trans Boxing is related to our belief that art can and should be socially engaged. In this way, L.H. Stallings' (2015) theory of funk in *Funk the Erotic: Transaesthetics and Black Sexual Cultures* characterises the everyday practice of Trans Boxing. Trans Boxing is an art project that works through tactility and impact. Participants are boxers. They train. They fight. It is a kinaesthetic, odiferous, sweaty, sometimes bloody, transfer of energy and intent. Trans Boxing is not art about boxing, but rather boxing as art. Thus, Trans Boxing is funky in the way L.H. Stallings develops in *Funk The Erotic*. Stallings quotes Robert Farris Thompson's etymology of funk:

> The slang term 'funky' in black communities originally referred to strong body odor and not to 'funk', meaning fear or panic. The Black nuance seems to derive from the Ki-Kongo lu-fuki 'bad body odor' and is perhaps reinforced by contact with fumet, 'aroma of food and wine' in French Louisiana. But the Ki-Kongo word is closer to the jazz word 'funky' in form and meaning, as both jazzmen and Bakongo use 'funky' and lu-fuki to praise persons for the integrity of their art, for having worked out to achieve their aims. . . . For in Kongo the smell of a hardworking elder carries luck. This Kongo sign of exertion is identified with the positive energy of a person.
>
> (Thompson, 1983, p. 66)

Thompson's etymology reveals that funk has always had a connection with the body, particularly its odour. This odour was not only reflective of hard work, in terms of mindless labour or toil, but it was also a sign of one who was fulfilled by their work to the point of performing it with excellence and intensity. Funkiness was always a positive sign delivered through a bad smell. A strong odour was reflective of vigorous exertion of the body. To be funky is to be in a state of enchantment, or what some sports psychologists call 'flow'. In Stallings' theory, funk becomes an episteme of the erotic because it has access to the transaesthetics of its effect. We could say funk offers a way for us to know about and tap into the use and power of erotic energy in bettering our whole, not merely sexual, condition. On its most basic level of conceptualisation, funk accounts for touch and smell, but more substantially the use of funk for Trans Boxing then has to do with an attempt to use the power of the erotic.

The erotic for Stallings, and Trans Boxing, is derived from Audre Lorde's 'Uses of The Erotic: The Erotic as Power' (2007). Lorde articulates how our understanding of the erotic sphere of human relation is underdeveloped as a consequence of its suppression and pornification in modern society. We find ourselves in a society that habituates the suppression of erotic energies in all but a few specific instances, many if not most characterised through pornotropy.[5] The importance of this force in the lives of individuals and groups was understood by Plato and the other ancients, but historical movements (including rationalism and puritanism) have left the average modern person radically separated from its full potential. Stallings writes:

> By looking at other black cultural products, we can glean funk as a philosophy about kinesthetics and being that critiques capitalism and the pathology of Western morality of the West while also possessing the wisdom to know and understand that the two are linked. Because funk sees the two as linked, it provides innovative strategies about work and sexuality that need to be highlighted. Black music scholarship has studied funk as a form that leads to dance and other music; I am examining funk as nonreproductive sex and transaesthetics of cultural art forms.
>
> (Stallings, 2015, p. 3)

Funk offers us a way to come into touch with the use and power of the erotic so that our lives may be improved via knowledge of what activities bring us pleasure and how that pleasure relates to personal excellence in our work. For Trans Boxing, being funky aligns with art as experience. As an art project, it acts on the experience of its spectators, thus affecting the conditions of its future possibilities.

We understand that some readers might be confused as to why we have chosen to completely omit stories of discrimination. After all, if transphobia didn't exist in life and boxing, then what would be the need for Trans

Boxing's founding? Of course, there is discrimination that propelled the club's becoming and its fighters' participation, but we feel it is more important to give some sense of who we are through a constructive mode. What we are strikes us as of more import than what we are not. Trans Boxing's founding is a response to transphobia. It is not reactionary to it. It is possible and necessary for resistance and art projects to be able to imagine what they are beyond what they are in resistance to. What we hope to have offered is an articulation of where Trans Boxing imagines itself in conversation with other human efforts. We accept the pragmatism of trans as an identity to organise under, but also desire to expand its definition. The 'trans' in Trans Boxing is descriptive of gender expression, but also of movement, as in to go from one state to another, to traverse space. Trans Boxing is transaesthetics by being a trans-aesthetic. Trans Boxing goes beyond the aesthetics defined by any one sensory mode; it works through a combination and negotiation of smell, taste, sight, touch, hearing, and proprioception. It is a transcendent object of human activity; an art project like funk that cannot be fixed into the limited framing of gender or form.

In this chapter, we have endeavoured only to make it clear that Trans Boxing is a co-authored art project, and what this means. For Trans Boxing to be co-authored means that its participants inhabit and share it in such a way that disallows participants to be rendered as means to an end, or as proper individuals able to own any part of the project. This simply means that like any land held in common, the improvement of the soil is to the benefit of all who hold it in common, not a sign of the proper ownership of the individual who might have fertilised the land. Instead, the project of Trans Boxing is held in common. For Trans Boxing to be a project means not only is it held in common, but that it is not concluded or realised to the point of becoming a work. After all, Trans Boxing was founded to increase the participation of trans and gender-variant people in boxing. There is no clause in that statement that indicates a culmination of that cause. That it is both held in common and cannot be completed are vital to how Trans Boxing imagines itself to be a project. Co-authorship can be seen everywhere in boxing. For example, Kronk Gym, as a project, was able to continue despite the passing of a figure as central as Emmanuel Stewart[6] because it was held in common. For Trans Boxing to be art means to be so in a way that preserves the possibility of being a project in common. It is to be an art, gilded by the trans-aesthetics of funk, toward a being-together that can only exist in the experience of being in a boxing club. Trans Boxing is a co-authored art project. Trans Boxing is a boxing club. Though it may not be the case for every club, Trans Boxing shows that a boxing club can articulate its being in such a way.

In its highest form of functioning, a boxing club is a site that is conducive to a multiplicity of self-expressions – a place to hold fighters as they negotiate a sometimes-adversarial collaboration with themselves and their environment, and make art from their heartache, failures, and hurt feelings. In the gym, there is the potential for the boxer to become liberated – however temporarily – from the task of having to determine how to be in/with themselves and others. For those who make it in, this can be a refuge from social contexts in which the rules of engagement are incomprehensible, implicit, incoherent, and veiled. This negotiation is precarious for most. For many, though, it is denied before they have the chance to enter the ring. This project is towards an end of a world where one could be kept away from boxing at all, but most acutely as a matter of gender expression.

Notes

1 Adrian Piper, *Funk Lessons 1–4*, was conceived and facilitated by herself in a number of institutions, including the New York Museum of Modern Art. Reference to the work can be found in Bishop, C. (2006) *Participation*. London: Whitechapel.
2 Public art performs a civic function. It seeks to make explicit linkages among the formal properties of a work, its ability to get us to pay attention to our surroundings, and how we value what we perceive. In this, the form and content of public art is fundamentally about how we live together with those around us. Art is treated as the embodiment of shared values and serves to integrate through its own legible forms those who might otherwise remain strangers to one another.
3 'Premier Boxing Champions (PBC) was created for television by Haymon Sports, LLC, in January 2015. PBC is a boxing series that returns the sweet science to its rightful place atop the sports pantheon. Featuring today's best and brightest stars in their toughest, most anticipated bouts, Premier Boxing Champions is broadcast and streamed live on SHOWTIME, FOX, FS1, and FOX Deportes'. Premier Boxing Champions Website 'About' Page (Accessed: 30 December 2022).
4 'The World Boxing Council' (WBC) was established as an initiative of the then president of Mexico, Adolfo López Mateos, to create an organisation that would unify all the commissions of the world and develop the expansion of boxing.
5 Coined by Spillers, H. (2003) 'Mama's Baby, Papa's Maybe: an American grammar book', in *Black white and in color: essay on American literature and culture*. Chicago: University of Chicago Press. 'pornotropy' is the reduction of one to the bare life of flesh (also a term coined in this essay) so that another can make that flesh a pure object for their own sexual/violent gratification.
6 Emanuel Steward (1944–2012) was a legendary boxing coach and trainer. He was the patriarch of the equally prestigious Kronk Boxing Gym in Detroit, Michigan. Steward helped a number of fighters become world champions, including Thomas Herns, Lenox Lewis, and Wladimir Klitschko.

Bibliography

Bishop, C. (2006) *Participation*. London: Whitechapel.
Bourriaud, N. (2002) *Relational aesthetics*. Dijon: Les Presses du reel.
Descartes, R. (2008) *Meditations on first philosophy*. Translated from the French by M. Moriarty. Oxford: Oxford University Press.
Dewey, J. (1934) *Art as experience*. London: G. Allen & Unwin.
Dewey, J. (1992) *Human nature and conduct: an introduction to social psychology*. New York: Holt.
Duze, J. (2022) Personal email to the authors, 6 October.

Garduño, S. (2022) Personal email to the authors, 8 October.
Gregory, A. (2022) Personal email to the authors, 8 October.
Hall, G. (2019) 'Extremely precise objects of ambiguous use', in Byrne-Sere, S. (ed.) *Over-beliefs: Gordon Hall collected writing: 2011–2018*. Portland: Portland Institute for Contemporary Art, pp. 15–18.
Hanson, N. (2021) *An effort to defend. Art exhibition*. Cincinnati, OH: Wave Pool Gallery, April 2021.
Lieberman, A. (2022) Personal email to the authors, 19 October.
Lorde, A. (2007) *Sister outsider: essays & speeches of Audre Lorde*. New York: Ten Speed Press.
Malatino, H. (2022) *Side affects: on being trans and feeling bad*. Minneapolis, MN: University of Minnesota Press.
Nalani, T. (2022) Personal email to the authors, 6 October.
Piper, A. (1982–84) *Funk lessons*. Berkeley: University of California.
Spillers, H. (2003) *Black, white, and in color: essays on American literature and culture*. Chicago: University of Chicago Press.
Stallings, L.H. (2015) *Funk the erotic: transaesthetics and black sexual cultures*. Champaign, IL: University of Illinois Press.
Thompson, F.R. (1983) *Flash of the spirit: African and Afro-American art and philosophy*. New York: Random House.
Trans Boxing Zine (2021) *Trans Boxing Zine Issue 01*. https://drive.google.com/file/d/12vEEOefTE-mXldHq9URCNZXzfWvluRgF/view?usp=sharing
Zank, B. (2022) Personal email to the authors, 5 October.

Chapter 8

Katie Taylor
Complicating a Boxing Identity

Emma Calow

Hailed the *manly art*, boxing is enmeshed in iron-clad stereotypes and dominant narratives about the boxer: 'Boxers are rugged, near-illiterate young men . . . parlaying their anger at the world' (Wacquant, 1992, p. 221). The boxing ring is a social and cultural space to perform violence in a certain way that is considered skilful, attractive even, to many. Boxing is thus largely constructed and conceived of as a male preserve where men enter the ring to perform their manhood (Matthews, 2016). As Joyce Carol Oates writes, 'boxing is for men, and is about men, and is men' (Oates, 1987, p. 392). Accordingly, the female boxer seemingly 'cannot be taken seriously . . . is parody . . . [and] is cartoon' (ibid). This dominant narrative has, however, been challenged in recent examples of female boxers across the world who, despite structural and cultural barriers, utilise boxing as a form of empowerment (Mitra, 2009). Specifically, as a longstanding supporter of and trailblazer for women's professional boxing, Katie Taylor, from Bray, Ireland, challenges the dominant narrative of what it means to be a boxer, thus complicating a boxing identity. This chapter looks at the interesting journey of Taylor's transition from disguising as a boy to compete in amateur bouts to being understood as the lead advocate for and the face of women's professional boxing.

Popular perceptions and cultural (re)productions of a boxing identity typically reinforce the idea that to be a boxer means to be physically and emotionally aggressive, prone to an enjoyment of physical violence, and to have certain personality traits that lend to boxing showmanship. For example, the persona performed by Laila Ali, the youngest daughter of the late Muhammad Ali, is often characterised as 'confident, charismatic, opinionated, strong-willed, fearless' – akin to her father (Springer, 2017). This is not to homogenise boxers but to reflect the commercial need for boxers to be more than just good fighters – they must actively engage with the showmanship of the boxing culture spectacle to succeed as professional boxers. Katie Taylor's performance of self in and out of the ring defies these expected showmanship requirements to succeed in boxing. In fact, her innate shyness is often perceived at odds with her boxing style. She is a self-proclaimed 'quiet person by nature' who is 'not really one for talking' – so much so that interviews for

DOI: 10.4324/9781003312635-11

Taylor are 'harder than the fights' (Taylor, 2012, p. 281). She is neither too outspoken, too feminine, too masculine, too political, too controversial, or too ambiguous to be considered a threat. And yet, she is taken very seriously within the professional boxing world. For example, her recent victory against Amanda Serrano – the first boxing match headlined between two women at New York City's Madison Square Garden – cements Taylor in the Irish and world boxing iconography. As a testament to Taylor's popularity and calibre in boxing, the match garnered 1.5 million viewers and witnessed a sold-out stadium (Gigney, 2022).

Taylor currently holds all four major world women's boxing titles, standing with a 20–0 record with no signs of retiring. (There have been whispers of a second fight against Serrano to be held in Croke Park, Ireland, when Taylor will be 36 years old.) As such, I argue that Taylor's performance of identity enables this transition, allowing her to occupy a space that is not parody or cartoon, that is not threatening to gender norms and expectations. I pose that Taylor is deemed as non-threatening due to her performance of gender and its nuanced relationship with identity (that is, a female boxer). Ultimately, in contrast to Oates' conceptions, I argue that being a boxer is not a unidimensional performance or identity.

Methodology

Culture is shaped by people as much as culture shapes them. Cultural studies examine cultural forms (such as movies, music, sport, media, literature) and cultural practices (like social justice movements, social media use, healthcare, rituals in sport) and how these shape social worlds and (inter)actions. Feminist cultural studies places gender at the centre of this analysis, allowing for deeper critical analysis of the often overlooked in everyday social and cultural life. As Emily Roper simply puts it: 'feminist cultural studies is focused on how gender is produced within society and how culture influences our beliefs about gender' (Roper, 2016, p. 275). Boxing is ritualised as a sport that deeply values characteristics traditionally associated with masculinity. Katie Taylor's presence and success in this sport disrupts these traditional gender norms by blurring the lines between feminine and masculine performances.

Using feminist cultural studies to study sport allows for a critical interrogation of the ways in which sport serves as both a site of empowerment and disempowerment for women, and how sport as a sociocultural institution reproduces gender inequality (Hargreaves and McDonald, 2000). To do so also requires an understanding of the historical and social context of modern sport as a domain made by and for white men as it relates to articulations and expressions of the superiority of masculinity and how this, in turn, impacts women's experiences in sport (Francombe-Webb and Toffoletti, 2018). Since I am using feminist methodology in this chapter, it is necessary for me to situate myself within the research (Krane et al., 2012).

As Vasupradha Srikishna puts it, 'feminist methodology calls for a deeper understanding of the researcher' (Srikrishna, 2020, p. 254). In this case, I am a Northern Irish white, abled-bodied, straight woman from a middle-class background. I am also a former elite athlete, having represented Northern Ireland and Ireland at junior and senior levels. My personal connection to the island of Ireland clearly influenced who and how I chose to write about for this body of work on boxing. For example, I'm not so much critiquing the larger inequities faced by Taylor as an Irish girl and woman in boxing as I am attempting to paint her story of an Irish woman performing and shaping her own success in boxing.[1]

The Early Days: Disguised as a Boy

> *It seemed that even at a young age, I was destined to break down barriers in how people perceive women in sport.*
>
> **(Taylor, 2012, p. 281)**

Taylor's love of and talent for boxing sport became evident at an early age. Taylor describes the beginning of her boxing career, 'not in a gym but in the kitchen of my house watching [her] Dad training' (Taylor, 2012, p. 476). Living in a household surrounded by men who boxed perhaps ignited the desire to become a boxer, or at least influenced her decision to pursue the sport. Taylor trained with her brothers, Lee and Peter, as she looked to father as a role model and coach who led her to local and regional wins disguised as a boy and to her Olympic gold medal as a young female adult. Before she became Ireland's first female European champion in 2005, boxing was non-existent for girls and women. Her desire to participate resulted in her needing to compete as a boy:

> From the beginning when I was starting out, I had to fight for the right just to be allowed to cliimb through the ropes as a woman and box. In those days, female boxing wasn't sanctioned by the boxing association, but my dad would tuck my hair up into my headgear and let me box against the boys. When asked what my name was, he would just say it was 'K. Taylor'.
>
> (Taylor, 2012, p. 120)

Living in a working-class, rural community meant do-it-yourself strategies were imperative, including building and organising a gender-inclusive boxing club that Taylor and her brothers could 'call home' (Taylor, 2012, p. 95). These active, self-affirming, sustained efforts to train for and participate in boxing resulted in her becoming the face of women's boxing in 2012 and beyond.

Taylor's story as a young girl in rural Ireland who was forced to pretend to be a boy for the right to fight is indicative of the cultural ideologies about where a girl or woman belongs in sport – and by extension, in society – and in what capacity. What about boxing has deemed it unfit or undesirable for girls and women to participate in, or indeed to identify as boxers? As Taylor notes,

> some of the local media were curious at the idea of a little girl boxing and it seemed to spark a bit of controversy . . . I didn't understand what all the controversy was about. As a child, the way I saw it my dad and brothers boxed, so why couldn't I?
> (Taylor, 2012, p. 98)

Because boxing is perceived to be 'most aggressively masculine' and is part of the sport culture cannon as a prominent form of proving one's manliness, to be a boxer is thus seemingly unnatural for/to women (Oates, 2011, p. 392). As a result, boxers who are women are seen as 'less than' their male counterparts (Schneider, 2021, p. 887). Moreover, women's boxing is relational to men's boxing, including various gender-marker strategies to differentiate the two – for example, there are less weight categories in women's Olympic boxing than the men's – subsequently devaluing women's participation as 'less important' (Tjønndal, 2016, p. 95).

Generally speaking, the wider public and men and women in boxing spaces (such as clubs, gyms, competitions) conceive of boxing as an inherently male space – so much so that women boxers are expected to control what they look like while boxing (for instance, minimal aggression and muscularity) (McGannon et al., 2019). To do so is to engage in the performance, or 'doing', of gender (Butler, 2004). That is, women doing gender as boxers means creating and maintaining a particular body image, controlling one's verbal and non-verbal bodily expressions, and dressing in stereotypically feminine ways to avoid the lesbian label (Krane and Mann, 2019). These constant negotiations of femininity and the need to establish one's womanhood in boxing dispels the heterogeneity of femininity in the larger context of sport, in turn reinforcing an essentialist construction of what it means to box/to be a boxer (McGannon et al., 2019). In other words, to compete in boxing requires a certain performance of gender (that is, men perform certain modes of masculinity), and when this performance is performed by the 'other' (that is, women performing certain modes of masculinity) the overall performance is complicated. As writer and fighter Melanie Joy McNaughton states, 'if sport is socially constructed as a stronghold for hegemonic masculinity, then to participate in sport as a woman is . . . a way of rewriting the performative code' (McNaughton, 2012, p. 5). Katie Taylor took it upon herself to rewrite these performative codes by performing – literally and symbolically – as a boy in the ring. The efforts she undertook as a girl to disguise herself as a male boxer at the beginning of her career speaks to her investment in securing the validity of women's boxing/women in boxing. Without this initial action of disguising as a boy to 'get a seat at the table', Taylor, arguably, would not be where she is today within the professional boxing realm.

In this way, a woman's physical presence and participation in boxing can serve as resistance to the systemic sexism and misogyny that characterises boxing culture (Lindner, 2012). That is, the body in boxing is a social and political tool (Paradis, 2012). For example, there's a hidden history of the sport being used as a platform among female indigenous as a tool for social and political commentary (Ross and Forsyth, 2021). As Jennifer Hargreaves writes:

> the body is the most important signifier of meanings, and in the case of women and boxing . . . these are constantly contested and are changing according to the broader contexts of boxing discourse and gender relations of power. Although strength and muscularity in boxing have symbolically been a source of physical capital for men, the diversities and complexities of representations of the female body in boxing make it difficult to assess the extent to which the sport is a subversive activity for women.
> (Hargreaves, 1997, p. 47)

The sport of boxing is not just a site of contention or constrain for women; it can also be a social and cultural space through women self-discover (Andersen, 2021) and articulate identity formation (Tjønndal and Hovden, 2021), which is seen through Taylor's investment in boxing as a participant and advocate. Such identity formation, however, is a riddled with complexities relative to the social context and circumstance, which comports women boxers into 'ambivalent positions: on the one hand, they challenge the existing gender order; on the other hand, they reinforce the status quo by displaying traditional modes of femininity' (Mennesson, 2000, p. 21). This tension of empowering/disempowering (McGannon et al., 2019) is almost always evident across most sports for women given their historical exclusion of modern sport based on pseudo-science and cultural ideals about the purpose of and place for women's bodies (Messner, 2007). Boxing, in this sense, is a gender regime to the extent that it is 'not necessarily a site of/for resistance for women because of the inherent structure of the sport that is rooted in ideals of hypermasculinity and power and labour' (Lafferty and McKay, 2004, p. 265).

This is arguably how Taylor transcends traditional ideas of who is/can be a boxer, and thus why her performance of gender is complicated. To disguise herself as a boy – to hide her long hair up under head gear, to change her name at competitions, and to perform athleticism that is traditionally associated with masculinity, to effectively 'fight like a boy' to win competitions – leads to a general acceptance of being in the ring in the first place and advocating for more access to and visibility of women's boxing.

The Golden Days: A Lead Advocate for and Presence in Women's Boxing

I think we stepped through those ropes not as girls trying their hand at a man's game, but as equals. We were simply boxers.
(Taylor, 2012, p. 1490)

In 2012, women's lightweight boxing was included in the Olympics for the first time in history. For women's boxing to gain acceptance into the Olympics was, according to Taylor, 'a struggle' (Taylor, 2012, p. 98). The fact that it took more than a century for boxing to become open to women at the elite level (Olympic Boxing) speaks to the persistent gender ideologies and power relations that plague the sport. That said, the introduction of women's boxing at the Olympics cemented Taylor in the boxing legends iconography by becoming the first *ever* female Olympic lightweight boxing champion at the Games in London after defeating Russian Sofya Ochigava. This win was twofold: a gold medal for Ireland and recognized as 'one of Ireland's greatest ever sporting moments', and a gold medal for an athlete who had been part of the years-long campaign for women's boxing to be included in the Olympics schedule (DeLaney, 2022, n.p.). Such a prolonged campaign – the length and existence of which is indicative of the attitudes toward women's belonging in the sport – involved demonstrative tournaments in front of members of the International Olympic Committee to convince the sport policymakers to make room for fighters who are not men (Rotella, 1999). Again, her continued activist efforts in fighting for inclusion, including turning professional in 2016, have inspired upcoming fighters, particularly in Ireland, who otherwise may not have had the same opportunities in and equal access to boxing.

This win in 2012 seemed to provide the catalyst for more wins. For example, Taylor made her professional debut in November 2016, defeating Karina Szmalenberg. In December 2017, she won the World Boxing Association Light Weight against Jessica McCaskill. In April 2018, she retained this title and gained another one, the International Boxing Federation Light Weight against Victoria Bustos (Boxing Records, 2022). Most recently, Taylor defeated Karen Carabajal to secure and defend her lightweight title (O'Halloran, 2022). Such consecutive victories are unprecedented and unmatched by any female boxer. Therein lies the epitome of what is possible when opportunity in sport is made accessible; to emerge from a working-class community in rural Ireland where boxing was once banned to becoming one of most prolific and successful professional boxers of all time speaks to Taylor's commitment, caution, and courage as a member of a marginalised group in the sport and larger society. Further, it challenges the notion that women boxers are a 'parody' and thus cannot succeed or make money in the sport (Oates, 1987, p. 73).

Like all professional sport, winning matters. Nobody forgets the winner: their victorious status propels athletes' desirability for commercial and sport sponsorship, increases public interest/attention in them, and elevates their position for future competition (thus drawing more money for promoters, event establishments, and managers). As evidenced, Taylor is not new to winning. More to the point, the result of her winning is more sentimental than money and status in that her constant presence and winning in boxing has paved the way for younger generations of boxers to have the necessary facilities, investment, and support needed to participate – and win. For example, 25-year-old Amy Broadhurst and 20-year-old Aoife O'Rourke won gold medals the 2022 World Boxing Championships in light welterweight and light middleweight, respectively (Watterson, 2022a). Moreover, at the European Championships in October 2022, Ireland secured three gold, two sliver, and two bronze medals – the first time an Irish women's team has conquered medals at this level (Watterson, 2022b). Clearly, magic happens when women athletes pave the way for and support the inclusion of fellow women athletes in a sport that historically excluded them.

Present Day: A Recognisable Face in Women's Professional Boxing

> *[I was just] the teenage girl from Bray who dreamed of being a boxer.*
> (Taylor, 2012, p. 1836)

Importantly, Taylor was able to get to this point through her 'non-threatening' performance of self that enables her to attain success as a professional athlete. In many ways, she presents a docile and compliant self-image that is branded non-threatening to the power structures and gender relations in the sport. For example, she keeps her hair long, speaks softly, is non-confrontational during pre-and post-fight interviews, is often seen smiling in pictures and promotional materials, and maintains an 'acceptable' body type that is not too muscular but muscular enough to meet the demands of boxing. She is neither outspoken, too feminine, too masculine, too political, too controversial, or too ambiguous to be a threat. These verbal and non-verbal behaviours fit neatly into characteristics that are traditionally associated with hegemonic femininity. In other words, Taylor performs gender appropriately as a woman who is a boxer – so much so that in 2021 she was voted Ireland's 'Most Admired Sport's Personality' for the fifth year in a row, thereby clearly illustrating the positive reception she garners (McCaughren, 2021). This reception extends beyond Ireland's borders; her story of 'the girl who once fought for the right to fight' captured the attention of journalists, boxing fans, and news outlets alike, especially in the lead up to her fight against Serrano in the U.S. (Mannix, 2022). The narrative of boxers as individuals overcoming obstacles to attain success is not an uncommon one, and one that attracts public interest.

This identity is complicated, however, when read against the activist and rebellious identities projected onto her at various moments of her boxing career. Competing as a boy, for example, and her role in the inclusion of women's boxing in the 2012 Olympics, defies the non-threatening identity she often presents. Moreover, there are moments in which her performance of gender contradicts traditional ideals of femininity and by competing (and winning) in professional boxing (Tjønndal, 2016). This nuanced relationship between gender and performance and sport thus complicates the boxing identity. Fundamentally, though, Taylor's performance of gender is non-threatening to the power structures and gender regime within boxing. As Carl Rotella argues, women's boxing, 'in an institutionalizing phase that resembles men's boxing a century ago, has plenty of room for female versions of the "gentleman" boxer – people who present solid middle-class credentials of education' (Rotella, 1999, p. 587).

Following her historic win over Amanda Serrano in May 2022, and as a two-weight world champion holding all four world women's boxing titles and currently undisputed lightweight champion, Taylor is afforded the title of 'Ireland's greatest athlete', thereby blurring gendered sport dichotomies (O'Donoghue, 2022). From competing as a boy to being one of the most prominent and profitable faces of women's professional boxing is a story not many have to tell. Moreover, to make a successful career out of a sport that was non-existent less than 30 years ago, including sponsorship and endorsement deals, is nothing short of legendary. To get there was, as noted, not an easy endeavour. Although Taylor is 'genuinely not trying to prove anything, [she] just wanted to be treated like any other boxer', it is hard not to acknowledge the work she has done to bring women's boxing into the conversation, proving that women can and do, in fact, belong in spaces from which they have previously been excluded (Graham, 2022). The empowerment that comes with making that decision is hard to ignore (Cooky, 2018). Her physical presence (and success) politicises women's boxing in the broader socio-political landscape of mainstream boxing. As a trailblazer of and one the most recognisable faces in women's professional boxing, Taylor's body in boxing signifies social and cultural change in the sport and professional women's sport in general, with cultural attitudes towards women as boxers shifting, slowly but surely, and leading the way for future generations of women boxers.

In her interview for *BBC Sounds* in March 2022, Taylor noted the:

> things I had to go through as kid and to get to where I am now and where women's boxing is right now . . . every single boxing gym in Ireland is packed with female fighters and that to me is my legacy.
>
> (Taylor, 2022)

She is a boxer who is 'going with and against the grain of history' (Rotella, 1999, p. 589). Her legacy, needless to say, goes beyond the increased participation of girls and women in the sport of boxing in Ireland and beyond. Taylor's boxing trajectory helps expand and explicate what it means to be boxer and be in boxing. Moreover, it politicises women's boxing in the broader socio-political landscape of mainstream sport. In contrast to previous theorisations and conceptions of boxers/boxing, her undeniable, history-making success in this traditionally male-exclusive sport signifies how her identities and story transgress these misconceptions about a boxing identity.

Taylor's performance of identity enables the transition of disguising as a boy to compete in amateur boxing competitions to being one of the most successful women boxers in professional boxing. This performance ultimately enables her to occupy a space that is not threatening to gender norms and expectations within and outside the sport. In this way, Taylor's performance of identity reflects the complexities of being a boxer who is not a man.

Note

1 Moreover, my love of and previous participation in (university club and fitness class) boxing also informed my decision to submit an abstract for this book. As such, I consider boxing as a source of empowerment for women as a social and cultural space in which women can express themselves in ways that other spaces may not otherwise acknowledge.

Bibliography

Andersen, W. (2021) 'Sport and self-love: reflections on boxing and the construction of selfhood', *Journal of the Philosophy of Sport*, 48(1), p. 129145.

Boxing Records (2022) *Katie Taylor*. Available at: https://boxrec.com/en/proboxer/778185 (Accessed: 31 August 2022).

Branch, J. and Pilon, M. (2012) 'Tebow, a careful evangelical', *The New York Times*, 27 March. Available at: www.nytimes.com/2012/03/28/sports/football/tebow-professes-his-evangelical-faith-carefully.html (Accessed: 31 August 2022).

Butler, J. (2004) *Undoing gender*. London: Routledge.

Cheng, J.E. (2019) 'Religiosity, integration and sport: Muslim women playing Australian rules football', *Journal of Australian Studies*, 43(1), pp. 55–70.

Clarke, D. (2018) 'Katie Taylor: "stepping away from my dad was difficult"', *The Irish Times*, 13 October. Available at: www.irishtimes.com/culture/film/katie-taylor-stepping-away-from-my-dad-was-difficult-1.3656030 (Accessed: 31 August 2022).

Cooky, C. (2018) 'Women, sports and activism' in Cooky, C. and Messner, M.A. (eds.) *No Slam Dunk: gender, sport and the unevenness of social change*. New Brunswick, NJ: Rutgers University Press. pp. 70–90.

Delaney, L. (2022) 'Ten years ago Katie Taylor won gold for Ireland', *Balls*, 9 August. Available at: www.balls.ie/boxing/ten-years-ago-today-katie-taylor-won-gold-for-ireland-520022 (Accessed: 31 August 2022).

Ellis, R. and Weir, J.S. (2020) 'In praise of god: sport as worship in the practice and self-understanding of elite athletes', *Religions*, 11, p. 677.

Fonow, M.M. and Cook, J.A. (eds.) (1991) *Beyond methodology: feminist scholarship as lived research*. Bloomingdale: Indiana University Press.

Francombe-Webb, J. and Toffoletti, K. (2018) 'Sporting females: power, diversity, and the body', in Mansfield, L., Caudwell, J., Wheaton, B. and Watson, B. (eds.) *The Palgrave handbook of feminism and sport, leisure, and physical education*. London: Palgrave Macmillan, pp. 43–55.

Fullager, S., Richa, E., Pavlidis, A. and van Ingen, C. (2019) 'Feminist knowledges as interventions in physical cultures', *Leisure Sciences*, 41(1–2), pp. 1–16.

Gigney, G. (2022) 'Katie Taylor vs Amanda Serrano drew in 1.5 million viewers', *Boxing News*, 9 May. Available at: www.boxingnewsonline.net/katie-taylor-vs-amanda-serrano-drew-in-1-5-million-viewers/ (Accessed: 31 August 2022).

Goudsouzian, A. (2017) 'From Lew Alcindor to Kareem Abdul-Jabbar: race, religion, and representation in basketball, 1968–1975', *Journal of American Studies*, 52(2), pp. 437–470.

Graham, B.A. (2022) 'Katie Taylor revels in "best night of career" after historic win over Serrano', *The Guardian*, 1 May. Available at: www.theguardian.com/sport/2022/may/01/katie-taylor-revels-in-best-night-of-career-after-historic-win-amanda-serrano-boxing (Accessed: 31 August 2022).

Hargreaves, J. (1997) 'Women's boxing and related activities: introducing images and meanings', *Body & Society*, 3(4), pp. 33–49.

Hargreaves, J. and McDonald, I. (2000) 'Cultural studies and the sociology of sport', in Coakley, J. and Dunning, E. (eds.) *Handbook of sports studies*. London: Sage Publication, Inc, pp. 48–54.

Hynes, R. (2022) 'Katie Taylor v Amanda Serrano prize money: how much will each fighter earn?', *Irish Mirror*, 30 April. Available at: www.irishmirror.ie/sport/other-sport/boxing/katie-taylor-v-amanda-serrano-26837299 (Accessed: 31 August 2022).

Jarvie, G. (2006) *Sport, culture and society: an introduction*. London: Routledge.

Krane, V. and Baird, S.M. (2005) 'Using ethnography in applied sport psychology', *Journal of Applied Psychology*, 17(2), pp. 88–91.

Krane, V. and Mann, M. (2019) 'Inclusion or illusion? Lesbians' experiences in sport', in Krane, V. (ed.) *Sex, gender, and sexuality in sport: queer inquiries*. London: Routledge, pp. 69–86.

Krane, V., Ross, S.R., Sullivan Barak, K., Rowse, J.L. and Lucas-Carr, C.B. (2012) 'Unpacking our academic suitcases: the inner workings of our feminist research group', *Quest*, 64(4), pp. 249–267.

Lafferty, Y. and McKay, J. (2004) '"Suffragettes in satin shorts"? Gender and competitive boxing', *Qualitative Sociology*, 27(3), pp. 249–276.

Lincoln, Y.S., Lynham, S.A. and Guba, E.G. (2018) 'Paradigmatic Controversies, contradictions and emerging confluences, revisited', in Denzin, N.K. and Lincoln, Y.S. (eds.) *The Sage handbook of qualitative research*. Thousand Oaks, California: Sage Publications, Inc, pp. 97–128.

Lindner, K. (2012) 'Women's boxing at the 2012 Olympics: gender trouble?', *Feminist Media Studies*, 12(3), pp. 464–467.

Magdalinski, T. and Chandler, T.J.L. (2002) *With god on their side: sport in the service of religion*. London: Routledge.

Mannix, C. (2022) 'Katie Taylor's long, strange journey', *Sports Illustrated*, 27 April. Available at: www.si.com/boxing/2022/04/27/katie-taylor-journey-ireland-amanda-serrano-fight (Accessed: 31 August 2022).

Marquees, M. (2017) *Redemption song: Muhammad Ali and the spirit of the sixties*. London: Verso Books.

Matthews, C.R. (2016) 'The Tyranny of the male preserve', *Gender & Society*, 30(2), pp. 312–333.

McCaughren, S. (2021) 'Boxer Taylor a hit with sponsors as popularity among public endures', *Independent*, 5 December. Available at: www.independent.ie/business/irish/boxer-taylor-a-hit-with-sponsors-as-popularity-among-public-endures-41116726.html (Accessed: 31 August 2022).

McGannon, K.R., Schinke, R.J., Ge, Y. and Blodgett, A.T. (2019) 'Negotiating gender and sexuality: a qualitative study of elite women boxer intersecting identities and sport psychology implications', *Journal of Applied Sport Psychology*, 31(2), pp. 168–186.

McNaughton, M.J. (2012) 'Insurrectionary womanliness: gender and the (boxing) ring', *The Qualitative Report*, 17(33), pp. 1–13.

Mennesson, C. (2000) ' "Hard" women and "soft" women: the social construction of identities among female boxers', *International Review for the Sociology of Sport*, 35(1), pp. 21–33.

Messner, M.A. (2007) *Out of play: critical essays on gender and sport*. New York: State University of New York Press.

Mitra, P. (2009) 'Challenging stereotypes: the case of Muslim female boxers in Bengal', *The International Journal of the History of Sport*, 26(12), pp. 1840–1851.

Oates, J.C. (1987) *On boxing*. NJ: Echo Press.

Oates, J.C. (2011) 'Rape and the boxing ring', in Kimball, G. (ed.) *At the fights: American writers on boxing*. New York: Library of America, pp. 392–397.

O'Donoghue, C. (2022) 'Katie Taylor's fight last weekend was seen by 1.5 million viewers worldwide and in 170+ different countries confirm DAZN', *The Irish Post*, May 4 2022. Available at: https://www.irishpost.com/sport/katie-taylors-fight-last-weekend-was-seen-by-1-5-million-viewers-worldwide-and-in-170-different-countries-confirm-dazn-233755

O'Halloran, C. (2022) 'Katie Taylor tops Karen Elizabeth Carabajal via unanimous decision in title defense', *ESPN*, 29 October. Available at: www.espn.com/boxing/story/_/id/34903902/katie-taylor-tops-karen-elizabeth-carabajal-via-unanimous-decision-title-defense (Accessed: 30 October 2022).

Paradis, E. (2012) 'Boxers, briefs or bras? Bodies, gender and change in the boxing gym', *Body & Society*, 18(2), pp. 82–109.

Pollack, S. (2022) 'From Bray to Madison Square Garden: The unstoppable rise of Katie Taylor', *The Irish Times*, 9 May. Available at: www.irishtimes.com/sport/from-bray-to-madison-square-garden-the-unstoppable-rise-of-katie-taylor-1.4873216 (Accessed: 31 August 2022).

Porter, K. (2018) 'Rory McIlroy sells his massive Florida home for $11.5 million after buying Ernie Els' property', *CBS Sports*, 7 November. Available at: www.cbssports.com/golf/news/rory-mcilroy-sells-his-massive-florida-home-for-11-5-million-after-buying-ernie-els-property/ (Accessed: 31 August 2022).

Roper, E.A. (2016) 'Cultural studies in sport and exercise psychology', in Schinke, R.J., McGannon, K.R. and Smith, B. (eds.) *Routledge international handbook of sport psychology*. Oxon: Routledge, pp. 274–281.

Ross, M.I. and Forsyth, J. (2021) 'A good fight: how indigenous women approach boxing as a mechanism for social change', *Journal of Sport and Social Issues*, 45(4), pp. 303–328.

Rotella, C. (1999) 'Good with her hands: women, boxing, and work', *Critical Inquiry*, 25(3), pp. 566–598.

Rothstein, M. (2022) 'The two sides of Katie Taylor: the success – and sacrifices – that took her all the way to the top of the sport', *ESPN*, 12 April. Available at: www.espn.co.uk/boxing/story/_/id/33810719/the-two-sides-katie-taylor-success-sacrifices-took-all-way-top-sport (Accessed: 31 August 2022).

Schneider, P. (2021) 'Sparring with patriarchy: the rise of female boxers in the Global South', *Journal of Gender Studies*, 30(8), pp. 887–900.

Schulberg, B. (2006) *Ringside: a treasury of boxing reportage*. London: Ivan R. Dee.

Springer, S. (2017) 'Laila Ali is undefeated – even against her father', *WBUR*, 16 June. Available at: www.wbur.org/onlyagame/2017/06/16/laila-ali-boxing-muhammad (Accessed: 31 August 2022).

Srikrishna, V. (2020) 'Practising feminist methodologies in applied research: the undone deal', *Indian Journal of Gender Studies*, 27(3), pp. 420–430.

Taylor, K. (2012) *My Olympic dream*. London: Simone & Schuster UK Ltd.

Taylor, K. (2022) 'Laura Whitmore: under the spotlight', *BBC Sounds*, 18 March. Available at: www.bbc.co.uk/sounds/play/p0bw854j (Accessed: 31 August 2022).

Thorpe, H., Barbour, K. and Bruce, T. (2011) '"Wandering and wondering": theory and representation in feminist physical cultural studies', *Sociology of Sport Journal*, 28, pp. 106–134.

Tjønndal, A. (2016) 'The inclusion of women's boxing in the Olympic games: a qualitative content analysis of gender and power in boxing', *Qualitative Sociology Review*, 12(3), pp. 85–99.

Tjønndal, A. and Hovden, J. (2021) '"Will God condemn me because I love boxing?" Narratives of young female immigrant Muslim boxers in Norway', *European Journal of Women's Studies*, 28(4), pp. 455–470.

United States Olympic & Paralympic Museum. *Olympic boxing*. Available at: https://usopm.org/hall-of-fame/boxing/ (Accessed: 31 August 2022).

Wacquant, L.J.D. (1992) 'The social logic of boxing in black Chicago: toward a sociology of pugilism', *Sociology of Sport Journal*, 9, pp. 221–254.

Walseth, K. (2006) 'Young Muslim women and sport: the impact of identity work', *Leisure Studies*, 25(1), pp. 75–94.

Watson, N.J. and Parker, A. (2013) *Sports and Christianity: historical and contemporary perspectives*. London: Routledge.

Watterson, J. (2022a) 'World champions: Amy Broadhurst and Lisa O'Rourke win gold medals', *The Irish Times*, 19 May. Available at: www.irishtimes.com/sport/other-sports/world-champions-amy-broadhurst-and-lisa-o-rourke-win-gold-medals-1.4883162 (Accessed: 31 August 2022).

Watterson, J. (2022b) 'Kellie Harrington, Amy Broadhurst and Aoife O'Rourke win gold for Ireland at European championships', *The Irish Times*, 22 October. Available at: www.irishtimes.com/sport/boxing/2022/10/22/kellie-harrington-amy-broadhurst-and-aoife-orourke-win-gold-for-ireland-at-european-championships/ (Accessed: 31 August 2022).

Williams, R. (1958) *Culture and society 1780–1950*. London: The Hogarth Press.

Woodward, K. (2007) *Boxing, masculinity and identity*. London: Routledge.

Chapter 9

Letting Down the Team?
Individualism, Selfishness, and Kinship in Women's Boxing

Sarah Crews

> If you're trapped in the dream of the other, you're fucked.
> (Gilles Deleuze cited in Žižek, 2008, p. 48)[1]

Professional women's boxing in the West has expanded exponentially between 2012–2022. The inclusion of women's boxing in the London 2012 Olympics changed the landscape for female participation in boxing dramatically. It brought about new audiences for the amateur sport and enabled promoters of professional boxing to capitalise on the vast media attention directed towards female Olympic athletes. Since 2012, UK-based boxing promoters in particular have started to invest in female boxers, developing partnerships and branding opportunities to market women's boxing to new and emerging audiences. The aim of promoters like Matchroom and BOXXER, and broadcasters Sky Sports Boxing, is to establish a regular viewership for the sport. Though improvements for female boxers have been made as a result of the platforms and practices established post-2012, little else has changed. Academic scholarship demonstrates how the inclusion of women's boxing in the Olympics legitimised the sport, opening up new discursive possibilities for boxing and its participants (Woodward, 2014). However, female athletes still navigate challenges that have dominated female experiences in boxing since the earliest instances of their inclusion in the sport – namely, rights to equal pay, requisite airtime and media coverage, and having to negotiate double standards pertaining to expectations of, and assumptions about, women in boxing. These underlying issues facing female boxers are rooted in the complicated nature in which female bodies are positioned and observed by boxing promoters, broadcasters, sports media journalists, and audiences. Boxing is an embodied practice – one in which women have benefitted greatly. Female boxing experiences captured in autoethnographic studies, autobiographies, biopics, and interviews frequently narrate the transformative potential found in and through the physical practice of boxing.[2] The socio-historical gains made by female boxers are also well documented and speak to a longstanding connection between boxing and female-centred activism.

DOI: 10.4324/9781003312635-12

But whereas female boxers access, embody, and perform modes of expression that are otherwise limited in the daily lives of women and girls, these same athletic bodies nevertheless negotiate an objectifying gaze. Boxing historian Kasia Boddy describes the contradictions that female boxers face in her essay 'Watching Women Box':

> Learning to box . . . could offer women an education in a particular cultural practice – that is, the disciplined expression of aggression (or, as it tends to be called empowerment). . . . It is perhaps, salutary to note that as the 2012 Olympic Games approached, most of the discussion about women's boxing has focused on the clothes the fighters will wear.
> (Boddy, 2014, p. 258)

This chapter explores what Lisa Downing describes as the restrictive and contradictory 'double bind' (Downing, 2019, p. 101) that punctuates how female expressions and behaviour are received in the public domain. This 'double bind' entraps 'Women' within 'totalizing . . . overwhelming' (2019, p. 101) and all-encompassing identity categories. Individuals who resist such categorisation are at risk of becoming intelligible as women altogether. Downing's term 'Women' refers to the generic but nevertheless harmful disciplinary standards that underscore popular readings of *all female-presenting bodies* – be that cis-gendered women or trans women. The restrictions imposed on those betwixt the 'category of Women' (2019, p. 101) include forgoing the same freedoms of individual expression afforded to male-presenting bodies. Downing's thesis is particularly important for understanding the debates and ambiguities surrounding the professionalisation of women's boxing post-2012, because the subsequent increase in media focus towards female boxers is forcing conversations about the gendered restrictions they experience. Shifting the discussion from *if* women should participate in boxing to *how* female boxing identities are constructed and received in popular discourse involves attending to gendered assumptions in and outside of boxing. Existing scholarship denotes both the positive cultural impact and the socio-economic failures of the London 2012 Olympics for women's sport broadly. This chapter builds on that research, focusing on the very urgent changes occurring in the recent history of professional women's boxing in the West.

Methodology: Barbie Girl in a Boxing World

I utilise feminist scholarship to analyse the latest trends, challenges, and discourses derived from reactions to increased female participation in boxing. Recognising how particular female boxers are *grouped* together and *distinguished* is important for understanding the current landscape of professional women's boxing. It is also imperative for charting the recent developments in the growth of the sport, and the future projections mapped out by boxing's gatekeepers – both of which rely heavily on narratives of Olympic alumnus. The expansion of social media has been instrumental in shaping and changing attitudes towards women's boxing. Platforms such as Twitter and Instagram have made it possible for female boxers to explore and publicly express their identities in and through boxing; these same platforms have made it easier (and indeed more creative) for female boxers to develop and sustain networks of support. Twitter has been foundational for connecting female boxers across global communities. Instagram has been core to establishing the far-reaching visibility of female boxers, documenting the careers and achievements of athletes away from mainstream media. This study engages content analysis of interviews and social media posts relating to specific boxing promoters and female boxers. UK-based Matchroom Boxing is said to be leading the way in promoting women's boxing since Chairman Eddie Hearn signed a long-term contract with Irish Olympic Gold medallist and professional boxer Katie Taylor following the 2016 Olympics. In addition to signing an exclusive partnership with broadcaster DAZN (described as the Netflix of sports broadcasters), Matchroom invested in several female boxers with the intention of generating global interest in women's boxing. Athletic abilities aside, Hearn is open about how the scale of a boxer's social media platform impacts their opportunities for signing with a company like Matchroom. To illustrate this, I have chosen to focus on a selection of in-depth interviews with Australian boxer and IBF Super Bantamweight World Champion Ebanie Bridges, as well as social media posts Bridges circulated between 2020–2022. I study the online activity and performances of Bridges – former maths teacher and competitive bodybuilder – who created vast social media interest in 2020, culminating in Bridges signing with Matchroom. Bridges describes her process of 'manifesting' her dream career in boxing during a podcast. On a trip to Vegas to see the third fight between British boxer and celebrity Tyson 'Gypsy King' Fury and American boxer Deontay 'Bronze Bomber' Wilder, Bridges experienced first-hand the support UK boxing fans show particular boxing personalities: 'there was just Brits everywhere and I thought "man, I need these . . . fans. I need to fight in . . . this kind atmosphere"' (Bridges, 2022b, *The Diren Kartal Show*). A self-proclaimed 'brand', 'businesswoman', and 'entertainer', Bridges (2022b) understands the importance of marketing and self-promotion to being a successful professional boxer. Making it her mission to 'get on Twitter' (Bridges, 2022b, *The Diren Kartal Show*), make boxing connections, and establish audience engagement, Bridges posted frequently during 2020 and conducted several interviews with boxing-related YouTubers. The aim was to ultimately travel to the UK and fight on a Matchroom show. Bridges gained a widespread fanbase within and outside of boxing, particularly individuals from what Bridges refers to as her 'adopted' hometown, Leeds (in West Yorkshire, England). However, Bridges also received backlash for some of the tactics she used to create attention – namely her unashamed awareness of her physical/visual appeal. Bridges has been accused of 'being bad for the sport' and failing to encourage viewers to watch women's boxing 'for the correct reasons'.[3] But her fans are ruthlessly supportive and champion Bridges' athletic improvement and overt ownership of her sexuality and femininity. Bridges understands she is a divisive figure in women's boxing. Describing the responses to her posts from pre-fight weigh-ins, whereby Bridges wears lingerie instead of the customary sportswear bra and brief set, Bridges states:

> British are like . . . who's this girl, this boxer . . . saying c*nt . . . in lingerie with these big titties . . . what's going on? And because the UK is so conservative . . . especially the boxing, you know? . . .. A lot of the boxers are . . . media trained, like institutionalised, I feel . . . everyone is the same.
> (Bridges, 2022b, *The Diren Kartal Show*)

Known by her alias the 'Blonde Bomber', Bridges proclaims to have the largest social media following for women's boxing across all platforms (Bridges, 2023). She *intends* on standing out as different and celebrates being 'herself' rather than what Bridges refers to as a 'cookie cutter' (Bridges, 2023) female boxer in an increasingly competitive marketplace. Critiques of Bridges, which include her generating appeal for women's boxing for the 'wrong' reasons and purportedly shining a negative light on other female boxers, are reliant upon the type of culturally enmeshed assumptions about women and female bodies that Downing draws attention to in *Selfish Women*. Accusations that Bridges is single-handedly compromising the gains made by other female boxers, thereby corrupting possibilities for further change, speak to archaic perceptions of women which insist that they cannot be *both* professional athletes *and* physically attractive – they cannot be independent thinkers *and* also invested in common, collective goals. Put differently, Bridges' self-propelled campaign for women's boxing is ether dismissed as silly and irrelevant, or Bridges is labelled as disruptive of the broader project of women's boxing – ergo she is selfish. During her six years as a boxer, Bridges has unsettled some of the dominant narratives underpinning the recent history (and future projections) of women's boxing. Bridges is not an Olympic alumnus like Katie Taylor, Claressa Shields, Savannah Marshall, and Natasha Jonas (to name only a few) – and therefore does not carry the same credence afforded to Olympic boxers, such as benefitting from 'empowerment' and 'trailblazing' rhetoric that accompanies much of the media attention directed towards Olympians who have chosen to turn professional.

Far from a marketing-friendly gimmick, though, I argue that Bridges is an important addition to the current and future landscape of women's boxing as her performance of self, and the reception to this from fans, media outlets, and other athletes exposes key myths about progress in boxing. Exploring how Bridges has been received makes visible the current state of play for female participants who have only recently been granted access to a male-dominated sport. Instead of problematising what Bridges' performance of self does to challenge rigidly defined markers of important, 'serious' contributions in boxing, I suggest viewing Bridges' activity in and outside of the ring as central to unpacking the restrictions female athletes navigate. A key legacy of 2012 is highlighting and celebrating the most visible 'firsts' in women's boxing: the first women to win gold (Nicola Adams); the first double Olympian (Katie Taylor, Claressa Shields, Adams); the first American boxer, female or male, to win consecutive medals (Shields). Such narratives persist in the post-Olympian careers of these athletes, cementing their place as 'history makers' and 'pioneers'. The issue with what I define as the 'trailblazer trend' in women's boxing is not just that continually defining these 'new' and 'first' achievements constructs individuals like Adams (GB), Taylor (Ireland), and Shields (USA) as *exceptional*, gravitating towards these narratives also undermines and erases other significant contributions to the sport. Against this backdrop, Bridges' activity is considered unconventional with respect to the professionalisation of women's boxing post-2012 and 2016. Her actions are at odds with the female-led activism marked by promoters, sports media, and fans as driving the all-important change for female participants in boxing. I study Bridges as her role in women's boxing highlights, in the most extreme way, the complex and contradictory 'double bind' governing the public profiles of female athletes. As a blonde, hyperfeminine body in a masculine space, Bridges complexifies stereotypes of female boxers. Female boxers are *either* 'parody' to their male counterparts *or* 'monstrous' in their performance of femininity, according to Joyce Carol Oates (1987, p. 73). They are *either* sexualised and at risk of objectification *or* considered serious athlete-activists – empowered and empowering – as recent popular narratives have put it.[4] 'Altogether too much has been asked' of female boxers, writes Boddy (2014, p. 259). Whether it is abiding by Angelo Dundee's description of boxer Barbara Buttrick: 'a perfect English lady outside the ring but a lioness when she climbed through the ropes' (in Boddy, 2014, p. 259), or being bound by 'discrimination and unequal treatment on the basis of gender' (Carty, 2015, p. 153), female boxers have a long way to escape the 'double binds' that limit their potential selves and experiences in boxing. Bridges, I argue, subverts recent tropes in women's boxing, revealing a host of resistances to female inclusion in boxing that the male-dominated institution continues to suppress and gloss over.

#Andthenew?

Narratives deemed important in boxing – those that carry cultural significance and capture media focus – typically feature boxers who understand their performances of self and social value through evidence of self-discipline and self-regulation. Assumptions of men's boxing foreground and are buttressed by narratives of heroic masculinity (Woodward, 2014). However, Lennox's research (2012) shows how 'Rather than explicitly seeking financial wealth, or the hallmarks of a tough, strong, masculine persona', male boxers also 'buy-in to modernity's grand narratives of self-control and docility' (Crews and Lennox, 2020, p. 35). Notions of docility and compliance are engrained in boxing narratives to the extent that these same qualities transfer onto depictions of female boxers. The remarks made by Bridges about British boxers appearing 'institutionalised' speaks to a notion that to be a 'good' ambassador of the sport, a boxer should embody a contained and disciplined public persona.[5] The 'trailblazer trend' in women's boxing is an example of where ideas about 'appropriate' behaviour remain tied to certain types of bodies. The relentless centring of Olympic boxers in sports media, and the marketing of these athletes as sole 'pioneers' and 'trailblazers' for women's boxing, not only limits the scope in which audiences access and engage with the diverse range of female participation in boxing, it also constructs a harmful binary that renders some female boxers as 'legitimate' and others as not. It seems there is *a correct* public image for women's boxing, which post-2012 binds 'correctness' to female Olympians. This observation in no way serves to discredit what Olympic athletes have achieved; rather, it means to recognise how the marketing of women's boxing on the shoulders of 'exceptional individuals'[6] encourages a singular perspective of what a female boxer *can* and *should* be. Professional boxer Ellie Scotney reflects on how training at an elite level with Team GB limited her self-expression in boxing: 'they kind of mould you into one sort of style and my character definitely didn't fit in . . .. I hated it, I was very down' (2023). Bridges takes this one step further, describing the Olympic trend as a threat to the careers of other female boxers:

> What happens if you're not a gold medallist . . . if you're not that style? What happens if you're not like quiet and shy and look like that? What happens if you are a very feminine woman, and you don't have a GB background or USA boxing background but you can fight? Or what happens if you do look like Barbie and you want to fight?
> (Bridges, 2023)

But understanding the possibilities of female fighters beyond Olympic 'trailblazers' requires paying attention to the sort of nuance in human behaviour and possibilities of social value that female public figures are rarely afforded. Though Taylor's athleticism, activism, and grassroots-level impact are unquestionable,[7] the positioning of a white, female athlete as a key trailblazer/pioneer for the sport is nevertheless pervasive, problematic, and inaccurate.

Shields is open about how her race and confident larger-than-life personality complicate notions of 'trailblazing' in women's boxing. Whilst Shields is a two-time Olympic gold medallist, her achievements outweigh most boxers, and her activism is far-reaching, Shields does not benefit from the same level of media support, public warmth, and appraisal that Taylor does. Shields' observation that her self-expression is not as palatable in the current media landscape as Taylor's (Crews and Lennox, 2020) affirms what Cooky and Antunovic suggest about the function of feminism in the careers of female athletes: sports media captures the activism of white female athletes at the cost of the labour of women of colour. 'Feminism circulates in an economy of visibility, where certain feminisms become more visible than others' (2020, p. 692). Therefore, in addition to rendering women of colour invisible, popular narratives of feminism in sport also undermine bodies and performances that do not fit a purportedly media-friendly image (Crews and Lennox, 2020). When Taylor is used as exemplar of success in women's boxing and her name leveraged to discredit other female participants, the repercussions are violent and damaging. If only specified female bodies are considered legitimate boxers and certain activist efforts identified, the work of female boxers broadly is devalued and possibilities for alternative performances of femininity are constrained. As Bridges states: 'because she's so successful, everyone is like "you need to be like Katie Taylor". . . . I'm Ebanie Bridges' (2022b, *The Diren Kartal Show*).

Bridges' brand of femininity may be considered unthreatening in that she benefits from her whiteness and how her core messaging of female empowerment, authenticity, and body confidence[8] align with popular discourse on female bodies. But whilst promoter Eddie Hearn is happy to capitalise on Bridges' commercial appeal, he nevertheless makes distinctions between who is *trailblazing* the way for future generations and who is not. Hearn publicly endorses Taylor's performance of self in boxing as exemplary, admiring her dutiful commitment to the 'next generation of young female athletes' (MMAFightingonSBN, 2022). Hearn does affirm Bridges as a legitimate athlete and World Champion, but his emphatic praise for Taylor indicates a preference of styles. 'As someone with 2 daughters', says Hearn, 'I look at Katie Taylor in a world of Instagram and TikTok and say "I want you to have a dream like Katie Taylor"' (MMAFightingonSBN, 2022). The trailblazer trend continues a legacy of distinguishing female bodies in boxing, which comes at the cost of embracing a diverse and complex breadth of 'changemakers' – Taylor and Shields included. The 10-year anniversary of women's boxing as an Olympic sport in 2022 marked the pinnacle of honouring the positive impact of female Olympians with two major events promoted by Matchroom and BOXXER, respectively, as 'firsts', moments for 'history', and 'legacy'. Matchroom's promotion of Katie Taylor and Amanda Serrano at Madison Square Garden (MSG) generated significant levels of enthusiasm, as did BOXXER's staging of the first legislated all-female boxing card in London. BOXXER pairing Olympic rivals[9] Claressa Shields and Savannah Marshall and the event at MSG demonstrated a gestural turn towards investing in future female athletes and boxing communities. These events moved towards wider-scale recognition and equity in professional women's boxing, but they also reinforced how organisations such as Matchroom and BOXXER are overpromising and underdelivering in terms of creating long-term, sustainable change for female participation in boxing. Former boxer Jane Couch (active between 1994–2007) argued that Shields v Marshall was 'massive, but boxing is still very anti-women' (in Davies, 2022). Couch continued:

> There are so many girls out there now that are fighting, trying to train, trying to hold down day jobs, who don't have any sponsors . . . there is still so much to do to put women's boxing on anything like an even keel with men's boxing.
>
> (in Davies, 2022)

Away from Olympian tropes of 'athletic supremacy' and 'national hero',[10] professional boxing remains an economic activity driven by commercial imperatives. Hearn himself justifies equal pay for women in the sector on commercial grounds, prompting US professional boxer Heather Hardy to condemn 'the systemic sexism that is so built into the sport of boxing that even gold medallists get on the stage and thank men for the opportunity to be there' (MMAFightingonSBN, 2022). The pervasive, much-vaunted project of 'trailblazing' in women's boxing, where 'trailblazing' refers to interpretations of leading by status quo put forward by boxing media, underscores what Woodward agues is an 'incremental' (2014, p. 242) effect of the Olympics, which produced only further uncertainty for female boxers. Moreover, Tjønndal suggests the broader impact of the Olympics on 'innovation, inclusion and exclusion' (2019) in elite level boxing is ambiguous. The focus on Olympic trailblazer narratives comes at the expense of critical consideration of the inequalities and access issues for women at grassroots, amateur, and professional levels within the sport.

Bridges destabilises trailblazer stereotypes presented in current and future visions of boxing for two reasons: 1) she is not an Olympian, therefore her activism is not recognised as advancing the sport. Bridges' priorities do not straightforwardly align with the 'history-making' and 'for legacy' initiatives driving narratives of change in women's boxing. 2) Bridges' overt confidence and hyperfeminine performance create conflict with future-orientated ideas about boxing, as her presence seemingly reactivates 'old' and 'outdated' modes of female expression in sport. For some, Bridges is guilty of reigniting battles that have already been fought and purportedly won for female boxers. Her support for ring girls on social media, for example, was viewed, by some, as regressing the progress made by other women in boxing. However, as Bridges' self-awarded title 'pioneer of . . . femininity' in boxing indicates, the historically complicated relationship between boxing, femininity, and the broader sexualisation of female bodies extends beyond Bridges: *it is neither new nor resolved*. Bridges' desire to teach 'little girls. . . . You don't have to be masculine and box' (2022b, *The Diren Kartal Show*), whilst at the same time defending ring girls' right to be involved in boxing, *confuses* her critics because these viewpoints disrupt binary distinctions used to justify how female bodies *should* participate in boxing. Bridges previously worked as a ring girl – namely because female participation in combat sports was illegal in Australia until 2008 and Bridges wanted to be part of the events. Bridges was also a competitive bodybuilder, meaning she understood, enjoyed, and was skilled at entertaining audiences with her body (2022b, *The Diren Kartal Show*). The backlash against Bridges' support for ring girls further reinforces the explicitly comparative and disciplinary rhetoric concerning female bodies in boxing. That female boxers are still subjected to scrutiny in terms of 'acceptable' and 'unacceptable' forms of femininity in boxing illustrates how deeply ingrained perspectives like Oates' 1987 remarks on women in boxing are. Such dismissive and reductive notions about femininity in boxing are evident in perspectives that celebrate Olympic and 'serious' boxers as 'empowered women' whilst simultaneously *blaming* rings girls (and their supporters) for supposedly stifling progress in women's boxing. The habit of pitting different styles of femininity against each other – and creating space for only a certain type of 'token women' within male-dominated spaces – is an example of where patriarchal-informed, value-based judgements make their way into feminisms, says Downing (2019, p. 142). In boxing, some female bodies (read: athletic and in keeping with the safe petametres of appropriate masculine/feminine physicality) are popularised as superior to others (read: the purportedly shameful and anachronistic 'body work') (Crews and Lennox, 2020, p. 66) of ring girls. Carlo Rotella, for example, argues that ring girls *let down other women* in boxing, displaying their bodies and 'strut[ing]' between rounds, eroding the innovative work of female boxers (Crews and Lennox, 2020, p. 66). Bridges opposes this rationale and fiercely defends the role of ring girls on the grounds that these women are genuine boxing fans and should not be shamed for how they choose to participate or earn money. Bridges' Instagram and Twitter posts picturing her with various ring girls highlight the reciprocal nature of the support they have for each other, gesturing towards a form of female kinship and respect in boxing, which unsettles hegemonic ideas about how relationships between women in boxing function.

Letting Down the Team

> Throughout history and indeed up to the present date, one of the messages that women in culture receive is that we're not supposed to prioritise ourselves . . . women and children . . . always go together. Women are infantilised. . . . Women are family.
>
> (Downing, 2019)

Cultural understandings of 'Women' see the central function of women in society as being 'for others' (Downing, 2019). This notion is consistent in recent readings of female boxers who are popularised by way of 'trailblazing' *for* other women, *for* the next generation. Instead of concentrating on long-term investment in professionalising women's boxing, organisations persistently rely on individual athletes and position their achievements as (short-term) collective gains for the sport. Furthermore, individual successes are rarely celebrated on their own terms – typically they are qualified as doing good for others. A question reporters frequently ask athletes: 'what would it mean to you to win', is, for female athletes, loaded with expectations that her labour will *contribute to something greater than her 'self'*. The weight of this assumption is evident in a pre-fight head-to-head discussion between Bridges and her UK opponent Shannon Courtenay, which saw Bridges defend her statement about wanting to win *for* herself and *by being herself*. Bridges told interviewer Adam Smith that she wanted to win for her 'own self-motivation', closely followed by her saying she also wanted to inspire her students, explaining her absence from school to them by stating 'your teacher is going to be a champion'.[11] The recruitment of self-sacrifice narratives for individual female boxers works to resolve cultural anxieties about how the demanding nature of athletic labour is at odds with homogenised ideas of female identity. Women who prioritise themselves over others – or who show too much independence – are labelled as selfish (Downing, 2019). Boxing narratives transcend time, place, and nation. For example, the stories boxers are 'fed', which 'lionize the defiant individual and portray the boxer as a lone warrior' (Crews and Lennox, 2020, p. 15). Gender, though, complicates how individuality and narrative intersect in boxing.

Historical examples of individuals going against the grain in women's boxing shows how self-determination for women reads as *letting down the team*. US boxer Christy Martin (active between 1989–2012) was (and still is) criticised for dismissing opinions that her actions in and outside of the ring were *feminist* in the sense that her efforts represent a conscious commitment to pursuing collective change for women in boxing. In 1996, Martin was featured in *Sports Illustrated*, making it clear that her sole motivation in boxing was personal gain. Posing with a vacuum cleaner, Martin declared that she is 'not out to make a statement about women in boxing. . . . This is about Christy Martin' (in Boddy, 2014, p. 257). Shields publicly shared her frustration with Martin (and Laila Ali) for not doing more to rid boxing of resistances towards women competing at the highest level: 'Who did Christy Martin give the blueprint too?' questions Shields, 'What about Laila Ali?' (2019). I have argued elsewhere that a defining characteristic of women's boxing is the cyclical nature in which the sport and its athletes disappear from public consciousness almost as quickly as they are visible. The *collective forgetting* of the histories and activist legacies of women's boxing is consistent, deliberate, and *strategic*: it speaks to the recurring threat of patriarchal values in boxing and broader culture. Women's boxing is nebulous in that it is built upon the transient and fragile shoulders of male and female *ghosts* who haunt the sport (Crews and Lennox, 2020, p. 106). Shields' assumption that these boxers could have done more to improve circumstances for future generations of women and girls might be naïve and unreasonable, but her upset towards navigating the same degradation of the skill and expertise that former female boxers withstood – not to mention the relentless questioning of women's right to be in the sport at all – is understandable. Shields asks the question: haven't we been here before? That some feel Martin *should* have been operating in the interest of *all* women – present and future – resonates with both the newly defined responsibility of female boxers to operate *for* other women, and Downing's thesis that female figures who go against the 'collective' interests of women, are, consequently, labelled *selfish*.

> For women, who are supposed . . . to be life-giving, to be nurturing, to be *for the other*, and therefore literally *self-less*, it is a far more serious transgression to be selfish while a woman – indeed it is a category violation of identity.
>
> (Downing, 2019, p. 1)

The rise in female empowerment discourse certainly captures more refined ideas about women's right to *independence, choice*, and *individual agency*. However, the frequent oversimplification of these ideas in popular debates ensures that female boxers remain trapped within a belief system that sees some of their behaviours and attitudes as *transgressive* of the broader category of women. Critiquing 1990s female boxers for not fulfilling an imposed moral obligation for female athletes to pave the way for future generations and leaving the sport better than they found it assumes that these athletes had the means, support, and opportunity to undertake this type of labour – not to mention the desire. Male athletes are rarely subjected to such grand and labour-intensive expectations because it is considered reasonable for male public figures to act solely out of self-interest. The fact that female boxers still experience what several women active in the 1990s have identified as promoters and organisations exploiting them for financial gain and for their niche commercial appeal demonstrates the lack of attention afforded to how 'progress' in boxing is identified and *who* it is benefitting. Boddy notes the patronising tone in which Laila Ali was referred to as a 'manicurist on a mission' during the build up to her fight with Jacqui Frazier, and the slurs used against 'fat girl' Freeda Foreman (2014, p. 258). Contemplating the torrent of abuse and ridicule directed towards female boxers in the 1990s, including media commentaries that made it 'difficult to tease out athletic from sexual objectification' (Carty, 2005, p. 147), resonates with global feminist projects 'Times Up' and #metoo. These movements have created awareness of the hostile, toxic, and misogynistic practices inflicted upon female bodies across media and in the workplace. But in the age of social media, everyday misogyny, ridicule, and exclusion of the grounds of gender expression remain a significant threat to female athletes.[12] One of the more complicated aspects to reconcile about how Bridges contributes to boxing is her links to tabloid outlets *The Daily Star* and *The Daily Sport*, whose brands were established upon their incessant objectification of female bodies. The same type of outlets reporting on 'butch' or 'unfeminine' (2014, p. 258) female boxers in the 1990s now celebrate Bridges boxing, galvanising her social media content and rewriting her posts in the same 'shocking' clickbait tone as before. A significant shift in this complex landscape, though, is that Bridges – for the most part – is dictating the narrative. On *The George Groves Boxing Club* podcast, Bridges shares a private message to her from *The Daily Star*, which reads:

> Thank you for embracing our content as much as you do . . . you have no idea just how valuable your stories are for our site. Last year the only topics that drove more traffic to our website was the world cup and Manchester United.
>
> (Bridges, 2023)

Bridges knows these media platforms benefit from her as much as she does from sharing their content to expand her profile and encourage broader appeal for women in boxing. For Bridges, critics fail to see that she is 'the most followed female boxer in the world on every single platform', and uses that platform 'to promote other women' (2023). Countering opinions labelling her 'bad for boxing', Bridges suggests that in establishing her own success, she also is working towards the common goal of getting 'women's boxing . . . seen' (2023). 'I want all of these women to be seen', says Bridges, 'I'm not selfish. . . . The more we shine and the more we support each other the bigger is all going to get. Our commercial value going to go up' (2023). The remaining issue for some female boxers is the manner in which women's boxing in *seen*, which is a valid concern in light of the historical status of female boxer as novelty – not to mention how female bodies are *either* measured against 'all-encompassing' criteria *or* defined via what Downing terms 'identity category violations' (2019). In a plethora of myopic perspectives on female boxers, Bridges' voice stands out as attending to the urgent need for women to be treated as individuals. It is remiss, therefore, to disregard Bridges' actions as letting down – or harmful to – other women in boxing. Instead, Bridges embodies what Downing defines as 'female self-fulness', whereby in operating out of self-interest, Bridges' opens up opportunities for female boxers to operate beyond binary distinctions, demonstrating where individuality and 'strategic common-cause-making can co-exist and flourish' (2019, p. 156).

What Fans? OnlyFans

Bridges irritates popular ideas about female boxers because her performance of self cannot be easily pinned down. In some respects, Bridges' self-expression aligns seamlessly with trends in popular feminism, including body/sex positivity and empowerment through individual choice. The public reveal of Bridges' sponsorship deal with renowned sex work platform OnlyFans, for example, draws links with the fraught (and seemingly irreconcilable) tensions between agency and exploitation of bodies in sex work and boxing.[13] Before stepping onto the scale at the public weigh-in for her 2022 fight with fellow Australian boxer Shannon O'Connell, Bridges removed her Leeds United football shirt to reveal a second T-shirt underneath. Bridges threw the second T-shirt – branded 'OnlyFans' and signed 'Blonde Bomber' – into the crowd as a memento. Posing in nude-coloured lingerie with black embroidery and an OnlyFans logo stamped across her tanned torso, Bridges capitalised on this media-rich opportunity to disclose what she knows to be a controversial move in partnering with OnlyFans. Even though several male combat athletes have chosen to work with the platform, Bridges anticipated how her aesthetic means her link with OnlyFans will be received differently to her male counterparts (read: negatively). Playing to this contention, Bridges pinned a version of the 'reveal' footage on her Twitter account, accompanied by music and lyrics to one of her chosen 'walk-out' songs: the 'You Don't Own Me' cover created for *Suicide Squad* character Harley Quinn. Lesley Gore's original 1964 lyrics, 'I'm not just one of your many toys. . . . Don't tell me what to do, don't tell me what to say', speak to the meticulous planning Bridges puts in to crafting and evolving her boxing persona. Whether aligning herself with other female figures considered controversial, such as pop singer Madonna and sex worker Kendra Lust, or subverting the 'dumb blonde' stereotype by celebrating her university qualifications and former profession as a high school teacher, Bridges is unapologetically her 'self' – refusing to adhere to reductive, binary expectations of women. In addition to embracing 'Barbie' references by choosing Aqua's 1997 hit 'Barbie Girl' for her ring walk, Bridges actively subverts typical boxing narratives.

Believing in a 'work with what you have approach'[14] to generating media interest, Bridges agrees with journalist Gareth A. Davies that enticing audiences for women's boxing requires 'capturing the male eyes that are on the sport' (iFL TV, 2023) already. However, unlike some, Bridges does not reduce her marketing skills to straightforward tactics of feminine appeal and 'banter'. Elsewhere, Bridges works to improve her athletic skills, and is forging relationships with women across sport and social media, creating opportunities to push back against limitations imposed on women and girls in boxing. Bridges' support for YouTube Channel Women's Fight News,[15] her championing of female sparring partners on social media, and financial investment in boxing prospects Stevi Levy and Nicola Hopewell demonstrate where Bridges participates in community-based, long-term aims. But the bonds between women in boxing are rarely recognised due to the frequent centring of 'novel', 'controversial', and 'overnight-success' tropes in female boxing stories. Boxing is broadly built on narratives of overcoming tragedy, striving for success, and reward for good behaviour; (Crews and Lennox, 2020) increased boxing content (long-form podcasts, YouTube videos, social media soundbites, and newspaper stories) only exasperates this focus on individual boxers and *their story*. Female fighters 'have narratives', says boxing journalist Steve Bunce to promoter Eddie Hearn, implying that narratives have value. Hearn responds by drawing on the periodic 'new' appeal of female boxers:

> That's what we're seeing from the media – the desire to sit down with these female fighters and understand their story, understand the barriers, understand what they've overcome . . . I still think there is a little bit of the unusual perception of a female fighting . . . people are quite fascinated by that . . . the narrative, the story, all of them are compelling.
>
> (in Bunce, 2023)

Bridges recognises the *value* of her 'self' and her story beyond traditional valued-based beliefs that demand women contribute to society in particular ways. Aware of the commodification of personal stories, and how these stories drive and are driven by media influence, Bridges actively controls how much – or little – she shares about her life in the public domain. Bridges understands the business of boxing and works to resist the expectation that boxers pour their bodies and life stories into promoting themselves for audiences. Prior to beginning her partnership with OnlyFans, which allows Bridges to *explicitly* negotiate when and where to share information with paying audiences, Bridges already exercised her agency over what visual content of her body to post on social media and what personal details to disclose in interviews. Partially opening up about 'traumatic times in her teens' (2022a, *Anything Goes*), Bridges tells podcaster James English that managing what she shares prevents certain details from resurfacing unexpectedly and potentially overshadowing her success. 'I don't need the sob story to help me get noticed or for people to . . . respect me' says, Bridges (2022a, *Anything Goes*). English replies, telling Bridges she should not feel ashamed as her 'sob story . . . can be the strength of someone else' (2022a, *Anything Goes*). Bridges agrees, but remains attentive to how this type of sharing limits her ownership of the information and reduces her ability to monetise her experiences post-boxing. Whilst Bridges aspires for longevity in boxing, she also understands the multifaceted requirements of sustaining a livelihood as a retried athlete. Bridges' retirement plan, then, involves running 'motivational seminars', telling 'her story and writ[ing] a book' (2022a, *Anything Goes*). In allowing only 'exclusive' access to intimate details of her life and training, Bridges can finance her time away from boxing while recovering from hand surgery and, ultimately, retiring.

Bridges' unrelenting self-promotion may be dismissed by some as pandering to the 'shocking', tabloid-generated perspectives of women's boxing that female boxers work to resist. But Bridges knows she cannot rely on the support of boxing organisations to build a career. For Bridges, women's' boxing is 'a product':

> You need to sell yourself. . . . it's not too hard for me because that's what I do but there are world champions out there who aren't even known because they're not selling themselves, they've got no-one pushing them.
> (2022b, *The Diren Kartal Show*)

As social media content on female boxers increases, 'empowerment' rhetoric begins to amplify – and to some extent, diversify. Though notions of 'empowerment' in boxing cannot escape what Banet-Weiser describes as the interlocking struggle between popular feminism and popular misogyny, individuals like Bridges – and the communities she connects with – are nevertheless effective in expanding perspectives on women's boxing and responding to the lack of nuance afforded to women in mainstream media narratives. Bridges persistently challenges gender norms on social media platforms – albeit, for the most part, 'through commodified and capitalist means' (Flood, 2019, p. 1198). For some, the commercial appetite for boxers like Bridges, and her connection to platforms like OnlyFans and *The Daily Star,* reignites historical resistances towards female boxers. But these critiques rely on false assumptions that sexism towards women in boxing went away. Bridges' overt ownership of her femininity and sexuality and how she uses this to draw 'eyes to the sport' is undoubtedly complicated – especially seeing as so many female boxers struggle to demonstrate their athleticism beyond objectification and ridicule. But Bridges – more than most – actively draws attention to the sexism and misogyny lurking in and around boxing. For example, amongst the wide-spread celebration of female Olympians and the genuine impact they have had, it is easy to overlook how the same type of institutional misogyny that debated if female boxers should wear skirts still exists across media platforms.

Bridges is accused of 'disrespecting the sport'. However, her drive towards getting 'eyes on the sport' is not solely derived from establishing her own success – it also comes from a place of respect and admiration for other female athletes. As 'disruptor' in women's boxing, Bridges destabilises the traditional balance of power between boxer, promoter, and press, gesturing towards where alterative gains for female boxers can be made. In championing the diverse entertainment value and athletic abilities of female boxers – and encouraging others to do the same – Bridges is successful in diverting focus away from dominant narratives in boxing that reinforce heteronormative white masculinity.

Conclusion: #Teamskankystripper

US professional boxer and former Olympian Mikaela Mayer strikes an honest, critically reflective balance between pursuing common goals in boxing whilst also prioritising personal achievement. BBC journalist Steve Bunce asks Mayer if women's boxing includes 'some sort of sisterhood . . . have you ever sat down with say Katie Taylor or Claressa [Shields], or Natasha [Jonas] or Savannah [Marshall] and had like chats about how you could build your sport?' Mayer responds:

> Umm, no. I mean, me and Claressa [who were Olympic teammates] obviously have had discussions but when it comes to these other women . . . at the end of the day, this is not a team sport. *It is really not*. We're all out gunning, trying to do the best we can and build our own brand and there is no playbook, like there is no recipe, right?[16]

Like Bridges, Mayer is realistic about needing to address – and indeed navigate – the longstanding obstacles that female boxers encounter. But Mayer's reply also speaks directly to the romanticisation of *women working collaboratively*. Female boxers might face the same (or similar) challenges, but perspectives like Bridges' and Mayer's are valuable in highlighting the importance of female boxers being recognised as individual athletic competitors working with extremely limited resources. It might suit the 'new' image of boxing to gravitate towards stereotypes of women working together – or toward the opposite extreme of comparing ostensibly 'good' or 'bad' individual examples of women – but doing so ignores the reality of individuals operating in a competitive, commercial sport that is ladened with additional pressures and gendered limitations. How Bridges creates audience engagement with women's boxing is troubling to some athletes and fans, and is dismissed altogether by others. In the build up towards her fight with O'Connell, Bridges and her opponent inspired a media frenzy because of their vehement dislike for each other. Bridges called O'Connell a bully for body shaming her on social media and O'Connell labelled Bridges a 'skanky stripper' – a title that Bridges embraced, which began trending on Twitter after Bridges won their fight. Celebrating her victory, Bridges provoked, 'not bad for a skanky stripper, eh?' What followed was an outpouring of support from fans and other professional female boxers who used #Teamskankystripper to affirm Bridges' place in boxing. O'Connell's accusation of Bridges having 'no morals' was constructed upon the same rhetoric used to shame female figures who express ownership of their femininity and sexuality broadly. O'Connell – and Bridges' previous opponent Shannon Courtenay – echoed arguments used in the 1970s and 1980s to distinguish anti-porn feminists from sex-positive feminists during the 'Sex Wars' (Downing, 2019, p. 136). Post-2000, ' "empowerment" via sex positivism is inevitably tainted . . . with distinct [internatilaized] misogyny', says Downing (2019, p. 136), which underlines the importance of individuals like Bridges who are dedicated to creating alternative possibilities to the uncompromising binaries that entrap women and demand uniform approaches to solving problems.

Bridges calls out the categorisation of 'appropriate' female bodies in boxing (athletic and 'good' role models) and purportedly 'inappropriate' forms of femininity (ambiguous and excessive), and in doing so unites female boxers in the hope that they can escape and begin to express themselves, beyond binarised judgement. Reflecting on the magnitude of popular engagement with women's boxing in 2022, Mayer retweeted Bridges' post, adding:

> U did a TON, Ebanie . . . you have defied odds to become World Champion and provided a hell of a lot of entertainment along the way . . . I truly feel that you brought a lot of us women together in the process.
> (Mayer, 2022)

It is possible to negate how Bridges' activism in boxing goes beyond opposing traditional rules that say 'You can't be sexy and . . . box' (2022b, *The Diren Kartal Show*). Reductive readings of Bridges' labour miss how she seeks to disrupt power structures in boxing and hit back against a culture of shaming women for their individuality and independent decision-making. This shame-based culture resides within and outside of branches of popular feminism and is rampant on social media. I have argued that Bridges' unconcealed sexuality and hyperfeminine performances might be read as an explicit reaction (some might argue overcorrection) to decades of boxing struggling, but nevertheless attempting, to define a one-size-fits-all approach to female boxers. Her work certainly butts up against the aims and intentions of other female boxers, but Bridges' efforts demonstrate a much-needed commitment to wrestling with – rather than ignoring – the complex status of female boxing bodies in the public domain. If, for Downing, the 'double bind' represents a cultural stronghold of distinctions that stifle female identity, separating 'good' female behaviour from 'bad', I propose that the 'clinch' in boxing – how boxers grapple at close quarters – offers a useful metaphor for the very active process in which female boxers engage with the historical (yet fragile) regulations that have suppressed female expression in boxing for over 300 years. The clinch, then, captures the creative labour of Bridges and other women in boxing who, in refusing to compromise their confident performances of self, untangle themselves from myopic opinions that overlook their athletic potential and undermine their labour.

Notes

1 Original translation: 'Si vous êtes pris dans le rêve de l'autre, vous êtez foutu'.
2 Sekules', K. memoir (2012) *The boxer's heart: a woman fighting*. New York: Villard Books; Merz's, M. (2011) *The Sweetest thing: a boxer's memoir*. New York:

Seven Stories Press; Merz's, M. (2012) *The boxing girls of Kabul*; Walsh's, L. (2008) *Fighting pretty*. Bridgend: Seren, as well as several other studies and documentary projects (including my own project 'Women's Boxing Wales: Past, Present and Future') pay close attention to the positive effects that boxing training has on women's and girls' confidence, and on their ability to tackle other issues in their lives.

3 Sky Sports Boxing (2021) *Fiery exchange! Shannon Courtenay and Ebanie Bridges come head-to-head before world title fight*, 9 April. Available at: www.youtube.com/watch?v=3oTAqyTKks8 (Accessed: 9 April 2021).
4 See (Crews and Lennox, 2020, pp. 94–95).
5 Further on what constitutes 'good' and 'bad', 'acceptable' and 'abject' boxing bodies is explored in (Crews and Lennox, 2020, pp. 42–76).
6 For more on how this term applies to the 'trailblazer trend', see Crews, S. and Lennox, P.S. (2020) '(Re)performing greatness', in *Boxing and Performance*. London: Routledge.
7 Katie Taylor's contributions to changing the landscape of women's boxing in the amateur and professional spheres is well documented. For further context of this, see www.espn.co.uk/boxing/story/_/id/33810719/the-two-sides-katie-taylor-success-sacrifices-took-all-way-top-sport.
8 See Banet-Weiser, S. (2018) *Empowered: popular feminism and popular misogyny*. Durham: Duke University Press; and Banet-Weiser, S. (2019) *Postfeminism and popular feminism*. Durham: Feminist Media Histories, p. 4.
9 Marshall and Shields were presented as amateur rivals, cementing the 'legacy' of their 2012 Olympic achievement. The all-female card, titled the 'legacy', featured genuine grassroots-level support for women and girls in boxing where BOXXER partnered with England Boxing to donate proceeds from ticket sales to local boxing communities. The show was staged at The O2 Arena, London, and content made accessible to audiences via social media platforms and streaming sites. www.boxxer.com/news/boxxer-partner-with-england-boxing/.
10 See Crews and Lennox, 2020, p. 66.
11 Sky Sports Boxing (2021) *Fiery exchange! Shannon Courtenay and Ebanie Bridges come head-to-head before world title fight*, 9 April. Available at: www.youtube.com/watch?v=3oTAqyTKks8 (Accessed: 9 April 2021).
12 For more on these trends and female-centred brands and influencer culture on social media, see Banet-Weiser, 2018 and Carty, 2015.
13 See Karandikar, S., Casassa, K., Knight, L., España, M. and Kagotho, N. (2021) '"I am almost a breadwinner for my family": exploring the manifestation of agency in sex workers' personal and professional contexts', *Affilia*, 37(1), pp. 26–41; and Wacquant, L.D.J. (1995) 'Pugs at work: bodily capital and bodily labour among professional boxers', *Body & Society*, 1(1), pp. 65–93.
14 Bridges' interview titled 'I'm not using sex to sell, I'm just using myself, and if I'm sexy then f**k it' includes further reference to my use of 'work with what you have'. https://inews.co.uk/sport/boxing/ebanie-bridges-interview-boxer-using-sex-to-sell-153746.
15 Women's Fight News are rare content creators in that they explore the status of women's boxing – past, present, and future – and seek to capture stories of female boxers that go beyond the general divisive, singular tone of popular media: https://linktr.ee/womensfightnews.
16 Quotes are taken from an episode of *5 Live Boxing with Steve Bunce* that has since been removed. Episode content was focused on promoting the fight between Mikaela Mayer and Alicia Baumgardner, which was on the undercard of the Claressa Shields v Savannah Marshall.

Bibliography

Banet-Weiser, S. (2018) *Empowered: popular feminism and popular misogyny*. Durham: Duke University Press.

Boddy, K. (2014) 'Watching women box', in Anderson, E. and Hargreaves, J. (eds.) *Routledge handbook of sport, gender and sexuality*. London: Routledge, pp. 258–259.

Bridges, E. (2022a) *Anything goes with James English: world champion Ebanie Bridges tells her story* [Podcast], 6 March. Available at: www.youtube.com/watch?v=JjaIGnJfNlw (Accessed: 7 March 2022).

Bridges, E. (2022b) *The Diren Kartal show #79 Ebanie Bridges* [Podcast]. Available at: https://open.spotify.com/show/4pWmhxHmzvp45NbfiPtKc3 (Accessed: 10 December 2022).

Bridges, E. (2023) *Ebanie bridges: marking a statement (part(s) one [and] two) the George Groves Boxing Club* [Podcast], 1 February. Available at: https://open.spotify.com/episode/0spaN1QEbukhB15IgL2IHg (Accessed: 1 February 2023).

Bunce, S. (2023) *Eddie Hearn 'for all the marbles in the garden' 5 live boxing with Steve Bunce* [Podcast]. Available at: www.bbc.co.uk/programmes/p0f0qljf (Accessed: 3 February 2023).

Carty, V. (2005) 'Textual portrayals of female athletes: liberation or nuanced forms of patriarchy?', *Frontiers: A Journal of Women's Studies*, 26(2), pp. 132–172.

Cooky, C. and Antunovic, D. (2020) '"This isn't just about us about us": articulations of feminism in media narratives of athlete activism', *Communication & Sport*, 8(4–5), pp. 692–711.

Crews, S. and Lennox, P.S. (2020) *Boxing and performance: memetic hauntings*. Abingdon, Oxon: Routledge.

Davies, A.G. (2022) 'Jane Couch: "Katie Taylor v Amanda Serrano is massive, but boxing is still very anti-women"', *The Telegraph*, 29 April. Available at: www.telegraph.co.uk/boxing/2022/04/29/jane-couch-katie-taylor-v-amanda-serrano-massive-boxing-still/ (Accessed: 30 April 2022).

Downing, L. (2019) *Selfish women*. London: Routledge.

Flood, M. (2019) 'Empowered: popular feminism and popular misogyny', *Feminist Media Studies*, 19(8), pp. 1198–1200.

Hardy, H. (2020) '"The business of boxing is systematically built against females" – Heather Hardy', *Sportshour on BBC World Service* [Podcast]. Available at: www.bbc.co.uk/programmes/w172x3c3nyx93l8 (Accessed: 14 November 2022).

iFL TV (2023) *'Does she not have powerful legs?' – Gareth A. Davies & Elle Brooke bizarre interaction*, 12 January. Available at: www.youtube.com/watch?v=DkCSyqFVXQY (Accessed: 13 January 2023).

Mayer, M. (2022) *U did a TON, Ebanie. No matter what anyone says, you have defied odds to become a World Champion & provided a hell of a lot of entertainment along the way. Not to mention, I truly feel that you brought a lot of us women together in the process. I admire you and your hustle* ♥ [Twitter], 31 December. Available at: https://twitter.com/MikaelaMayer1/status/1609308570784342016 (Accessed: 1 January 2023).

MMAFightingonSBN (2022) *Katie Taylor vs. Amanda Serrano full press conference with Jake Paul, Eddie Hearn | MMA fighting*, 28 April. Available at: www.youtube.com/watch?v=UC0HyhlwDto (Accessed: 31 March 2023).

Oates, J.C. (1987) *On boxing*. New York, NY: Harper Collins.

Scotney, E. (2022) *The George Groves boxing club: Scotney the 'Cockney'* [Podcast], 30 November. Available at: https://open.spotify.com/show/28kDHdS2BCqXE9QQ8NgShq (Accessed: 30 November 2022).

Shields, C. (2019) 'It's ridiculous all the hate I get for being great! Same women who hate on me praised Rousey! Then they make up reasons to dislike me. "Oh, she calls herself the GWOAT, it's disrespectful to the women who came before her!" How is that? I never said the pioneers couldn't fight! Or they are bums or even say they are not self-made. All I did was speak life into myself and women's boxing! How can you hate on someone's hard work and accomplishments? Some of these pioneers in women's boxing make me sick. The thing is, they should be grateful that I'm dedicating my life to this sport and pushing it forward! Because before me it was dead for damn near 20 years! Who did Christy Martin give the blueprint? What about Laila Ali? Those women barely speak positive about women's boxing! It was always about themselves! So don't be mad at me I actually love everything about boxing and give props to other female fighters!' [Facebook], 22 April. Available at: https://en-gb.facebook.com/claressa.shields.7/ (Accessed: 30 November 2022).

Sky Sports Boxing (2021) *Fiery exchange! Shannon Courtenay and Ebanie Bridges come head-to-head before world title fight*, 9 April. Available at: www.youtube.com/watch?v=3oTAqyTKks8 (Accessed: 9 April 2021).

Tjønndal, A. (2016) '"I don't think they realise how good we are": innovation, inclusion and exclusion in women's Olympic boxing", *International Review for the Sociology of Sport*, 54(2), pp. 131–150.

Tjønndal, A. (2019) '"I don't think they realise how good we are": innovation, inclusion and exclusion in women's Olympic boxing", *International Review for the Sociology of Sport*, 54(2), 131–150. Available at: https://doi.org/10.1177/1012690217715642

Woodward, K. (2014) 'Legacies of 2012: putting women's boxing into discourse', *Contemporary Social Science*, 9(2), pp. 242–252.

Žižek, S. (2008) *Violence: six sideways reflections*. New York, NY: Pictor.

Chapter 10

Alfonso 'Mosquito' Zvenyika and the Dominant Narratives on Boxing in Post-Colonial Zimbabwe

Manase Kudzai Chiweshe and Gerald Dandah

Introduction

This chapter employs a social biography methodological approach to trace the life history of one of the most talented yet 'controversial' boxers to emerge from Zimbabwe. The 'Rumble in the Jungle' between George Foreman and Muhammad Ali in 1974 brought global attention to boxing within the African continent. The bout between Foreman and Ali in Zaire (now the Democratic Republic of the Congo) supported the rise in the popularity of boxing in Zimbabwe. Following Zimbabwe's independence in 1980, fighters such as Langton 'Schoolboy' Tinago and Proud 'Kilimanjaro' Chinembiri drew thousands of local and global audiences to their fights. These boxers contributed to boxing being one of the most popular sporting disciplines in the early years after independence. However, a few years after the popularity of both Kilimanjaro and Tinago had waned, a slim pencil boxer from one of the country's old high-density suburbs of Mbare in the country's capital Harare emerged (Flood, 2016). Alfonso 'Mosquito' Zvenyika rose from obscurity to having a glittering boxing career. Zvenyika overcame adversity and became an embodiment of the power of sport to change lives and turn one into a role model for millions of people in the country. His career took him to places such as Glasgow, Scotland, and Melbourne, Australia, proving how sport can create cultural heroes whilst also serving as a way out of poverty (Gennaro and Aderinto, 2019, pp. 1–13). Despite enjoying his flirtation with success, Zvenyika's once efficacious life did not last long after his career; he now lives in squalor struggling to make ends meet.

The chapter is novel in that there needs to be more literature on boxing in Zimbabwe. It is based mainly on newspapers and grey literature to document the seemingly larger-than-life story of Zvenyika. This narrative highlights how the bodies and lives of sporting figures become public to the point that they no longer own their account. In that light, the paper employs a sociological analysis as an entry point into the hidden dynamics of sportspersons' lives, with Alfonso Zvenyika being utilised as a case study. Many sports persons in Zimbabwe are often castigated and caricatured at the end or near of their lives. They have little to show for their once promising and successful careers. In Zimbabwe, many sports stars die paupers despite enjoying the trappings of celebrity, fame, and fortune during the pinnacle of their careers. The chapter also highlights how local and global political affairs can conflate to deny sportspersons opportunities to showcase their talents.

Boxing worldwide has historically provided many stories of fighters who grew up in poverty and found success and wealth, only to end up broke again. Fitzsimmons (2013) outlines a list of ten soldiers that were once wealthy and lost their money. Talking about Mike Tyson, Fitzsimmons details how Tyson amassed between $300–400 million during his pro career before filing for bankruptcy in 2004 with outstanding debts of $23M and $17M in taxes (2013). These stories of rags to riches and back to rags highlight the problematic nature of boxing as a tool for social mobility. Writing for *The Dispatch Live* in South Africa, Mesuli Zifo (2022) notes the long history of boxers who have died paupers in the country. In Kenya, Mwendwa (Mwendwa, 2021) highlights that many former medal-winning boxers struggle with mental health and live in poverty without assistance. Around the world, there is a recurrent theme of fighters living out their lives in poverty. It is, however, important to note that boxing is not unique, as many sports also have similar stories. For example, *Sports Illustrated* (Torre, 2009) published a study showing that 78% of American football players have gone bankrupt or are under financial stress two years after retirement and that within five years, 60% of National Basketball Association players are close to breaking.

There have been other fighters of note to emerge from Zimbabwe, such as Thamsanqa Dube, who won the African heavyweight title but was to be stripped of the belt because he could not get a sponsor to organise a fight for his title defence. The long list of reputable fighters to emerge from Zimbabwe with no particular emphasis on fight division includes Mordecai Donga, Ambrose Mlilo, Elvis 'Bomber' Moyo, Arigoma Chiponda, Chamunorwa 'Sting' Gonorenda, Sipho Moyo, and Misheck Kondwane. Charles Manyuchi is the latest fighter of international calibre to emerge from the country after his capture of the World Boxing Council silver welterweight championship after defeating Russian Dmitry Mikhaylenko on his home turf, Yekaterinburg, Russia. The thread that holds all these stories together is how (except for Manyuchi, who is still fighting) none of these fighters could transform their lives through boxing. The sport might have provided fame and trinkets of the good life at the peak of a boxing career, but without any sustainable wealth beyond retirement. This also fits nicely into the narrative of a largely dormant sport in contemporary Zimbabwe due to the economic hardships affecting all aspects of the economy. The sport is reeling as promotion companies, such as Rampage Ring Promotions, Blow by Blow, and Mau Mau have disappeared from the radar. Boxing in Zimbabwe is currently comatose, with its profile not even spoken of, talked of, or written about (Kariati, 2021). Matches amongst local pugilists are now few and far between. The purses handed out are pitiful whenever they are there, with training facilities way below the expected standards; hence, the public interest in the sport has dwindled to alarming levels. Boxing in Zimbabwe is going through a period of definitive decline and, currently, there are no heroes or role models to talk of within the sport (Kariati, 2021).

History of Boxing in Zimbabwe

Mosquito's story has to be understood within a historical context in which boxing amongst Black athletes was relegated as a tool for social control and not a vehicle for social mobility. We highlight this history to show that his story is not unique, but an oft-repeated narrative of Black boxers in colonial and post-colonial Zimbabwe. Pre-colonial Zimbabwe, just like other African traditions and cultures, valued public displays of masculinity often demonstrated in combat sports such as wrestling, fighting, and hunting as traditional rites of passage into manhood. The late Nigerian novelist Chinua Achebe (1958), in his classic novel *Things Fall Apart*, documents the traditional masculine and manliness cultures of Africa in his characterisation of Okonkwo in the pre-colonial south-eastern Nigerian Igbo community. This shows that wrestling and fighting were integral to the African way of life Sikes (2016). Fighting in Africa through wrestling and traditional forms of boxing was a way to avoid social ridicule accompanying any perceived appearance of weakness, indolence, and effeminate qualities. Bravery and fighting were typical features and qualities inextricably expected in and from men in African societies. Our world is premised on the gender binary of masculinity and femininity; hence, it has normative assertions of what men ought to be and how they should act and represent themselves to others (Lindsay and Miescher, 2003). This inevitably becomes the social construction and representation of gender emanating from a mostly patriarchal inclination linked to hegemonic masculinities (Alankaar Sharma and Das, 2016), where manhood is culturally defined as dominance, toughness, and honour (Flood, 2013).

Sport sociologists and historians Michelle Sikes and Peter Alegi document how wrestling and fighting contests were widespread across pre-colonial Africa, with some still in practice even today. The Yoruba practised *gidigbo*; the Hausa had *dambe* (Iyorah, 2018); the Canary Islands, *lucha canaria*; whilst Madagascar and other islands on the southeast coast had *moraingy* (Sikes, 2018). In the Venda culture, a conflation of both South African and Zimbabwean tribes, *musangwe* still serves as a traditional rite of passage where boys are expected to box or fight. These fighting cultures of bare-knuckle fistic and violent combats merged with European fighting to create boxing on the continent. These historical narratives are essential to show that Africa has its unique history of combat sports that are often ignored when discussing the history of fighting games. On the other hand, modern boxing emerged after the European annexation of Africa primarily as a way for social control and to 'discipline and civilise' Africans according to Western ideals, norms, and values.[1] The traditional and historical trajectory of fighting cultures shows that boxing has a long and rich history in Africa. However, the historical narratives of the sport of boxing promote erasures and silences of how these African traditions and ways of fighting knowledge contributed to the growth and development of the sport as we know it today. This highlights how sport on the continent received little attention despite its scale and significance in people's everyday lives (Sikes, 2018; Gennaro and Saheed, 2019). For example, Novak (2012) particularly notes how boxing spread organically in urban metropoles of Southern Rhodesia without direct European influence.

The rich histories of African combat sports were silenced or ignored by colonial and imperial power structures and the violent use of European boxing practices as a form of social control (Alegi, 2010). This certainly attests to the white racial superiority central to how societies were organised (Seda, 2021). Sport, in the case of colonial Zimbabwe, was a means to engage in social activity for indigenous communities. Still, the overarching goal was to foster social acculturation and identity formation according to white racist ideology (Novak, 2012; Sikes, 2018). Anecdotally, the authors of this chapter both grew up in Mbare, where in post-colonial Zimbabwe, boxing was popular. In the late 1980s and 1990s, Mbare hosted informal boxing matches that usually took place on Sunday afternoons. People frequented the raised platformed dusty patches of earth which generally served as a ring on Sundays. The fighting at this venue was called *"wafa-wafa"* (do or die), as it was typically unregulated fights with 'one size fits all' gloves. It is in this space and suburb that Alfonso Zvenyika emerged. Fighters usually had no protection, such as mouth or head guards, to protect them from serious injury. The fights usually had no limits, ending when one fighter conceded defeat. In case of serious injury, there was usually no medical staff on standby to help those injured. The fighting was just for the collective and societal sense of pride and honour. Such narratives seem to shape the historical view of boxing as a sport with a mainly social function and not as a viable space to accumulate wealth and change the lives of the boxers. This thinking is apparent in the case of Zvenyika, which is explored in this chapter and is also evident in other fighters before and after him.

The historiography of African wrestling and fighting cultures is critical for a fuller understanding and contextualisation of the nuances of boxing in Zimbabwe as the country emerged from colonial domination. Fighting is inherent to the African way of life (Sikes, 2018). Boxing, through its "manly" art of displays of masculinity, proved to be a prevalent pastime and a site of resistance to colonialism amongst African men. The men, especially those working in colonial urban centres, saw boxing as a space for leisure and social recreation where men could drink beer and smoke *marijuana*, although colonial authorities had outlawed it (Novak, 2012; Seda, 2021). Novak (2012) highlights how sport in what was then Rhodesia was a sphere for contested control, hence the colonial regime's need to arbitrate on all forms of sport as part of measures to control the gathering and manage political protest. Furthermore, gender discrimination was highly manifest in these public spaces of socialisation and interaction, as the presence of women was prohibited. This will be explored in detail later as Zimbabwe female boxers have, throughout the years, struggled for acceptance and recognition.

Boxing in Zimbabwe was mainly an offshoot from South Africa. The colonial history of the sport is essential to situate the dominant narratives that shape Zvenyika's story in post-colonial Zimbabwe. The public perception and view of the sport were shaped mainly in this colonial period. It was primarily relegated to the periphery as an activity that unemployed and poor youths practice. It was constructed as a pastime of little significance to social mobility for Black athletes by a colonial administration that viewed the sport as nothing more than a means to maintain social order. The Zimbabwean colonial administrators leaned on South Africa for advice and guidance on properly managing and regulating the sport for social good (Novak, 2012). South Africa was the de facto body of control for sport, as it had the first evidence of European sport on the continent (Sikes, 2018). The Rhodesian government established the Wrestling and Boxing Control Act in 1956, modelling its law from a similar one in South Africa passed in 1954 (Hakata, 2019; Seda, 2021). The two laws, which were carbon copies of each other, were meant to regulate Africans' participation in boxing whilst outlawing interracial fights (Seda, 2021). The issue of banning interracial fights was based on institutionalised racial discrimination, especially in colonial and imperial domination areas (Novak, 2012; Sikes, 2018). This mantra acquired global significance in the boxing history of the United States (US), from where it was steeped in the history of racial exclusion from slavery (Lamb, 2021). The plausible explanation was that it was meant to shield white bodies from harm at the hands of the colonised. There was perhaps an innate and inherent fear of powerful Black men for white people. Jack Johnson's famous victory over the white, formerly undefeated heavyweight champion James Jeffries in the 'Fight of the Century' on July 4, 1910, sparked racial tensions at the height of racial segregation in the US. The fight attracted hype and popularity, as it was deemed a referendum on racial superiority (Lamb, 2021). Johnson's triumph saw bloody confrontations between Blacks and whites that left about a dozen people dead (mainly Blacks), hundreds injured, and many more arrested (Lamb, 2021). The ideas about white racial superiority were complicated to sustain in a world where a Black man was the heavyweight champion.

Another vital narrative to emerge in this colonial context around boxing is the belief in superstition and the influence of the supernatural in the sport. Boxing in colonial Zimbabwe was filtered with superstitious indigenous 'medicines', *'juju'*, or *muthi'*, such as *mangoromera* (Seda, 2021), which are distinctive African traits still in use today. The use of *muthi* in sporting activities is also evident in football. In boxing, this belief permeated the story of the most famous boxers that emerged in Zimbabwe. The stories of these boxers are instructive in highlighting how Zvenyika is by no means a unique case. In Zimbabwe, Langton 'Schoolboy' Tinago and Proud 'Kilimanjaro' Chinembiri are two Black Zimbabwean boxers who garnered global acclaim for their fighting skill (Mhlanga, 2021). Tinago was crowned Commonwealth champion three times, winning the lightweight title twice and the featherweight crown once, and earning himself a place in the *Guinness Book of Records*, a rare feat for a boxer from the low-income suburb Mambo in Gweru. To many boxing analysts, Tinago is arguably the finest boxer ever produced in Zimbabwe, as he could have achieved and could have been more had it not been for the ban on international sport placed on Rhodesia during the period of a unilateral declaration of independence (UDI). The white settler minority regime led by then Prime Minister Ian Smith sought independence from the British Empire in 1965, excluding Rhodesia from international sporting platforms (Ziwira, 2020). Tinago's story highlights the global fame that boxing brings without the socio-economic transformation for the boxer. Whilst the colonial context can help explain the failure of Tinago to transform economically through boxing, a distinct narrative emerges on how fighters face difficult times past their prime.

Another example is the story of Kilimanjaro, 'the man mountain,' as Chinembiri was affectionately called because of his physical build. Chinembiri came to dominate the heavyweight boxing scene soon after independence in Zimbabwe and Africa (Dielhenn, 2020). His moniker Kilimanjaro came from a gigantic mountain in East Africa. Chinembiri won the Zimbabwean boxing heavyweight championship in April 1982 after defeating the then-champion Ringo Starr in 29 seconds in Masvingo (Dielhenn, 2020). Kilimanjaro's finest hour came at a packed Rufaro Stadium in Mbare when he knocked out Ghanaian boxer Adama Mensah to claim the African heavyweight championship (Dielhenn, 2020; Zililo, 2020). Kilimanjaro, before finding solace in boxing, according to Wellings, was a 'professional mugger' with a 'bad reputation' for street fighting at the slightest provocation (Dielhenn, 2020). Kilimanjaro dominated the African Boxing Union championship between 1982 and 1987 and between 1988 and 1990 (Mhlanga, 2021). Kilimanjaro was ranked number nine by the World Boxing Council (WBC) at his peak (Dielhenn, 2020; Zililo, 2020). Kilimanjaro's trainer, Dave Wellings, in the memoirs of his travails across Africa, *The Bengu Years* (Wellings, 2010), notes his protégé's life as 'a tale of poverty, thuggery, mythology, wasted potential and ultimately tragedy' (Dielhenn, 2020). Again, the recurring narrative of a boxer who fails to capitalise on the fame of their peak and later lives in poverty and obscurity. Kilimanjaro missed a chance to fight then-Olympic gold medallist Lennox Lewis when he failed to provide satisfactory medical records in Britain on the night of the scheduled fight. He later died on February 15, 1994, at the young age of 36. These stories further illustrate the aim of this chapter to use

Zvenyika's career as a case study of how boxing has been constructed as a sport whose stars essentially end up in tragedy.

Boxing in Zimbabwe is a masculine and male-dominated sport, historically and in contemporary times. Despite African and European political ideologies running contrary, their patriarchal ideologies seemed to conflate and resonate in curtailing sporting opportunities for African women (Alegi, 2010). Boxing, like other sports, such as football, was predominantly male, with women denied participation opportunities (Seda, 2021). Since colonial times, boxing as a sport has generally struggled to recognise women legally (Munetsi, 2022). This standardised and institutionalised discriminatory practice hinged on sexism perhaps explains the low uptake of the sport amongst girls and young women across the country. It was only after the appeal of the first female professional fighter in Zimbabwe, Monalisa Sibanda, that the sports ministry took notice. However, the legislation is still vague on the participation of women in boxing. Monalisa Sibanda defeated Kenyan Joyce Awino by a unanimous points decision to clinch the vacant Women's International Boxing Association (WIBA) title in Nairobi in April 2019 (Nyakwenda, 2019), Kudakwashe 'Take Money' Chiwandire made history when she became the first Zimbabwean to win the World Boxing Council (WBC) super bantamweight gold title. The side-lining of female boxers despite their overwhelming success, even mainly by the dominant and mainstream sports media, has traceable consequences on the public's recognition of men's and women's sports (Hargreaves and Anderson, Routledge, 2014, pp. 3–18). Most male pugilists have cult-like status, yet female boxers are viewed as largely disturbing the 'natural' and established gender order.[2] This microcosmic analysis of the current women's place in Zimbabwean boxing highlights the heteronormative and heterosexual restrictions on the female athletic body (Hall, 1988). Bulky and muscularly toned women participating in sport are generally frowned upon in society, as the heteronormative expectations of women are centred on their frailty, weakness, and helplessness.

Methodological Note: Social Biography Method

The study is based on a social biographical design which utilises desk research to analyse the lived experiences of Alfonso Zvenyika. Burke III (2019) notes that social biographies explore the connections between the dense specificity of individual lives and the larger contexts in which they are embedded. The individual narrative of the person is based on the social context within which the person is located. As such, this approach allows the researcher to understand the connections between the profoundly local and individual on the one hand, and the global and world-historical on the other (Burke III, 2019). In the case of Alfonso Zvenyika, the experiences of this one boxer provide important insights into a sociological study of boxing as a livelihood option and vehicle for social mobility for athletes from poor communities and backgrounds. There is a dearth of academic literature focusing on boxing in Zimbabwe; thus, newspapers, in this instance, serve as important and accessible repositories of information. Newspapers, especially about this chapter, offer detailed descriptions with concrete events and dates of concerns and debates of the past about boxing (Sikes, 2016). A lot of scholarly attention in Zimbabwe has been given to team sports, such as football/soccer, with little to no work done to focus on presumed minority, individual sports, such as boxing. The study thus focused mainly on newspaper reports as a data source, as most of the reports contain interviews with the boxer. Newspaper articles are great starting points for research and can sometimes be invaluable information vaults. Earl et al. (2004) concluded that newspaper data were sound and that researchers could proceed cautiously. Newspaper stories were purposively sampled to focus mainly on Alfonso Zvenyika, boxing in Zimbabwe, nd former boxers' lives globally. An internet search was utilised to ensure access to varied sources that speak to the lived experiences of Zvenyika and other former fighters. The collected stories were thematically analysed to provide a nuanced analysis of the life of a boxer.

Findings and Discussion

Alfonso Zvenyika: The Early Years

Alfonso Zvenyika was nicknamed 'Mosquito' because of his 50-kilogram fighting weight and skills (Zoe Flood, 2021). Zvenyika was born on November 25, 1975, in the suburb of Mbare, established by British colonial authorities in 1907 (Zoe Flood, 2021). He grew up in poverty, and he had a tough childhood. Zvenyika grew up eking out a living through trading and vending to make ends meet. This has become part of the daily 'struggle to put food on the table in a country where up to 90% of working-class adults are not formally employed' (Zoe Flood, 2021). Zvenyika grew up scraping for survival on the margins and was only enrolled in primary school at the very late age of 11, when most of his mates were already preparing for secondary school. As a result, he could only proceed up to grade two, the most basic education level equivalent to early childhood education (*Sunday Mail*, 2015). Zvenyika's struggles and failures justify societal beliefs that a lack of schooling often leads to poor life decisions. Concerns raised by most of society over a lack of education become justified when juxtaposed against the life of Zvenyika. His lack of a formal educational background to inform some of his actions and decisions led him to a tragic life.

Boxing Fame and the Life of the Celebrity

Professional sport, especially globally, often gives its proponents a claim to fame and walks in the much-desired pantheon of celebrity life. Boxing is no different, as most pugilists have become success stories. Zvenyika rose to fame and celebrity life following his famous Commonwealth boxing title victory over Paul Weir in Scotland. He noted, 'Beating Paul Weir of Scotland on January 28, 1998, was the highest point of my career because suddenly I became an internationally recognised boxer' (*Sunday Mail*, 2015). Victory in Scotland ensured Zvenyika pocketed a sizable sum (Sanganyado, 2014), allowing him to drive around in nice cars, eating and dining with the rich and famous. Zvenyika later defeated another Scottish boxer, Keith Knox, in less than two minutes in a subsequent bout before losing his Commonwealth title to Damien Kelly of Northern Ireland in December 1998. Zvenyika, offered citizenship in South Australia (*Sunday Mail*, 2015), was affected by the fame he seemed unprepared for, leading to poor lifestyle decisions. Zvenyika noted,

> Those victories came with both money and fame. As you know, where there is a combination of those two (money and fame), there are also many risks. When you are a celebrity, there are so many forces against you, women will come to you, beautiful ones, and sometimes you cannot resist. It happens to most men. Maybe I needed more proper guidance; being someone who never really went to school, I probably took things for granted.
> (*Sunday Mail*, 2015)

Sporting prowess without a grounding in managing fame and money often produces situations in which sports persons from poor backgrounds fall prey to the mismanagement of funds. Long and Sanderson (2002) argue that there is a lack of robust evidence or research that sport necessarily leads to social mobility. Sport does not offer a panacea for social problems (Spaaij, 2010), such as poverty, because they are based on complex socio-economic and political factors beyond the scope of the sporting sector. Boxing and all its rewards could not transform the socio-historical context which shaped the life, decisions, and mindset of Alfonso Zvenyika.

The Downfall of a Boxing Legend

Zvenyika's story is a case study of a sportsperson who enjoys wealth and glamour but tragically ends in poverty and, subsequently, crime. The situation was so dire that at one time, the boxer attempted suicide by overdosing on malaria medication (Ntuli, 2021). Zvenyika now has little to show for his triumphs in the boxing ring (Zoe Flood, 2021). Zvenyika regrets his extravagance and obsession with opulence that affected his wealth, leaving him in squalor (Mhara, 2016). Zvenyika, just like Kilimanjaro before him, had many flaws that might explain his impoverished background. Still, again, just like Kilimanjaro, both were doyens of the sport representing the halcyon days of Zimbabwean boxing. Zvenyika supports this by noting, 'I am a former two-time Commonwealth champion, but I do not have a gym, no gloves, no head gears and yet people call me a legend' (*Sunday Mail*, 2015). Flood further quotes Zvenyika, saying, 'I'm shy to say it but I can't afford to feed my family properly. We eat bread without butter, we drink tea without milk' (2021). The everyday struggle for survival highlights how the boxer has turned into a case for charity. The boxer admits that:

> There was a time when I had things, people came to me and pretended to love me, pretended to be my friends, but because of blindness, I did not see it. And when I got broke and was incarcerated, they all ran away.
> (Madzokere, 2017)

Zvenyika, speaking of his plight, concludes, 'All the money I made I spend it. If only I earned that money with my current knowledge, I would be somewhere. Life has been my greatest teacher. The only asset I have is my life'.

Struggles for survival later forced Zvenyika back to a life of crime. The construction of an image of success and opulence of the once famous boxer is far removed from the reality of Zvenyika, the criminal. He admits to making a wrong decision that saw him having a 20-month stint in jail for stealing a boom box (radio/stereo set) (Madzokere, 2016; Sanganyado, 2014). Zvenyika noted, 'I was in prison because of wrong movements because I did not have anybody to show me [the way]' (Madzokere, 2017). Zvenyika has been 'in prison, in hospital, in a hooligan's cell' (Zoe Flood, 2021). The boxer also suffered a stroke whilst in prison. Zvenyika's actions challenged the crafted persona of a sporting inspiration and role model. The construction of role models often happens outside the athlete's control, who often undergo complex internal struggles that fall short of society's expectations. In 2019, Zvenyika was also beaten up by his children, who accused him of using witchcraft and *juju* in his boxing career, which in turn caused their poverty. One of the children was quoted saying,

> Yes, we beat him up because our lives are miserable due to the effects of the lucky charms he took for boxing. We are four girls but only one is married and the rest our marriages are just collapsing because of his juju. We are also made spiritual wives by his things.
> (*Zimbabwe Morning Star*, 2019)

Another child accused him of failing to get documentation for the children, which affected their ability to continue with schooling. What is clear through this episode is how the boxer's misfortune has been played out in public due to the fame and high profile he achieved in his career.

The Contemporary Iteration of Alfonso Zvenyika

Narratives around Zvenyika are dominated by the view that he is an also-ran who got cheated of his riches by the allure of fame, booze, and women. This narrative has built negative impressions of the boxer's life as a failure which cannot be changed. Yet by 2021, Zvenyika had started a new venture as a boxing trainer at his Mosquito Boxing School of Excellence with a self-obligation to teach youths the art of fighting in the ring and critical life skills for survival. This initiative is essential for the boxer as a way of giving back to young people in the poverty-stricken suburb of Mbare, which also has a negative perception of a failed community. Zvenyika argues, 'People paint a bad picture of Mbare, but it's a talent hub. People always have the misguided belief that everyone from Mbare is rogue, delinquent, and stubborn' (Flood, 2016). These efforts to teach the next generation of fighters is a welcome development, as it helps keep young people away from social vices, such as drugs and crime (Mavhunga, 2021). Drug abuse has become endemic in most of Harare's low-income areas (Zoe Flood, 2021). Illicit alcohol (*tondoni* or *kranko*), marijuana, and *guka* or *mutoriro* (crystal methamphetamine) are all popular among the youth in Mbare (Chingono, 2021). These highly addictive drugs and illicit substances are a significant talking point currently inviting condemnation of leaders and communities as they have seen the destruction of young lives.

Zvenyika's efforts have been largely ignored, as there is little support for the initiative from corporate sponsors. This is perhaps mainly because of the narrative of failure that has defined his post-boxing legacy. He highlights,

> No one is willing to help me revive this sport; no company is willing to assist me. When I approach them asking for financial support, all they see in me is that notorious Mosquito from Mbare, they doubt me . . . yes, I erred but don't I deserve a second chance.
>
> (*Sunday Mail*, 2015)

The legacy of failure seems to follow the boxer beyond past mistakes. Redeeming a public persona is difficult for people who were formerly popular. Yet this new initiative focusing on the youths in Mbare has the potential to reshape Zvenyika's legacy. On his part, the former boxing champion notes,

> I'm in this project because I wanted to remove kids from drug abuse and womanizing and stealing because there is a lot of crime committed by these young guys. When you are drunk, dozed by those drugs, it isn't very good. So, I decided to open this club to rehabilitate them, to teach them life. They have got life. When someone is not schooling it's tough to deal with. The moment he catches up to what you are saying, then he will come back to sense.
>
> (Mavhunga, 2021)

Zvenyika is becoming part of the solution on his self-redemption journey; perhaps society should now judge him differently. The discussion around the contemporary iteration of the boxer is to highlight how powerful narratives of the downfall of sporting heroes often overshadow any attempt at redefining their lives after the loss of fame and fortune.

Takeaways from Zvenyika's Case Study

The case of Alfonso Zvenyika highlights the complex space between fleeting fame and fortune for boxers emerging from areas of deep poverty. It provides fascinating insights into how famous sports personalities often lose their identities to narratives created in the media and by the public. Such narratives become potent representations of the person. In the case of boxers such as Alfonso Zvenyika, the narratives of failure and poverty overwhelm their achievements in the sporting arena. His story highlights the social dynamics around sporting heroes who emerge from underprivileged communities only to return to these communities after a short spell of success. Zvenyika often argues,

> I didn't get proper guidance and look where I am now. Invest your money, and create a solid financial plan for when you can no longer fight. This career is concise, so you must be careful with your finances. Be very disciplined and remain humble.
>
> (Mhara, 2016)

Boxing talent and skill are not enough if it is not accompanied by the capacity-building of sports stars to understand financial literacy and management. Boxers from poor backgrounds are left at the mercy of promoters, hangers, and other predatory characters who often benefit at the expense of the sports star. Building sport as a viable livelihood and social mobility option requires understanding these limitations and promoting a sustainable way of creating success beyond the active days of the athlete. This case has shown how athletes become pawns of narratives that judge their actions harshly without fully understanding the context within which they performed, lived, and celebrated success.

Conclusion

The chapter utilised the case of Alfonso Zvenyika to highlight some of the dominant narratives around boxing in Zimbabwe. It showed that one of the significant narratives is constructed around the precarious nature of boxing as a career in Zimbabwe. It has highlighted how Zvenyika's case is not unique, but the norm, especially in Africa, where boxers that emerge into stardom often return to poverty due to various factors, including the lack of proper financial management. Zvenyika's social biography provides two key sociological insights into our social understanding of boxing and sport. Firstly, the role of sports, such as boxing, in social mobility is limited due to the complexity of lived experiences of fame and fortune of individuals that grew up in poverty. Secondly, public perceptions of failing former sporting stars are shaped by the dominant narrative usually created by the media and is out of their control. The sporting personality has little ability to shift or change this narrative. This chapter also highlights the need for sustained scholarly attention on boxing in Africa as part of the field's sociological and cultural analysis and documentation, as there is currently a dearth of knowledge of this field.

Notes

1 Mangan, J.A. (1988) *The games ethics and imperialism: aspects of the diffusion of an ideal*. London: Frank Cass; Novak, A. (2012) 'Sport and racial discrimination in colonial Zimbabwe: a reanalysis', *The International Journal of the History of Sport*, 29(6); Sikes, M. (2018) 'Sport history and historiography', in *Oxford research encyclopedia of African history*. Available at: https://doi.org/10.1093/acrefore/9780190277734.013.232 (Accessed: 20 May 2022); Seda, A.T. (2021) 'Jack Johnson and Africa: boxing and race in colonial Africa", *Black Perspectives*. Available at: www.aaihs.org/jack-johnson-and-africa-boxing-and-race-in-colonial-africa/ (Accessed: 20 November 2021).
2 Griffin, P. (1998) *Strong women, deep closets: lesbians and homophobia in sport*. Champaign, IL: Human Kinetics; Messner, M.A. (1988) 'Sports and male domination: the female athlete as contested ideological terrain', *Sociology of Sport Journal*, 5(3).

Bibliography

Achebe, C. (1958) *Things fall apart*. London: William Heinemann Ltd.
Alegi, P. (2010) *African Soccerscapes: how a continent changed the world's game*. London: Hurst and Company.
Burke III, E. (2019) *Social biographies as world history*. Available at: https://cpb-us-e1.wpmucdn.com/sites.ucsc.edu/dist/f/704/files/2019/05/Writing-Social.Biographies.pdf (Accessed: 20 September 2021).
Chingono, N. (2021) 'We forget our troubles', *The Guardian*, 16 March. Available at: www.theguardian.com/global-development/2021/mar/16/crystal-meth-mutorirodrug-use-rises-zimbabwe-lockdown (Accessed: 20 March 2021).
Dielhenn, J. (2020) 'Proud Kilimanjaro was Africa's best heavyweight and earned a fight with Lennox Lewis but could have been much more', *Sky Sports News*, 19 April. Available at: www.skysports.com/boxing/news/12183/11973957/proud-kilimanjaro-was-africas-best-heavyweight-and-earned-a-fight-with-lennox-lewis-but-could-have-been-so-much-more (Accessed: 20 May 2021).
Earl, J.M.A., McCarthy, D.D. and Soule, A.S. (2004) 'The use of newspaper data in the study of collective action', *Annual review of Sociology*, 30, pp. 65–80.
Fitzsimmons, L. (2013) '10 big boxing names who went bankrupt', *Bleacher Report*, 29 May. Available at: https://bleacherreport.com/articles/1654741-10-big-boxing-names-who-went-bankrupt (Accessed: 20 April 2021).
Flood, M. (2016) 'Involving men in ending violence against women: Facing challenges and making change', *Graduate Journal of Social Science*, 12(3), pp. 12–29.
Flood, Z. (2021) ' "I was born a fighter": the champion boxer changing young lives in Zimbabwe', *The Guardian*, 18 October. Available at: www.theguardian.com/global-development/2021/oct/18/i-was-born-a-fighter-the-champion-boxer-changing-young-lives-in-zimbabwe (Accessed: 20 May 2021).

Gennaro, M. and Saheed, A. (2019) *Sports in African history, politics and identity formation*. London: Routledge.

Griffin, P. (1998) *Strong women, deep closets: lesbians and homophobia in sport*. Champaign, IL: Human Kinetics.

Guni, S. (2021) 'Take money explodes, takes WBC gold', *H-Metro*, 28 February. Available at: www.hmetro.co.zw/take-money-explodes-takes-wbc-gold/ (Accessed: 9 March 2021).

Hakata, S. (2019) 'Time to revive boxing', *The Patriot*, 7 February. Available at: www.thepatriot.co.zw/old_posts/time-to-revive-boxing/ (Accessed: 9 May 2021).

Hall, M.A. (1988) 'The discourse of gender and sport: from femininity to feminism', *Sociology of Sport Journal*, 5(4), pp. 330–340.

Hargreaves, J. and Anderson, E. (eds.) (2014) *Routledge handbook of sport, gender and sexuality*. London: Routledge.

Iyorah, F. (2018) 'Dambe: how an ancient form of Nigerian boxing swept the internet', *Aljazeera*, 18 June. Available at: www.aljazeera.com/features/2018/6/18/dambe-how-an-ancient-form-of-nigerian-boxing-swept-the-internet#:~:text=Dambe%20began%20when%20clans%20of,has%20become%20an%20internet%20sensation (Accessed: 10 May 2021).

Kariati, M. (2021) 'Boxing on the rebound but . . .', *The Standard*, 21 February. Available at: https://thestandard.newsday.co.zw/2021/02/21/boxing-on-the-rebound-but/ (Accessed: 10 May 2021).

Lamb, C. (2021) 'When a black boxing champion beat the "great white hope", all hell broke loose', *The Conversation*, 30 June. Available at: https://theconversation.com/when-a-black-boxing-champion-beat-the-great-white-hope-all-hell-broke-loose-163413 (Accessed: 4 May 2022).

Lindsay, A.L. and Miescher, S. (2003) *Men and masculinities in modern Africa*. Portsmouth, NH: Heinemann.

Long, J. and Sanderson, I. (2002) 'The social benefits of sport: where's the proof?', in Gratton, C. and Henry, I.P. (eds.) *Sport in the city*. London: Routledge, pp. 199–215.

Madzivanzira, A. (2018) 'Commonwealth Games . . . raw deal for sportsmen and developing nations', *The Patriot*, 3 May. Available at: www.thepatriot.co.zw/old_posts/commonwealth-gamesraw-deal-for-sportsmen-and-developing-nations/ (Accessed: 20 January 2022).

Madzokere, M. (2017) 'Mosquito's ultimate fight', *The Standard*, 2 April. Available at: https://thestandard.newsday.co.zw/2017/04/02/mosquitos-ultimate-fight/ (Accessed: 9 June 2022).

Mangan, J.A. (1988) *The games ethics and imperialism: aspects of the diffusion of an ideal*. London: Frank Cass.

Mavhunga, C. (2021) 'Former boxing champion tries to "knock out" drugs in Zimbabwe', *Voice of America*, 26 November. Available at: www.voanews.com/a/former-boxing-champion-tries-to-knock-out-drugs-in-zimbabwe-/6328724.html (Accessed: 7 June 2022).

Mazangaizo, S. (2021) 'Zimbabwean boxer dies after "blows to the head" in the ring', *The Times*, 5 November. Available at: www.timeslive.co.za/news/africa/2021-11-05-zimbabwean-boxer-dies-after-blows-to-the-head-in-the-ring/ (Accessed: 7 October 2022).

Messner, A.M. (1988) 'Sports and male domination: the female athlete as contested ideological terrain', *Sociology of Sport Journal*, 5(3), pp. 197–211.

Mhara, H. (2016) 'Mosquito warns Manyuchi', *The Newsday*, 16 June. Available at: www.newsday.co.zw/2016/06/mosquito-warns-manyuchi/ (Accessed: 9 March 2022).

Mhlanga, E. (2021) 'Kili, Schoolboy, Mosquito set the benchmark in boxing', *The Herald*, 7 April. Available at: www.herald.co.zw/kili-schoolboy-mosquito-set-the-benchmark-in-boxing/ (Accessed: 9 March 2022).

Mthetwa, S. (2015) 'Lack of promoters kills boxing', *The Southern Eye*, 18 February. Available at: www.southerneye.co.zw/2015/02/18/lack-promoters-kills-boxing/ (Accessed: 10 March 2021).

Munetsi, G. (2022) '"Take money" gets crack at first WBC world title', *The Herald*, 15 February. Available at: www.herald.co.zw/take-money-gets-crack-at-first-wbc-world-title/ (Accessed: 9 March 2022).

Mwendwa, M. (2021) 'Lost bout: Kenyan boxers' struggle with depression and poverty', *Al Jazeera*, 8 April. Available at: www.aljazeera.com/sports/2021/4/8/depression-poverty-khat-kenyan-boxing-stars-struggle (Accessed: 9 March 2022).

Novak, A. (2012) 'Sport and racial discrimination in colonial Zimbabwe: a reanalysis', *The International Journal of the History of Sport*, 29(6), pp. 850–867.

Ntuli, D. (2021) *Sharuko on Saturday – so we went to Ghana, riding on a wave of words*, n.d. Available at: https://sportsmagic.co.za/2021/05/22/sharuko-on-saturday-so-we-went-to-ghana-riding-on-a-wave-of-words/ (Accessed: 20 November 2021).

Nyakwenda, L. (2019) 'The boxing queen who ruled at last', *The Sunday Mail*, 5 May. Available at: www.sundaymail.co.zw/the-boxing-queen-who-ruled-at-last#:~:text=THEY%20say%20the%20best%20is,realising%20a%20long%20cherished%20dream (Accessed: 20 November 2021).

Nyakwenda, L. (2020) 'The Mbare boxer who ruled Africa', *The Sunday Mail*, 29 March. Available at: www.sundaymail.co.zw/the-mbare-boxer-who-ruled-africa (Accessed: 20 November 2021).

Sanganyado, E. (2014) *The Good Shepherd: grace sets back your setbacks*. CA: Grace Revealed! Books.

Seda, A.T. (2021) 'Jack Johnson and Africa: boxing and race in colonial Africa', *Black Perspectives*, 12 October. Available at: www.aaihs.org/jack-johnson-and-africa-boxing-and-race-in-colonial-africa/ (Accessed: 20 November 2021).

Sharma, A. and Das, A. (2016) 'Men, masculinities, and violence', *Graduate Journal of Social Science*, 12(3), pp. 7–11.

Sikes, M. (2016) 'Print media and the history of women's sport in Africa: the Kenyan case of barriers to international achievement', *History in Africa*, 43, pp. 323–345.

Sikes, M. (2018) 'Sport history and historiography', in *Oxford research encyclopedia of African history*. Available at: https://doi.org/10.1093/acrefore/9780190277734.013.232 (Accessed: 20 May 2022).

Spaaij, R. (2010) 'Using recreational sport for social mobility of urban youth: practices, challenges and dilemmas', *Sociétés et jeunesses en difficulté*. Available at: http://journals.openedition.org/sejed/6641 (Accessed: 20 May 2022).

Sunday Mail (2015) 'Boxing: the "dark" past Arifonso can't shed', *The Sunday Mail*, 8 February. Available at: www.sundaymail.co.zw/boxing-the-dark-past-arifonso-cant-shed (Accessed: 9 March 2021).

Torre, P. (2009) 'How (and why) athletes go broke', *The Vault*, 23 March. Available at: https://vault.si.com/vault/2009/03/23/how-and-why-athletes-go-broke (Accessed: 9 March 2021).

Vickers, S. (2021) 'Taurai Zimunya: questions asked as Zimbabwean boxer dies after fight', *BBC Sport Africa*, 3 November. Available at: www.bbc.com/sport/africa/59156447 (Accessed: 9 March 2021).

Wellings, D. (2010) *The Bengu Years*. Tustin, CA: Book Pal Publishers.

Zifo, M. (2022) 'Yet another boxer dies a pauper', *Dispatch Live*, 22 February. Available at: www.dispatchlive.co.za/sport/boxing-mecca/2022-02-22-yet-another-boxer-dies-a-pauper/ (Accessed: 20 May 2022).

Zililo, R. (2020) 'Lack of corporate support stifles boxing: Bulawayo Bomber', *The Chronicle*, 4 August. Available at: www.chronicle.co.zw/lack-of-corporate-support-stifles-boxing-bulawayo-bomber/ (Accessed: 9 March 2021).

Zimbabwe Morning Star (2019) 'Former Commonwealth champion seeks counsel of prophets after he is floored by his children', *Zimbabwe Morning Star*, 8 August. Available at: www.zimmorningpost.com/former-commonwealth-champion-seeks-counsel-of-prophets-after-he-is-floored-by-his-children/ (Accessed: 9 March 2021).

Ziwira, E. (2020) 'Sport harnessing talent for the collective good', *The Manica Post*, 3 April. Available at: www.manicapost.co.zw/sport-harnessing-talent-for-the-collective-goo (Accessed: 9 March 2021).

Chapter 11

Political Symbolism of Mary Kom from the Manipuri Autobiography to the Indian Blockbuster

Myriam Mellouli

Introduction: To Be Some (Political) Body

Being a boxer is being a body that matters (Crews and Lennox, 2020): it is a signifier inscribed in the real world (Butler, 1993). Each hardship endured by the bodily matter gains purpose and meaning thanks to the sporting goals and their symbolic nature in terms of socio-political identity. The representation of the boxer struggling to survive belongs more to the image of boxing than to the daily socio-cultural reality of boxers. The real-life boxers are more at the threshold of the middle class, according to Loïc Wacquant: 'to become a boxer requires a regularity of life, a sense of discipline, a physical and mental asceticism that cannot take root in social and economic conditions marked by chronic instability and temporal disorganization' (2004, p. 44). This makes boxing narratives based on social exclusion, such as those of Mary Kom, Indian six-time world champion in the light fly division in amateur boxing, described as an Indian boxer but identifying primarily with her native Tibeto-Burman region of Manipur in her autobiography, all the more exceptional and worthy of decipherment. She claims her transformation from 'nobody' to 'somebody' thanks to the hard work and mental strength that helped her overcome the struggles of her class and ethnic background: 'Look at me. I am a nobody who became a sporting icon only because of my consistent hard work' (Kom and Serto, 2013, p. 17). In other words, she became 'somebody' thanks to the performance of boxing in the ring – she has transformed herself into a body that counts thanks to boxing understood as a 'cultural performance' (Cohen, 1979, p. 106). Boxing is a 'drama', the term being meant in the most restricted sense by the anthropologist Abner Cohen in his foundational article on 'Political Symbolism':

> A drama is a limited sequence of symbolic action, defined in space and time, which is formally set aside from the ordinary flow of purposeful social action. In this sense, the drama is not an imitation of life but a symbolic construction . . . the drama selects a few elements that are not obviously related in ordinary life, indeed that are often contradictory, and integrates

them within a unity of action and of form, a *gestalt* that temporarily structures the psyches of the actors and transforms their relationships.

(Cohen, 1979, p. 105)

The spectacular transformation of the boxer M.C. Mary Kom is made possible thanks to a mythology around her rural and Manipuri origins in her collaborative (Thoudam, 2022, pp. 70–81) autobiography, *Unbreakable* (2013), co-written with Dina Serto, and the mystification of womanhood as an allegory of India (Hirji, 2021) in the biopic *Mary Kom* (Kumar, 2014). Between the individual struggles she had to face and her identity ambitions, Mary Kom constitutes a political symbol because of her bifocality, rewording Abner Cohen, since 'normative symbols are . . . essentially bivocal, satisfying both existential and political ends' (1979, p. 102). For the boxer from Northeast India, the drama of boxing allows her to link her individual inspirations with her socio-political identity. She becomes more of a symbol of a people than a mere human being – a myth, as she states that she crystallizes the identity of a whole community:

> My community was proud that I was now an international-level boxer. It was the first sporting achievement of its kind by anyone in our small tribe. To be honest, one of the greatest motivating forces for me has been my desire to assert the identity of my tribe 'Kom' within my own country and the world over. We are just a few thousand people. I hoped that by coming up in sports and getting known worldwide, I'd be able to popularize the culture and ethos of my tiny tribe.
>
> (Kom and Serto, 2013, p. 30)

Myth adds a transcendental[1] aspect to the political symbol (Fourtanier et Chelly-Zemni, 2018), and art is the privileged promoter of myths (Kovacevic, 2007) thanks to its storytelling powers (Addis, 2007). The term 'mythology' could be understood as a rewriting of reality by applying fantasies and giving meaning to sometimes unrelated events. Mary Kom transforms her fate, working in the fields, thanks to her body that could be seen as the vessel of her mythology and a transformative force (Crews and Lennox, 2020). For her, myth could be seen as her own deep truth and links it with her belonging to her local, regional, and national origins (Bonzel, 2020), the Kom community, Manipur, and, finally, India. As David Rowe states:

> it is clear that they [mythologies and ideologies of sports] share a profound attachment to the idea that sports constitute a subsystem of signs that can be scrutinized for their capacity to reveal or represent 'truths' – direct or indirect, literal or metaphorical – about the social world.
>
> (2014)

In her collaborative autobiography (Thoudam, 2022), Mangte Chungneijang 'Mary Kom' wrote her fighting narrative in a simple and direct style in English with the help of Dina Serto and her editor, Atijha ('Acknowledgments' in Kom and Serto, 2013). 'Mary' refers to her Catholic beliefs in a predominantly Hinduist country, and 'Kom' stands for the rural origins of the Kom tribe that belongs to the Meiteis, an ethnic minority in India but a majority in Manipur, far from the urbanity where one might think most of the boxers stem from (Heiskanen, 2012). The work that first builds the representation of Mary Kom on the public stage is the autobiography of Mary Kom co-written with Dina Serto. It tracks the local and regional origins down as she considers herself as a woman formed and strengthened thanks to a masculine work as a child in the fields with her father. From the beginning, the reader is immersed in the village of Kangathei where she was born. She speaks about her parents, her grandparents, and her siblings. She insists on the reader knowing where she's coming from; they are the roots of her identity. Then, she tells us the struggles of a young female boxer in a rural area of Manipur and narrates with pride how she overcame them. She develops the discovery of social relationships with her future husband, but also the deep connection she feels with her managers and the institutions – not with some bitterness – where she evolved. Finally, she proudly exhibits all her wins and the backstage of the international competitions she was part of. She interestingly transfers her identity from the individual point of view to the collective (the regional, the national, the international community of the sportswomen). In the final chapters, she is more of a symbol of a generation of Northeastern and Manipuri women who overcame struggles to achieve their sporting goals. She even suggests solutions for the integration of more and more people *like her*, raising the question of representation. She sets herself as a role model, as she opened a boxing school for young Manipuri boxers living in rural areas.

The artwork that made her story mainstream not only in India but worldwide – since it is still streaming on Netflix in 2023 – is the filmic adaptation of her autobiography by Omung Kumar. When the director came to the female boxer, her reaction was symptomatic to the lack of importance given to Manipuri and women's boxing:

> Initially, I didn't believe it when the director Omung Kumar came to meet me in Manipur where I stay. This is before I won bronze at the 2012 Summer Olympics. When Omung came to me I was a five-time World Amateur Boxing champion. I was surprised why he would want to make a movie on me and thought he was joking or gone mad! Boxing, especially in women's section, is not so well known in India as it's hardly reported, and no one recognized me as Mary Kom.
>
> (KBR, 2014)

To be a source of recognition equivalent to esteem (Heinich, 2009) in the competitive world of sports, the film adaptation is highly glamorized and conforms to the dominant ethnicity of India with the Hindi actress Priyanka Chopra in the title role, even if the boxer told reporters that her life story and the actress' are similar for the sake of national unity. Thanks to the film and above all to her wins in the 2012 Olympics (bronze), 'Magnificent Mary' is recognized as a national hero and even as a national pride in India (*The Hindu*, 2014). The film builds an Indian and even a Hindi heroine, consequently masking the Manipuri origins of the boxer. She becomes a Bollywoodian star in the biopic. The film, both blockbuster and author film, was considered problematic as it wasn't screened in any theatre in Manipur due to a ban by insurgency outfits (*The Hindu*, 2014). It opens with the chaos of the Manipuri village she lived in as a child, Kangathei. A boxing glove is found in the ruins of a plane crash. Her boxer's fate seems inscribed in the dramatic scheme: the assumed insult issued against her – 'female Mohamed Ali' – when she defends her friend from an aggressive boyfriend functions like an omen. Then, a typical boxing film unfolds thanks to the figure of the manager, the training sequences, and the bouts. She marries and has children after that. At this point, the features of her Manipuri identity look picturesque in the film. They are reduced to some folkloric details. Her motherhood is highlighted and her dedication to her ill child's health is exemplary. All along her wins, she's yelled at as India's pride and the final scene confirms that perception of Mary Kom in the film. Through sound and sight, India looks over her as the Indian National Anthem is played and the gigantic Indian flag is raised before her watery eyes after her win during the Fifth Women's Amateur World Boxing Championship in Ningbo, China (*The Times of India*, 2008). Drawing on the concept of political symbolism developed by Abner Cohen, this chapter explores the political substance of boxing drama in the boxing narratives of Mary Kom's autobiography and its film adaptation. From the abstracts of both the autobiography and film, we understood how putting the drama of boxing into words and into motion pictures participates in the sacredness and 'traditionalizing effect' (Apter, 1963) of boxing as a secular ceremony. The boxing would be a ritual performance of which the body would be the monument and the incarnation of the socio-political identity the meaning. Both the autobiography and the biopic about Mary Kom show a characteristic alternation of the political symbol between individual, 'particularistic' aspirations and collective, 'universalistic' aspirations. By wanting to box like Bruce Lee, as the young London footballer of Indian origin Jesminder 'Jess' Bhamra wanted to *Bend it Like Beckham* (2002), the Manipuri boxer embodies difference. In the autobiography, transnational inspirations like Chinese martial arts film heroes support her in highlighting her regional identity. In contrast, in the biopic, Mary Kom's Manipuri identity is supplanted by a national reappropriation of the political symbol. This difference in the treatment of the political symbol leads to a reflection on auctoriality in the writing of 'Our Kom-mitment to the Nation', to use the catchphrase of an advertising campaign in which she was the star. The source of the representation determines the nature of the political symbol. A collective writing is led by an original Manipuri voice in the autobiography while the biopic directed by the male director Omung Kumar testifies to a representation of the woman typical of Bombay cinema seeing her as an allegory of the nation. Through the mediatisation of the figure of Mary Kom, these contemporary accounts of boxing testify to the decline of the heroes of the ring in favour of the rise of the status of entertainment stars.

Boxing Like Bruce Lee

Manipur and the Manipuri are at the core of the Mangte Chungneijang 'Mary Kom' autobiography. References to India are highly counterbalanced by 'silences and fissures' that work like 'subversions' (Thoudam, 2022) in the collective boxing narrative. She embodies Manipur and Bruce Lee more than the Indian flag she supposedly fights for in a work exuding an oral literature aesthetics and consequently expresses a voice, the embodied expression of language. The Northeast region of India marginalized spatially and is the space of political tension between the Indian government and the rebels (Baruah, 2012). However, the boxer who represented India in the Olympics in 2012 is strongly attached to her region, the Meitei, and more particularly her tribe, the Kom. Being *here* (Woodward, 2015) as a Meitei is an absolute priority for Mary Kom, as she embodies the Meitei and gives a voice to this 'subaltern' (Spivak, cited in de Knock, 1992) people in India. In Spivak's words, the Manipuri boxer constitutes a 'subaltern' (2010) voice and Mary Kom embodies difference and gives her voice to the collective autobiography. Through the collective writing characteristic of Indian outcastes narratives as the Dalits' (Thoudam, 2022), the boxer leads the autobiography like a performer. Even if the autobiography is censored by the editors to serve the Indian *ethos*, its authenticity and liveliness is due to Mary's voice and Mary's performance. As Pipkin states, quoting the baseball player Kareem Abdul-Jabbar, the 'athlete's role in the collaborative process' is 'the verbal equivalent of what an actor does' (Pipkin, 2008). She is the leader of a 'subaltern' writing of a minority in India, 'in other words, the autobiography is a site where the subject performs him/herself and the cowriter' (editor or translator) remains 'a listener or reader' (Thoudam, 2022, p. 78). Their voice is quieted and, as Spivak outlines concerning the status of the subaltern:

> Subaltern is not just a classy word for 'oppressed', for the other, for somebody who's not getting a piece of the pie. . . . In post-colonial terms, everything that has limited or no access to the cultural imperialism is subaltern-a

space of difference. Now who would say that's just the oppressed? The working class is oppressed. It's not subaltern.

(de Kock, 1992)

She strongly links her political marginalization and her sporting status of underdog in the boxing arena. She objectively exposes her aloneness as a representative of her region:

> Being a boxer from the Northeast, and particularly from a remote region in Manipur, I was always worried about being dropped from the selections. Because of this, I never once let my guard down in any sporting event or space.
>
> (Kom and Serto, 2013, p. 102)

In competitions, she mostly had to be somebody on her own, the isolated body of some people of the North-eastern India. She was not given enough attention by coaches and she fought very hard for the Olympic berth and for the Olympics (Kom and Serto, 2013, p. 102).

The hostility of the socio-political environment where Mary evolved encouraged her to find refuge in the 'heterotopia' (Foucault, 1984) of the boxing world and in the ritual performance of the pugilistic practice. This transnational (Taylor, 2013) sport goes beyond borders and creates in gyms and boxing clubs local spaces where success becomes possible. The term 'heterotopia', coined by Michel Foucault, defines an accessible space in which norms and rules drastically differ from the world surrounding it. Paradoxically, her situation built her personality and individuality, since she had to affirm it. Rejection created a defence mechanism: the revendication of her identity. That's why the 'embodied culture' (Csordas, 1990) of the boxer expresses itself through transnational references, whether they come from Christianism, an unwelcomed religion in India especially when the conversion comes from outcastes (Jörg, 2018), or popular culture, thanks to Chinese martial arts cinema. The status of the underdog held by Mary Kom contributes to the drama of boxing. She pairs her boxing status with the biblical David and Goliath duel when the future king of Israël beats the giant Goliath (*Bible*, Samuel, 17–58). She is put aside by the Indian institutions during the competitions. She has a 'do or die' attitude (Kom and Serto, 2013) and compares herself to a 'tigress', already transgressing her human nature. She is all by herself and has only her tiny body to spare, like a David with her fighting spirit and God:

> With the coaches, whether from Manipur or Haryana, favouring their own boxers, I knew I was alone in my fight. Comments about my eligibility began flying thick and fast: 'Mary is so small, how can she win?' 'She won't stand a chance against the bigger, stronger boxers in that category' or 'She has fighting spirit and technique, but her height and weight are against

her.' I steeled myself to prove them all wrong and prayed to God to keep me calm.

(Kom and Serto, 2013, p. 108)

She adapts David and Goliath's fight for the boxing ring. That leads her to a deep faith in her success. Boxing like David against the established boxers and the institutions, she had other male and non-Indian role models during her childhood: martial arts actors. They are characterised by a double 'cultural performance': the boxer's and the actor's. Indeed, she is inspired by the protagonists of the cinematic martial arts – Bruce Lee, Jet Li and Jackie Chan – to progressively create her *persona* from a young age. Her down-to-earth attitude nevertheless keeps her grounded. Her life is real, her projects are realistic, but identifying with actors and fictional characters was the starting point of the construction of her identity:

> My favourite movies were the action-packed martial art films starring Bruce Lee, Jet Li and Jackie Chan. Hindi films were boring. We didn't understand the language, and after the blanket ban by militant groups on Hindi films in 2000, they weren't available anyway. When anyone in the village happened to acquire a new video cassette, news of it travelled very quickly. We all visited the home with the cassette and packed into a room to watch the movie. Afterwards all of us kids would imitate the hero and aim kicks at each other. I wanted to be a fighter like those martial arts heroes and my cousin Chungjalen was the usual recipient of my Bruce Lee kicks.
>
> (Kom and Serto, 2013, pp. 21–22)

Staged performances and childhood identificatory processes train the corporeality of the aspiring boxer: she not only identifies with the martial arts film actors, she also becomes their double. They look more *like her* and represent her more than the Hindi film actors. In this sentence, she raises the representativity issue in Bollywood since the lack of representation in Hindi films is patent and the representation of minorities is highly stereotypical, if not absent (Sahu, 2010). She punches her cousin with signature kicks that she appropriated since she mentioned that her cousin was 'the usual recipient of [her] Bruce Lee kicks'. What is more interesting here is the importance of other fighting narratives in the construction of her own. Most of these films are targeted to a Western audience or at least the quoted actors are considered transnational (Szeto, 2008). In the film adaptation, the specificities of her fighting narratives are erased, going from the choice of the actress to the highlighted Indian references.

'Our Kom-mitment to Nation'

In the biopic, Mary Kom's Manipuri identity is supplanted by a nationalist reappropriation of the political symbol. The film debut of the director functioned like a statement for Omung Kumar, who walks knowingly in the footsteps of the nationalist epic drama *Mother India* (Mehboob Khan, 1957) filled with Hindu mythology.[2] The difference in the treatment of the political symbol between the autobiography and the film leads to a reflection on auctoriality in the writing of 'Our Kom-mitment to the Nation', whether it is expressed authentically by herself in her *Unbreakable Autobiography* or used for a 'greater good' in *MK*. The source of the representation determines the nature of the political symbol and the nature of the representatives of the 'we' implied in 'Our Kom-itmment to the Nation'. A collective writing is led by an original Manipuri voice in the autobiography, while the biopic directed by the male director Omung Kumar testifies to a representation of the woman typical of Bombay cinema, seeing her as an allegory of the nation:

> *Mary Kom* ends with a prolonged focus on the Indian flag and the Indian anthem as Mary weeps in gratitude for her athletic victory as well as the recovery of her young son – a none-too-subtle nod to the ways in which motherhood and nation are inextricably joined, while gliding over the racism and marginalization experienced by Indians from the northeast.
> (Hirji, 2021, p. 116)

The climactic training sequence of the film is accompanied by a song that explicitly transfers the personal emotion to a greater good of the Indian nation since the song is entitled *'Salaam India'*. The director's artistic liberties were there to add a 'masala'[3] touch, a dramatic effect that would appeal to the audience in reference to melodramatic Indian TV movies. Mary Kom hopes for a more rigorous work around her pugilistic techniques if a second episode of *MK* would see the light of day.[4] The emotion is not hers alone, it is collective (von Scheve and Salmella, 2014), as her rising is appropriated by a whole nation and her struggles are meant to be felt by all the Indians. As the lyrics of *'Salaam India'* put it, she is willing to sacrifice her body to an India that she salutes with worship, and the relationship of Mary Kom to the Indian nation is imbued with Hindi spirituality in the biopic: 'My head bows down in front of You/Your lap is my home/I salute You, O my India!'[5] The flag is the symbol of this national religion since it is mentioned in the song that 'they' as a collective entity will 'redecorate the skies with the tri-colour flag'. She is represented as emotionally linked with the whole nation as close shots of her isolated body parts are filmed one by one, with her gaze filled with determination. Then, her body is inscribed in the luxuriant nature of Manali and these shots show the strength of Mary Kom as they exhibit the natural wonders of the Indian North that belong to the whole country. A shot of her doing push-ups on rocks by the river symbolizes this communion between her and the whole nation, natural sites and people included. She is pushed by India as she makes progresses with each training shot filmed. Thanks to the supposed Indian/Hinduist spirit embodied by her trainer filmed in a yoga position (lotus position or Padmasana) while watching her train, she is lifted up and the transformation of her body strength is made visible for example with various shots where she has to keep balance with her arms on a vertical bar above the vacuum. With the 'Indian spirit' in her, she finally makes it. This boxing discipline is what makes her a boxer, body and soul. In the autobiography, discipline is deeply personal and really specific to her, whereas the biopic interprets the training sequences in favour of the construction of an Indian identity. While she deeply connects her personal life and its specific circumstances to her boxing identity in the autobiography, the film makes boxing a medium for expressing a national identity. Her womanhood, and all the more her motherhood, is allegorical of the nation and its strength. Femininity is highly performed in the biopic to counterbalance the masculinity exuded in the boxing ring and generally associated with men. The presence of nail polish (Davis, Khoza and Brooks, 2019) could symbolize this balance between her femininity and her masculinity, seen as not that threatening with this 'feminine touch'. She painted her nails from the beginning of the film. When dull tints predominated in the beginning, the Indian tri-coloured flag is worn proudly before a championship in Ningbo, China, in 2008 in the last half-hour of the film:

ONLER: 'Where is your concentration?'
MARY KOM: 'Painting my nails'.
ONLER: 'Nail polish, before a fight? I can never understand your logic'.
MARY KOM: 'Painting nails is a woman's birthright'.

More than womanhood and femininity, her motherhood is strongly tied to the power of the Indian nation. Womanhood and motherhood are considered strengths by Singh, who gives her the sacralised traditional cloth (Singer, 1960) as he has given the boxing gloves previously in the film. It sounds like a ritual. As he states: 'A woman becomes even stronger after becoming a mother'. Here, she is seen as having a superior force: strong women, as goddesses (Newman, 1995) in the Graeco-Roman mythology, are often idolized and seen as exceptions of the female kind. Through the mediatization of the figure of Mary Kom in the advertising campaign, these contemporary accounts of boxing testify to the decline of the heroes of the ring in favour of the rise of the status of entertainment stars. Mary Kom is no longer an 'outsider' heroine. The 'Mary' interpreted by Priyanka Chopra is seen more as privileged; more as 'chosen' by the Indian nation than a disadvantaged boxer responsible for her own success. Kath Woodward mentions the transformation of the bodily capital for the sake of the boxers:

> Boxing combines the aspirations to heroism which attract boxers with the embodied practices and the daily physical grind of training. Dreams of success are, however, firmly grounded in a material reality of embodied social, economic and cultural disadvantage.
>
> (Woodward, 2008, p. 540)

The 'outsider' characteristics of Mary Kom are obliterated to offer a consensual image of the Indian boxer and sportsperson, one that could be branded in the name of India. With the bankable actress Priyanka Chopra and a conservative personal branding characterised by the re-enactment *ad nauseam* of identity performances of Indianness and traditional womanhood, I could state that *Mary Kom* is an Oriental film that internalizes Orientalism (Schirato, 1994). The term coined by Edward Said refers to all the discourses, political or artistic, that represent the Oriental as the other and *de facto* stereotype it or give them attributes that build a binary vision of the world where the Oriental, and by extension the other, is seen as the evil when the self is seen as the owner of the good in imperialistic thinking. In Omung Kumar's film, the Manipuri pride is highly hidden and the landscapes, the dishes, and the Oriental looks are almost considered picturesque. As 'picturesque representations', paintings that stereotypically show the costumes and manners of a given people, the film reduces her culture to aesthetic purposes, to details attractive to the eye. Her culture is relegated to the private spaces and personal ceremonies. It doesn't have public impact or even political importance. When the boxing sequences and the Indian nation are both put under the spotlights, the shots showing her culture are at best part of a 'cinema of intimacy' (Roche and Schmitt-Pitiot [dir.], 2014), where the viewer discovers the characters in their private spaces and unfolds their vulnerability, bodily and emotionally. By the 38th minute, her Manipuri identity is somewhat reduced by the airport advertising poster *Magnificent Manipur*, referring to the sporting nickname given to Mary Kom, 'Magnificent Mary'. After winning the finals of the World Boxing Championship (Turkey, 2002), she comes back to her village and is welcomed with great fanfare. The traditional scarf with the typical Manipuri motifs (bold colours, geometrical patterns, lasingphee as quilted cotton material) on her suit, costumes, and traditional dances illuminated by a sunny sky are what mainly constitute Manipur in the film. They are not what 'motivates' her. They are not associated with strength and power. Meitei culture is associated with the softness and the deliciousness of a traditional plate she prepares for the journalist, the Iromba. Sitting on the ground, the playful tone dominates when the reporter says: 'Mohamed Ali before and now M.C Mary Kom'. Subliminally, her culture is even what hinders her from going up in her boxing evolvement, since she married according to her Christian faith and that stopped her training with M. Singh, who refused to train her after her marriage with Onler (58'51"). In boxing, Manipur is marginalised as the clandestine fight is only a way to gain money and the rebels are considered remote fans. They are not represented at the front of her social support system. Understanding some racist tendencies and colourism – a discrimination made on the basis of the skin complexion, generally in favour of the fairest ones – in Bollywood, it is possible to consider that Mr Sharmila – as a representative of the regional government – is not a representant of the 'real India' according to the film, as he is represented with a very dark complexion, mainly used in

Bollywood to determine the evil characters (Sheth, Jones and Spencer, 2021). The film avoids in a way claiming the systemic racism to favour the highlight on the messages of country unity and of good triumphing over evil. On the contrary, the 'good' Indian is embodied by Priyanka Chopra's glamorous figure. The choice of the actress was highly controversial and a Manipuri actress would have been preferred by her community; the Hindi traits of Priyanka Chopra erase the 'oriental looks' of Mary Kom and consequently the discrimination that the Manipuri people suffer at a national level that she highlights in her autobiography:

> There was also the fact that I was not always recognized as Indian in my own country. Because of our oriental looks, people from the Northeast are often mocked in other parts of India. We're called Nepalis, or Chinkies, and people call us names like ching-ching chong-chong. In a country where people speak all kinds of languages and have varied kinds of looks, why is such treatment meted out to us? When I used to say that I am from Manipur, many people didn't even know where it was. To be honest, in Manipur too we refer to people from mainland India as 'Mayangs', or non-Manipuri, and that too makes me sad. Whether or not I look 'Indian', I am Indian and I represent India, with pride and all my heart. Often, when I travelled abroad, the Chinese, Korean, Mongolian, Vietnamese or Thai athletes would mistake me for one of their own. Each time, I would explain that I was Indian. But you look like us, not like them, they would say, pointing at my team-mates.
>
> (Kom and Serto, 2013)

Mary Kom is an Oriental film – as it is considered as a film produced by an ancient British colony – that internalizes Orientalism by displacing it to a regional level, making it a 'Regional Orientalism'[6] in a country characterised by its regional and linguistic diversity. As she explains it, she is not fully 'recognised' in her otherness in India. Her region is even considered as nowhere. The other is the Manipuri here, but most of the time the film tries to silence the otherness of the boxer – since here the other is good and it does not fit with the Bollywood ideology around Hindi goodness – and the Manipuri 'good characters', highlighting the Indians' and national unity (Dundoo, August 2014), even with the rebels. The Manipuri rebels let her go when she was pregnant by calling her '45 seconds' (referring to the great feats she did in the last minute of her boxing performances) and tell her that 'she is still gutsy'. They support her by listening to the comments on her bouts when she represented India. In the biopic, Priyanka Chopra is more important than the original Mary Kom, as the boxer is seen as a star and stardom as a source of fantasies and desire (Gledhill, 1991). This interpretation of 'Mary Kom' erases the 'Kom-mitment' to privilege the 'commitment' to a sanitised image of India and to the brand of the Indian nation.

Conclusion: Branding Identity

This chapter attempted to comprehend the figure of the boxer as a political symbol. Mary Kom, in her representations in *UA* and *MK*, corresponds to Abner Cohen's definition of the political symbol and her boxing contributes to the 'traditionalizing effect' described by David Apter. It acts here in the appropriation of an Anglo-Saxon martial art coming from a former colonising Britain. By looking first at the 'embodied culture' of the boxer, this chapter invites us to reflect on the boxer's narratives not as 'realistic reality' but as a personal truth, a drama where personal crises intertwine with collective ones. If 'in all societies, nearly all crises are ceremonialized' (Cohen, 1979, p. 98), the *agon*, the contest between life and death instincts, is staged in a very spectacular way in the ring. Loss puts at stake the whole identity of the boxer, as the knockout could be understood as a symbolic death. As Normand Berlin puts it, with the impulses of life and death at stake, 'Boxing is theater, primary, raw theater' (Berlin, 2006, p. 23). The passage from autobiography to film participates in the transformation of the political symbol: the fantasies and desires of the director and the target audience are projected and injected into the corporality of Mary Kom. The body is transformed from a living matter of political claim to a bodily capital undergoing nationalist instrumentalisation. Screened again and again under the semblance of Priyanka Chopra, Mary Kom's body loses its Manipuri force. It is reduced to a brand image, to a 'Kommitment to the Nation' that has nothing to do with the Kom but everything to do with the Indian nation.

Notes

1 Translation from French: 'Traditionally, one seeks "transcendence by starting from invisible and immaterial elements, such as the soul, the spirit or God knowable by reason. The tendency is rather to locate in the body a bridge between philosophy and theology"' (Tommasi, 2018).
2 Basu, M. (2014) 'I wanted Mary Kom to be the mother India of my career', Omung Kumar, *KOIMOI*, August 2014. Director Omung Komar, whose first film was *Mary Kom*, wanted it to be a film of the same impact as *Mother India* (Mehboob Khan, 1957), which focused on the lives of impoverished peasants and was considered a fresco of rural India. The musical film contains many pieces that punctuate the work of the body in the fields. The moving couples evolve with the upheavals of their love story.
3 Deprez, C. (2003) 'La télévision indienne: un modèle d'appropriation culturelle', *Questions de communication*, 3(1), pp. 169–183. Translated from French: Definition of masala ('spice mix') films: 'Masala' ('spice mix') films combine all the ingredients of the previous film genres by combining comedy, action, romance, dance, and song. Popular cinema plays on easily recognizable stereotypes: viewers must be able to construct a fictional familiarity with the works they are watching. These films also rely on cultural references, as evidenced by the use of slang, Indian jokes and puns, and costumes. In the world cinematographic landscape, the singularity of masala films is also due to the permanent evolutions they undergo, from conception to public reception.

4 The Official Website of the Olympics. *A movie on me must have more fights, less masala: Mary Kom.* Available at: https://olympics.com/en/news/indian-boxer-mary-kom-movie-biopic-masala-drama-bollywood-true-story (Accessed: 10 August 2020).
5 Translation from Hindi, Latin transcription: ' "huke" Tere Aage Sar/Teri God Mera Ghar/Hai Tujhe Salaam India'.
6 I came to these conclusions and coined the term after thoroughly reading the meticulous dissertation of Abderrahmene Bourenane on Orientalist cinema and its variations and derivations: Bourenane, A. (2022) *The orientalist legacy in Hollywood cinema' (1900–2018): ideological issues and aesthetic practices*. PhD dissertation. Le Mans, France.

Bibliography

Addis, H. (2007) *In search of the holy story: an exploration of storytelling in relation to Heidegger's phenomenological model of art, and the power of storytelling to re-enchant the world*. PhD thesis. University of Wales Trinity Saint David Lampeter.

Aitchison, C.C. (2007) *Sport & gender identities. Masculinities, feminities and sexualities*. London: Routledge.

Apter, D.E. (1963) 'Political religion in the new nations', in Geertz Glencoe, C. (ed.) *Old societies and new states*. New York: London, Free Press, Collier-Macmillan.

Baruah, S. (2012) *Beyond counter-insurgency: breaking the impasse in Northeast India*. Oxford: Oxford University Press.

Berlin, N. (2006) 'Traffic of our stage: boxing as theater', *The Massachusetts Review*, 47(1), pp. 22–32.

Bonzel, K. (2020) *National pastimes: cinema, sports, and nation. Sports, media, and society*. Lincoln: University of Nebraska Press.

Bourenane, A. (2022) *The orientalist legacy in Hollywood cinema (1900–2018): ideological issues and aesthetic practices*. PhD dissertation. Le Mans, France.

Butler, J. (1993) *Bodies that matter: on the discursive limits of sex*. London: Routledge.

Cohen, A. (1979) 'Political symbolism', *Annual Review of Anthropology*, 8, pp. 87–113.

Crews, S. and Lennox, P.S. (2020) *Boxing and performance: memetic hauntings*. Abingdon, Oxon: Routledge.

Csordas, T.J. (1990) 'Embodiment as a paradigm for anthropology', *Ethos*, 18(1), pp. 5-47.

Davis, L., Khoza, L. and Brooks, J. (2019) 'Nail art, nail care and self expression: gender differences in African Americans' consumption of nail cosmetics', *Fashion, Style and Popular Culture*, 6(2), pp. 159–175.

de Kock, L. (1992) 'New nation writers conference in South Africa', *Ariel: A Review of International English Literature*, 23(3), pp. 29–47.

Deprez, C. (2003) 'La télévision indienne: un modèle d'appropriation culturelle', *Questions de communication*, 3(1), pp. 169-183.

Dundoo, S.D. (2014) 'The story of a biopic', *The Hindu*, August 2014.

Foucault, M. (1984) 'Des espaces autres', Conférence au Cercle d'études architecturales, 14 mars 1967', *Architecture, Mouvement, Continuité*, 5, pp. 46–49.

Fourtanier, M. et Chelly-Zemni, A. (2018) *Le mythe dans la pensée contemporaine*. Paris: L'Harmattan.

Gledhill, C. (1991) *Stardom: industry of desire*, London: Routledge.

Heinich, N. (2009) 'The sociology of vocational prizes: recognition as esteem', *Theory, Culture & Society*, 26(5), pp. 85–101.

Heiskanen, B. (2012) *The urban geography of boxing: race, class, and gender in the ring*. New York, NY: Routledge.

The Hindu (2014) 'Mary Kom disappointed as Manipur misses film show', *The Hindu*, 7 September. Available at: www.thehindu.com/entertainment/mary-kom-disappointed-as-manipur-misses-film-show/article6388361.ece (Accessed: 5 May 2022).

Hirji, F. (2021) '(Indian) girl rising? Challenging traditional femininity in contemporary Bollywood films', *Global Media Journal: Canadian Edition*, 13(1), pp. 108–122.

Jörg, F. (2018) 'Outlandish Christendom: the Catholic Church in India and China', *A Journal of Church and State*, 60(4), pp. 681–704.

KBR, U. (2014) 'Priyanka Chopra's story is similar to mine: Mary Kom', *Daily News India*, 17 August. Available at: https://web.archive.org/web/20170406043022/http://www.dnaindia.com/entertainment/interview-priyanka-chopra-s-story-is-similar-to-mine-mary-kom-2011078 (Accessed: 5 May 2022).

Kom, M. and Serto, D. (2013) *Unbreakable: an autobiography*. Uttar Pradesh: Harper Sport.

Kovacevic, I. (2007) 'Art and the analysis of myth', *Zbornik Matice srpske za drustvene nauke*, pp. 151–163.

Kumar, O. (2014) *Mary Kom*. United States: Viacom 18 Motion Pictures.

Morris, C.R. (ed.) (2010) *Can the subaltern speak?: reflections on the history of an idea*. New York: Columbia University Press.

Newman, B. (1995) *From virile woman to woman Christ: studies in medieval religion and literature*. Philadelphia: University of Pennsylvania Press.

Pipkin, J.W. (2008) *Sporting lives: metaphor and myth in American sports autobiographies*. Minneapolis: University of Missouri Press.

Roche, D. and Schmitt-Pitiot, I. (eds.) (2014) *Intimacy in cinema: critical essays on English language films*. Jefferson, North Carolina: McFarland & Company, Inc. Publishers.

Rowe, D. (2014) 'If you film it, will they come? Sports on film', *Journal of Sport and Social Issues*, 22(4), pp. 350–359.

Sahu, G. (2010) 'Representation of minorities in popular Hindi cinema', *Media Watch*, 1(1), pp. 27–32.

Said, W.E. (2003) *Orientalism*. London: Penguin Classics, Penguin.

Scheve, C. and Salmela, M. (eds.) (2014) *Collective emotions: perspectives from psychology, philosophy, and sociology*. Oxford: Oxford University Press.

Schirato, T. (1994) 'The narrative of orientalism', *Southeast Asian Journal of Social Science*, 22, pp. 44–52.

Sheth, S., Jones, G. and Spencer, M. (2021) *Bollywood, skin color and sexism: the role of the film industry in emboldening and contesting stereotypes in India after independence*. Brighton, Massachusetts: Harvard Business School.

Singer, M. (ed.) (1960) *Traditional India: structure and change*. Jawahar Nagar, Jaipur: Rawat Publications.

Szeto, K. (2008) 'Jackie Chan's cosmopolitical consciousness and comic displacement', *Modern Chinese Literature and Culture*, 20(2), pp. 229–261.

Taylor, M. (2013) 'The global ring? Boxing, mobility, and transnational networks in the anglophone world: 1890–1914', *Journal of Global History*, 8(2), pp. 231-255.

Thoudam, N. (2022) 'Mary Kom's collaborative autobiography: negotiating authorship', *Journal of Comparative Literature and Aesthetics*, 45(3), pp. 70-81.

The Times of India (2008) 'Mary Kom gets fourth consecutive world championship gold', *The Times of India*, 29 November. Available at: https://timesofindia.indiatimes.com/sports/boxing/mary-kom-gets-fourth-consecutive-world-championship-gold/articleshow/3772993.cms (Accessed: 5 May 2022).

Tommasi, F.V. (2018) 'Transcendance et corps', *Diakrisis*, 1, pp. 97-110.

Valentino, L., Tafuri, F. and Caso, F. (2022) 'Boxing as a discipline in the young athlete's training', Research Journal of Humanities and Cultural Studies E-ISSN 2579-0528 P-ISSN 2695-2467 Vol 8. No. 1 2022 www.iiardjournals.org 8(1), pp. 1–5.

von Scheve, C. and Salmella, M. (dir.) (2014) *Collective emotions: perspectives from psychology, philosophy, and sociology*. Oxford: Oxford University Press.

Wacquant, L.J.D. (2004) *Body & soul: notebooks of an apprentice boxer*. New York, NY: Oxford University Press.

Woodward, K. (2008) 'Hanging out and hanging about: insider/outsider research in the sport of boxing', *Ethnography*, 9(4), pp. 536–550.

Woodward, K. (2015) *The politics of in/visibility: being there*. London: Palgrave Macmillan.

Chapter 12

Turn the Volume Up! Boxing Hearts and Beats

Kristína Országhová

I often get asked what music I listen to during boxing training or what the music of 'my field' is. My (simplified) answer is that it is mainly Justin Bieber and turbo-folk. People often associate boxing spaces with hyper-masculinised hip-hop music. Both are linked, through social imagination, to the struggle of marginalised communities or those at the lower end of socioeconomic status (Boddy, 2008). Just as Muhammad Ali fought his way out of poverty, Jay-Z worked his way out of drug dealing through music. The association is emphasised by the claims of hip-hop artists or rappers who liken their music to boxing. Jay-Z comments: 'Hip-hop in itself perfectly blends poetry and boxing. Most artists are competitive, of course, but hip-hop is the only art I know that's built on direct confrontation' (2010, p. 70). While hip-hop is present in the soundscapes of the boxing gymnasium in post-socialist Central Eastern Europe (CEE) where my research takes place, it is not the dominant music genre played in these spaces. The soundscape of this environment is better characterised by pop and turbo-folk music.

The main narrative of a *boxer* in academia and popular culture presents itself clearly as the story of a marginalised (often male and racialised) body, seeking its way out of poverty, social exclusion, or the wrong side of town and attempting to forge new social connections. This story functions in society as what Roland Barthes (1982) referred to as a myth. According to Barthes, myth is a speech and a system of communication. It is not an object, concept, or idea, but a mode of signification. While myths are culturally constructed, their main function is 'naturalisation', which means that despite being social constructs, myths survive by presenting themselves as 'natural' or 'naturally occurring'. Hence, myths are prone to escape critical analysis. The myths about boxing anchor it in the social imagination as a masculine activity of predominantly working classes. Working classes participating in boxing are often perceived through stereotypes attached to both working-class and boxing culture. Crews and Lennox (2020) warn us that these myths being recited, re-enacted, and reiterated perform a very partial narrative meaning of boxing, notably by establishing identities available to boxing bodies that are deemed appropriate, and limiting alternatives. These identity-producing narratives or

DOI: 10.4324/9781003312635-15

myths of boxing identity are shaped and circulated through oral histories, media images, and, I suggest, music and the images music evokes.

Methodology

This chapter analyses music in boxing spaces. It aims to explore what the music played in boxing spaces can tell us about myths of boxing, highlighting the ways music is co-constitutive of these myths. In my analysis, I focus on the relationship between boxing myths, music, and gender. I draw on more than two years of ethnographic research among amateur boxing communities in Central Eastern Europe. During this time, I spent more than 1,000 hours in the field training, travelling, and sharing free time with the members of these communities in six different countries – Slovakia, Czech Republic, Poland, Hungary, Serbia, and Bulgaria. I became a pugilist, a friend, and a boxer. I generated around 450 minutes of field recordings. Additionally, in my field notes, I paid particular attention to the sound dimension of these spaces – to the voices, tonalities, punching sounds, and music played. The case studies presented later in this chapter are linked to a specific boxing gymnasium in Slovakia in which I spent time, socialised, and trained over two years.

I refer to where my research takes place – Central Eastern Europe – as the CEE region. In its broadest sense, CEE can be understood as the area stretching from the Baltic states, Poland, the Czech Republic, Slovakia, Ukraine, and Hungary to Croatia, Slovenia, and to the countries of the Balkan peninsula, such as Romania and Bulgaria (Podraza, 1997). The region has been referred to as 'the part of Europe situated geographically in the center, culturally in the West, and politically in the East' (Kundera, 1984, p. 33) or 'neither East nor West; it is both East and West' (Konrád, 1995, p. 157). It consists of diverse ethnic and religious minorities and is marked by instability, fluidity of state borders, and frequently changing social and political systems throughout history (Murzyn, 2016). Moreover, the latest shared fate of the countries of the CEE region is their falling under the sphere of influence of the Soviet Union and its dissolution in 1989, followed by wars, struggles for independence, and processes of privatisation (Murzyn, 2006). The common cultural landscape of the CEE is in the boxing world of the region manifested through the cooperation between its boxing communities. Boxers often represent teams of different nationalities at local competitions (for instance, Slovak and Romanian boxers representing various Bulgarian teams at the National boxing Championship of Bulgaria or Polish or Czech boxers representing Slovak teams at local tournaments in Slovakia). To a certain extent, the shared regional identity is present in the popularity of the sometimes regionally specific music genres played in the CEE boxing gyms.

In this chapter, I focus on what music *does* socially and politically, especially in relation to our understanding and interpretation of gender in boxing within the spatiotemporal frame of training. I analyse three artists repetitively played in one of the boxing gymnasiums of the CEE region where I have conducted my fieldwork between 2020 and 2022: 1) Justin Bieber, a contemporary pop idol; 2) turbo-folk and the 1989 turbo-folk song 'Jugoslovenka' by the Yugoslav singer Lepa Brena; and 3) 'Orlík', a 1980s Czech nationalist skinhead band. These songs were chosen since they initiated social interactions in the boxing spaces. While the analysis of Justin Bieber's songs serves as an ethnographic vignette to illustrate the possible interactions triggered by music in the gym, the music of Lepa Brena has been repeatedly played in the gym by the coach. Orlík, on the other hand, was the music choice of one of the boxers. I consider this a moment worth particular attention because boxers in this gymnasium rarely actively select the music themselves. Furthermore, all three artists, whether chosen (Lepa Brena, Orlík) or occurring accidentally in the space (Justin Bieber), were the only three songs addressed directly by members of the boxing community. Their comments particularly hint towards their perception of gender in and through music.

Listening to Gender

When we imagine ballet training, what music do we *hear*? What music do we *hear* when we think about boxing training? The music we associate with these physical activities represents and reproduces myths about them, which shapes the identities of their practitioners. While ballet often tells the myth of the elegance, purity, and nobility of the white body, the myth boxing communicates is linked to narratives of masculinity, toughness, passion, violence and criminality, and aggression and wildness. However, the sounds of these activities and of the spaces they are exercised in not only represent the environment, they also co-construct the identities of their participants.

In the last decade, music has become almost inseparable from sporting environments, with the formalising of opening and closing ceremonies at stadiums, workout playlists in gymnasiums, or even in swimming pools through underwater speakers. Music has become closely associated with athletic activity. The use of music in sporting environments is at least two-fold. It is linked to the ability of music to increase arousal either as a response of physiological processes to the rhythmical components of music or through musical associations. In other words, music inspires thoughts that increase (or regulate) physical performance.[1] The associations that music evokes (for example, how the tone of Survivor's 'Eye of the Tiger' conjures the image of fictional boxer Rocky Balboa) are constructed by repetition and circulation of images in which television, the internet, and media play a significant role. This socially constructed association may work as a conditioned response that triggers a specific mindset or mood (Karageorghis, 2015).

Music also plays a role in the ways we forge, reproduce, but also potentially undermine our – including gender – identities; it is a tool for self-representation, self-affirmation, and expression of belonging to a group or culture. Nicola Dibben (2002) argues that while it is problematic to draw conclusions on the ways gender identity is formed through music, it is possible to identify some general processes of gender identity construction: 'the musical activities people participate in, through their musical preferences and through their beliefs about what constitutes gender-appropriate musical behaviour' (Dibben, 2002, p. 130). It is well established that music preferences are intertwined with other identity markers, such as age, socioeconomic status, and ethnicity (Dibben, 2002, p. 130). Therefore, it would be misleading to attribute our musical behaviour to gender alone, yet it is important we recognise its impact on music choices. Schäfer and Sedlmeier (2009) claim that men tend to listen to louder music with more bass, while women prefer softer, more rhythmical and romantic music. These differences are tied to social constructions of femininities and masculinities (Dibben, 2002) where social context also plays a vital role.[2]

Music choices of boxers might also be aligned with choices deemed appropriate for their gender. These choices, I will show, cannot be associated with music considered 'too feminine' or else they run the risk of threatening their boxing identity. At the same time, what is considered 'too feminine music' or 'too masculine music' varies according to the boxer's class belonging. Gender also affects our listening, how and what we hear, and how we draw meaning from what we hear (Tagg, 1989). Thus, the music played in the boxing gym can hold different meaning for the boxers according to their gender. Normative gender identities, then, not only ascribe particular aesthetics and behaviours to bodies, but they also ascribe soundscapes. It is not enough to look like a woman (or a man) or behave like a woman (or a man). You need to sound like one as well. Non-conforming or non-normative soundscapes thus also have the potential to disrupt gender binaries.

Gender is not only something we can recognise through visual signifiers in that gender is not only *seen*, but also *heard*. Moreover, our relations to sounds are highly gendered. My analysis aims to emphasise the need to understand the specificities of reinventing and re-enacting gender identities through music in the context of the boxing gyms in the CEE region. The majority of boxing scholarship on gender has focused on the ways gender identities are negotiated in social interactions, but not *musical* social interactions. I wish to look at the ways gender and boxing identity can be analysed through music played in boxing gymnasiums. How can the analysis of music played during the training session help us understand the ways gender is done, performed, perceived, negotiated, and disrupted in these spaces? What does the music suggest and what does it mean? What can it tell us as an additional source of data that we would not or might not be able to grasp otherwise?

Boxers, Bieber, Beliebers

Me: Hey, Hana, could you turn the volume up? They are [the radio station] playing Justin [Bieber]! It would not be training without Justin.

Hana nods in response to my question, goes to the stereo system, and turns the volume up.

Male boxer: You like Bieber?
Me: Yes. Why?
Male boxer: Nothing, I would just never guess that. You just do not seem like someone who would listen to Bieber.

(Országhová, 2021, Unpublished)

This excerpt is from field notes I took at the evening training of mixed-sex boxing practitioners in a boxing gym in the CEE region. The mixed-sex group training in this gym usually takes place on Fridays at 5 pm and consists of various numbers of competing male and female boxers with a balanced group gender structure. This training, unlike the sex-segregated one, requires both male and female boxers to hit and punch each other and create spatiotemporal conditions in which they can potentially revisit the ideas about gendered bodies, their capabilities, and behaviour expectations (Maclean, 2016). A simple sound system can be found in the corner of the boxing gym right next to the wall of mirrors on the right side of the entrance. For many, the sound system becomes the first spot they approach as soon as they enter the gym and take off their shoes. As if the silence of the space intensified the anticipation of labour, sweat, and suffering to come and the music had the capacity to break through it, to disrupt or divert it, to let one postpone the training time or help one transition from the sweat, labour, and violence of the outside world to the spatiotemporal reality of the boxing gymnasium. The playing of music then serves as a tool for transitioning between social worlds and social realities. It is a guardian of the passage from one world to another. Once the sound system is turned on, the familiar pre-set radio station starts to play. It is the mainstream radio station playing a selection of songs mainly from international contemporary pop idols like Dua Lipa, Justin Bieber, and Miley Cyrus. The playlist remains the same for several weeks with very few alterations and a number of songs being played several times a day. The coach, who spends most of the day in the gym, is sometimes heard humming pop-music hits, although it is not the music he would select himself. His repetitive exposure to it throughout the day results in the tones settling in his body and manifesting in his humming reaction once he hears it. Songs by Justin Bieber are played regularly several times a day. The excerpt from the beginning of this subchapter refers to the song Peaches played during one of the training sessions. As I heard the familiar tones of Bieber´s song, I asked one of the other female boxers to turn the volume up to both enjoy the song and get into the training mindset. The response of one of the male boxers after realising that I might like listening to Justin Bieber suggested that the image of this pop idol, the image of a female boxer represented by me, and his perception of those who listen to Bieber were somehow in conflict. Justin Bieber is a Canadian pop star. His soft and gentle physique and celebrity image represent 'feminised' and trivialised forms of cultural consumption expressed in accusations of his 'cheesy' status. His (often young) female followers or fangirls are called 'Beliebers', a mocking term when used by people outside of the group Allen, Harvey and Mendick, 2015).

Moreover, Bieber is often located outside of the appropriate adult modes of masculinity. His 'brat-like' behaviour, childlike, soft feminine body, and tender visual appearance often prevent him from being recognised as a 'bad boy' and from allowing him to escape his child-star image. As Bieber's image is defined by its insufficiencies to fulfil the image of 'traditional' masculinity, so are the images associated with those who like his music – especially girls and women – reminiscent of the historical positioning of teenage girls and women as inappropriate and othered consumers of culture (McRobbie and Garber, 2006). The image of the female boxer – a strong and muscular woman often touching the boundaries of respectable and accepted femininity (McNaughton, 2012, p. 33) – is then in contradiction with the image of a 'girly infantile Belieber'. As Bieber's image of male femininity disrupts mainstream assumptions about male gender identity, so does a traditionally feminine female boxer disrupt mainstream ideas about boxers' performance of gender identity. While Bieber's music evokes images of the infantile femininity of its fans, images of female boxers are accompanied by the anxiety of insufficient femininity. Female boxers touch the boundaries of respectable and accepted femininity. It is hard to be a boxer and a girl on account of the seemingly opposed or contradictory gendered identity performances required of each position. To embody the dual positions of boxer and female, individuals need to reconcile the ways these terms contradict each other and constantly navigate between the expectations of both.

This ethnographic vignette shows how the encounter of the contesting gendered images of female boxers and female Bieber fans may open space for the negotiation of their gendered perceptions and the normative binary gender identities. While the images evoked by, travelling through, and associated with music can reinforce gender norms and stereotypes, they might also create cracks in socially fixed and fixated ideas about gendered boxing bodies and allow for leakages, reformulations, and transformations. Building on the intersectionality's premise that gender should never be treated as a standalone category, in the next section, I argue that in the boxing gyms in the CEE region it is particularly important to pay attention to the ways class produces gender (Lutz, 2015).

Working Class Femininity and Skinhead Subculture

During one of the morning sessions, a female boxer was sitting on the bench getting ready for the last series of bench-press exercises when I noticed a notebook placed in the corner of the room. It took me a while to realise that the sounds I could hear were coming from the open tab of the YouTube channel. Soon I could identify what at first sounded like humming. It was the music of the Czech band Orlík. Another boxer was standing behind ready to help her in case the weight would be too much. He looked at me and pointed toward the fact that 'I must surely know the band playing'. The female boxer further commented: 'She is too young for that. She can't remember' (Field notes Gymnasium 5, 2022, Unpublished). The comment referred to the fact that the band reached the peak of its popularity before I was born. The band Orlík was a skinhead music[3] band established during the 1980s in the former Czechoslovakia. Both Orlík and the skinhead subculture it represents and boxing are considered male preserves (McNaughton, 2012; Smolík, 2015).

While the growing number of scholarship on gender and skinhead subculture or gender and boxing (Borgeson, 2003; Paradis, 2012; Tjønndal, 2019 problematises, demystifies, and expands our knowledge on the nature, motivation, and negotiation of femininities among female participants in these subcultures, in the mainstream imagery both remain dominated by the male figure and male masculinity.[4]

The band Orlík rose to prominence especially after the 1989 revolution. Despite the decline from early 2000 in skinhead groups in the Czech Republic, the Orlík band managed to keep its legacy on the skinhead musical scene (Smolík, 2015). The band was represented by the figures of Daniela Landa and David Matásek, the former being a boxer and Thai boxer himself, which supports the findings of qualitative research on this subculture that show its mingling with other masculine subcultures, such as football and boxing Smolík and Novák (2019). Although diverse in their socioeconomic status in the early years of Orlík's fame, the fans of Orlík after the mid-2000s are mainly manual workers or apprentices (Daniel, 2016).

The music of Orlík is part of the working-class culture and habitus. With its roots in anti-communist and often racist ideology, the music still stands as representation and expression of anti-regime sentiments more generally and discriminatory attitudes, especially towards Romani people and migrants. The social interaction the music triggered between the boxer and me made me as a researcher more sensitive to the conversations among the boxer and others. As an additional source of data, it helped me recognise and understand the subtle hints in conversations that pointed towards racist and anti-regime attitudes, but were not explicitly articulated. Music (sound) therefore played an important role in a more complex understanding of the social reality of the boxing gym. Furthermore, the music was also vital in understanding the complex ways femininities are constructed in relation to class status. As the female boxer is listening to the Orlík music – music perceived as masculine – it might pose a threat to her femininity. Yet I wish to argue that listening to masculine music (even for a female boxer) in the boxing gymnasium does not result in undermining her femininity. In the context of the boxing gymnasium, it is read primarily through her working-class identity while her gender identity becomes secondary. Class then produces sound dimensions of gender in a particular way. The interlocking systems of gender and working-class identity and their soundscapes need to be in the space of a post-socialist boxing gym understood in relation to their particular construction during state socialism.

Despite the changing class structure of the gymnasium, the majority of the competitive boxers (both male and female) in the boxing gymnasium where this female boxer trains belong to the traditional working class. They work as clerks, waitresses, workers in car factories, or car mechanics. The struggle of the working classes creates the everyday fabric of this training space. Daily conversations in the gymnasium address working conditions, and criticise and express frustration and anger in regard to the state's neglect of its labour force. Over these narratives of working-class struggles linger in the post-socialist boxing gymnasiums residues of socialist ideology and theories of physical culture that saw women and men as equals. Li Xiaojiang and Li Hui (1989) illustrate how women under socialist ideology were equal to men as labourers and workers, not women with their particular experience of gender identities. Women were equal to men as socialist constructors deployable for the building of the socialist nation-state. The image of the socialist female worker was probably best depicted in the figure of the female co-operative farmer in Vera Mukhina's 1937 sculpture 'Worker and Kolkhoz Woman'. Their labouring bodies were theorised as gender neutral. Similarly, within the heavily ideologized theories and concepts of physical culture framed by socialism, as Oates-Indruchová argues, 'the unity and equality of some concepts – like male/female – was politically desirable to preclude the dissipation of purpose and power, which would occur if various groups struggled for various conflicting interests' (2003). The equality of men and women in a socialist state happened almost overnight. Yet this equality imposed from above by the ideology of the state took place in an environment with lingering patriarchal discourses formed in the past. Thus, any sporting endeavours of the individuals were part of the collective project of building a socialist society while upholding patriarchal culture. In such a project, men and women shared the equal role, although the two sexes may not have recreated the world in the same way (Oates-Indruchová, 2003). While the revolution of 1989 marked the end of the socialist experiment in the CEE countries, I argue that myths of strong working-class female figures still shape the understanding and perception of gender in the boxing spaces. Here lingering narratives of post-socialist ideologies allow for their interpretation as strong, respected, and hard-working mothers, workers, and athletes. What then could be understood as an activity

– as listening to masculine skinhead music – that deviates from gender normative behaviour and appropriate music preference norms assigned to gender is read through the female boxer's working-class identity. Differently classed bodies allow for different understandings of what it means to sound 'feminine enough'. While listening to music associated with masculinity might undermine the femininity of the white middle-class female body, it does not pose a threat to already masculinised female working-class identity.

However, it would be wrong to conclude that working-class women then enjoy a greater range of femininities available to them than the middle-class ones, causing less disturbance to the natural gender order. On the contrary, already othered bodies of working-class women cannot escape the naturalised class identity that codes them as 'naturally' more powerful and often more masculine and thus also more masculine sounding – in short, less civilised than the middle-class ones. As women boxers engage in transgressive body practices, it is the traditional notion of the white middle-class feminine body and the music associated with it that is privileged in assessing what the *right* gender performativity (Butler, 2009) and right sound attributed to such performativity are.

Your Car is What Our Love is All About (It Knocks Me Out)

While the previous sections focused solely on the representation of gender identities in images evoked by music, in the following case study I also shift the attention to gendered ways of listening. During my field trips to various boxing gyms in Balkan countries, the figure of Lepa Brena and the turbo-folk music genre that she represents became a recurring theme within the spaces of boxing communities. Her music was often played during training sessions or tournaments. She is also a frequently played, listened to, and discussed singer in the boxing gym in Slovakia, which is the focus of this chapter. The main reason of the popularity of her music outside of the Balkan boxing communities is that the boxing gyms in Central Europe are often attended by Croatian, Serbian, or Bulgarian migrant workers for whom turbo-folk is a part of national culture.

Even though the turbo-folk genre itself is changing, interestingly, women remain its main performers and are usually referred to as 'divas' (Jelača, 2015), and Brena is one of them. With her 1989 song 'Jugoslovenka' (A Yugoslav Woman), she created a popular hymn to Yugoslavism that helped to uphold the dream of common Yugoslavic identity amidst the eroding communal ties of the 1990s (Zlatan, 2020). The song portrays the optimistic myth of Yugoslav nationhood, the unity of its nations, and the celebration of its cultural differences. As 'Jugoslovenka' plays in the gym while boxers are jumping the ropes during the warm-up routine, when the verse 'my heart is the Slavic soul' (Setna mi je duša slovenska) comes, the coach turns the volume up.

It is one of his favourite songs. *Turbo-folk* can be most easily described as a hybrid of regional newly composed folk music and Eurodance that peaked during the Yugoslav wars. The beginnings of this music genre can be traced back to the 1980s and they are closely tied to the nationalist regime of the Serbian president Slobodan Milošević. With the songs full of devotion to the nation, the Milošević government found in turbo-folk a perfect tool to promote the assumed superiority of the Serbian people (Tarlac, 2003). Turbo-folk songs were listened to on the battlefields of Yugoslavian countries and served as a source of motivation for the Serbian military (Tarlac, 2003). Since the early 2000s, turbo-folk genre underwent a significant social, visual, and aural change. The contemporary turbo-folk genre visually resembles mainstream hip-hop and is sonically closer to pop music. Also, the nationally specific musical instruments and voices of particular nation-states of Balkan have been largely lost from the genre (Dumančić and Krešimir, 2017). To address this shift in turbo-folk music and for the clarity of the text, I will follow the example of the scholars Dumančic and Krolo and refer to the contemporary form of turbo-folk as *pop-folk*.

Despite its troubling political past, pop-folk remains a popular genre across Balkan countries listened to by Slovene, Croat, and Bosnian youth alike (Volčič and Karmen, 2010). Among Slovene teenagers at the beginning of the 2000s, pop-folk was the third most listened to genre after pop and rock (Volčič and Karmen, 2010). The pertaining popularity of pop-folk stirs a cultural panic among the elites and generation which remembers the war times because it triggers images quintessentially tied to atrocities of war and Milošević's nationalistic propaganda. The historian Rory Archer (2012) argues that pop-folk's political orientation is much more complex. According to him, contemporary pop-folk performers unify the formerly divided Balkan nations in a shared cultural space by celebrating the peripheral position of the Balkan in Europe. In his interpretation, Balkan is not merely a place or a spot on the map, but also a mental space (Archer, 2012). Contemporary pop-folk then represents a common sociocultural region and potentially creates a shared regional identity that both includes nation-states and transcends ethnonational borders through forging of the transnational solidarity. In the context of the boxing gym, pop-folk music and 'divas' as its main performers might hold different meanings and interpretations according to the gender identity of the listeners. While the men in the boxing gym emphasise the national (and nationalistic) importance of the music and perceive divas as objects of sexual desire, for female boxers, divas and their songs are a source of empowerment.

One of Us

The main performers of pop-folk are called *divas* – female singers visually characterised by hyperbolic femininity (plastic surgeries are not uncommon among divas) (Jelača, 2015, p. 201). In popular culture, divas are portrayed as strong women who always maintain control over their life despite historical tragedies and personal sufferings (Volčič and Karmen, 2010). 'A strong woman who can survive all the pains in life' (Volčič and Karmen, 2010, p. 112). Often coming from disadvantaged backgrounds (poverty, rural areas), a diva represents a self-made, strong, individual woman for whom a relationship with a man can be stripped of the idea of romantic feelings and serve as a tool of material improvement (Volčič and Karmen, 2010, p. 112). As turbo-folk performer Dragana Mirkovič sings in her 1994 song 'Red Ferrari', 'Your car/Is what our love is all about (it knocks me out)' (Jelača, 2015, p. 40).

In the CEE boxing gyms, divas as female boxers often share the narrative of coming from disadvantaged backgrounds (Volčič and Karmen, 2010). A diva is – as some female boxers might aspire to be – a self-made, successful woman. Through entrepreneurship, she rises from poverty or low socio-economic status to become a wealthy businesswoman (Jelača, 2015). At the same time, she is from the *folk*, the ordinary woman, and thus could become a potentially empowering figure for the female boxers as she is *one of them*. Even though divas are perceived as the ones in control, they are portrayed as loving mothers, loyal wives, and objects of men's desire. They are a perfect combination of a mother, a businesswoman, and an artist (Jelača, 2015). Such a portrayal of a diva in a mainstream culture neatly blends neoliberal feminism with patriarchal nationalism – succeeding both in societal reproductive demands based on her gender and the traditionally masculine sphere of labour without jeopardising her femininity (Volčič and Karmen, 2010). Divas represent women who made it in the masculine world of entrepreneurship and remained *women*. Similar desires can be found among female boxers who wish to succeed in the male-dominated world of boxing while protecting their femininity. Divas thus become an important source of individual empowerment for many socioeconomically disadvantaged women – as they are from the *folk* – and women trying to succeed in masculine environments, such as female boxers. At the same time, for male boxers, divas represent something else. Rather than their empowering potential, they emphasise divas' sexualised images.

When we [boxers] gathered around the computer screen where the video from Lepa Brena's concert in Belgrade was playing, the coach and the male boxers commented on sexually attractive visuals of Brena making it clear that she is an object of their desire (Field notes, Gymnasium 3, 2021, Unpublished). On the other hand, the Serbian female boxers on several occasions referred to the pop-folk singers as being, 'beautiful, strong, and wild' and expressed the feeling that if they [divas] could do it, they can too (Országhová, 2022, Unpublished). These comments align with the findings by Volčič and Karmen (2010) in the study on turbo-folk audiences. While for male boxers, divas are sexual objects, for female boxers they might become a source of empowerment. In the social imagination, the figure of a diva as a female boxer is emotional, wild, strong, and authentic without seizing to be the object of male desire. Despite the romanticised projection of the image of *wildness* upon the body of a diva and a female boxer, I wish to argue that the image of the *wild* attached to their bodies both holds them captive in masculine imagination, but also hints toward a potential of the transgression of gender and sexual categories. Halberstam in their discussion on *wildness* refers to it as 'undomesticated modes of life, disorderly behaviour, the lack of moral restraint, excess in all kinds of forms' (2020, p. 216). Wild can be understood as a set of conditions under which unpredictability can thrive (Halberstam, 2020, p. 216). According to Halberstam, throughout history, wild has been used as an umbrella term for various subaltern groups – children, racialised bodies, animals, working class – to signify certain unruliness to the otherwise civilised order of things, often causing bewilderment. In such a reading of the concept of the 'wild', what can it tell us about the figures of divas and women boxers?

Bodies of both these figures carry the idea of the wild held captive by masculine (lack of) imagination. Nonetheless, the idea of the wild hints toward something unruly in the figure of the diva and the female boxer. This disorder or unruliness is best seen in the bewilderment of the many for whom the female boxer is a monstrous caricature of the woman (Oates, 1987) and diva is the representation of the class of the *tasteless low culture* as opposed to the *tasteful high culture* (Jelača, 2015). If boxing is seen by some as a tool of upward social mobility for the lowly classes, then diva could be interpreted as a particular representation of femininity and the upward mobility for the boxing women from these classes. Through pop-folk music thus travels particular ideas and images of gender. These can be interpreted as both transgressive forces against prevailing gender norms and at the same time tools to strengthen them. I wish to argue that for the women in the boxing spaces in the CEE, these images might serve as the source of empowerment while for men they might further reproduce the perception of female bodies as sexualised objects. These different ways of interpreting the music support the claims that listening to music is a gendered practice.

Conclusion

While significant attention has been given to the material, spatial, and visual aspects of the social world of boxing, its sound dimension has remained widely overlooked and neglected. In my analysis, I looked at different soundscapes produced around boxing to try to understand how this auditory approach can potentially bring us a different understanding of the cultures and social world studied. The analysis focused on three songs played in a particular boxing gymnasium that characterise a significant part of its soundscape: 1) Justin Bieber, a contemporary pop idol; 2) 'Orlík', a 1980s Czech nationalist skinhead band; and 3) pop-folk. In this chapter, I propose a different reading of what the soundscape of the boxing gym suggests and what it actually means socially and culturally with a particular focus on gender and gendered experience of music.

As some of the women boxers are recognised as fans of Justin Bieber and his music, I suggest that the contesting images of femininity of Bieber's female fans and female boxers undermine the narratives of normative gender identities. The image of the female listener of Bieber is associated with 'being girly', and the image of the female boxer associated with toughness in the space of the boxing gym is disrupted and open for reinterpretation. Listening to skinhead music – associated with masculinity – might undermine the femininity and heterosexuality of a female boxer. Yet in the space of the boxing gymnasium, it is primarily read through the lens of working-class culture and identity that side-lines the doubts about the 'right' gender performance and the music associated with it. Turbo-folk (pop-folk) and hyper-feminine divas can be perceived by male boxers as objects of sexual desire, yet for the female boxers, they might be a representation of upward social mobility and a source of individual empowerment. This chapter attempts to analyse gender in boxing through what can be heard in the boxing spaces of the CEE region. I look at the music played in boxing gymnasiums through two perspectives – how the music is used and interpreted by boxers and what the similar social processes are in boxing and music. Music played in boxing gyms can become an important tool for interpreting what it 'does' to our understanding of gender in the boxing social worlds, lead to its more complex reading, and produce alternative myths about it.

Notes

1 Synchronised (artistic) swimmers can hear the music underwater through underwater speakers that are connected to the main sound system above the water.
2 See Richards, C. (2013) *Teen spirits: music and identity in media education*. London: Routledge, and Koizumi, K. (2002) 'Popular music, gender and high school pupils in Japan: personal music in school and leisure sites', *Popular Music*, 21(1), pp. 107–125.
3 Skinhead subculture is often – erroneously – perceived by the mainstream public as aggressive and violent and associated with the ideas of Neo-Nazism or extreme right-wing politics (Sobotková Nielsen et al., 2014). That is not to say that the skinhead subculture is not tied to right-wing politics, but that it cannot be encapsulated by one narrative (Smolík, 2015). Its political ideology ranges from the extreme right to the extreme left. Having said that, the skinhead band Orlík is in the cultural space of former Czechoslovakia strongly connected to nationalism, right-wing politics, and racism.
4 See Borgeson, K. (2003) 'Culture and identity among skinhead women', *Michigan Sociological Review*, pp. 99–118; Paradis, E. (2012) 'Boxers, briefs or bras? Bodies, gender and change in the boxing Gym', *Body & Society*, 18(2), pp. 82–109; and Tjønndal, A. (2019) ' "Girls are not made of glass!": barriers experienced by women in Norwegian olympic boxing', *Sociology of Sport Journal*, 36(1), pp. 87–96.

Bibliography

Allen, K., Harvey, L. and Mendick, H. (2015) ' "Justin Bieber sounds girlie": young people's celebrity talk and contemporary masculinities', *Sociological Research Online*, 20(3), pp. 124–138.
Archer, R. (2012) 'Assessing turbofolk controversies: popular music between the nation and the Balkans', *Southeastern Europe*, 36(2), pp. 178–207.
Barthes, R. (1982) *A Barthes reader*. London: Vintage Classics.
Boddy, K. (2008) *Boxing: a cultural history*. London: Reaktion Books Ltd.
Borgeson, K. (2003) 'Culture and identity among skinhead women', *Michigan Sociological Review*, 17, pp. 99–118.
Butler, J. (2009) 'Performativity, precarity and sexual politics', *AIBR. Revista de Antropología Iberoamericana*, 4(3), pp. i–xiii.
Crews, S. and Lennox, P.S. (2020) 'Boxing, Bourdieu and Butler: repetitions of change', *Studies in Theatre and Performance*, 40(2), pp. 145–161.
Daniel, O. (2016) *Násilím proti "novému biedermeieru". Subkultury a většinová společnost pozdního státního socialismu a postsocialismu* [*Violence against the "new Biedermeier". Subcultures and majority society of late state socialism and post-socialism*]. Příbram: Pistorius & Olšanská.
Dibben, N. (2002) 'Gender identity and music', in MacDonald, R.A.R., Hargreaves, D.J. and Miell, D. (eds.) *Musical identities*. Oxford: Oxford University Press, pp. 117–133.
Dumančić, M. and Krešimir, K. (2017) 'Dehexing postwar West Balkan masculinities: the case of Bosnia, Croatia, and Serbia, 1998 to 2015', *Men and Masculinities*, 20(2), pp. 154–180.
Halberstam, J. (2020) *Wild things: the disorder of desire*. Durham: Duke University Press.
Jay Z (2010) *Decoded*. New York: Random House.
Jelača, D. (2015) 'Feminine libidinal entrepreneurship: towards a reparative reading of the sponzoruša in turbo folk', *Feminist Media Studies*, 15(1), pp. 36–52.
Karageorghis, I.C. (2015) 'The scientific application of music in exercise and sport: towards a new theoretical model', in Lane, A. (ed.) *Sport and exercise psychology*. London: Routledge, pp. 276–322.
Koizumi, K. (2002) 'Popular music, gender and high school pupils in Japan: personal music in school and leisure sites', *Popular Music*, 21(1), pp. 107–125.
Konrád, G. (1995) 'Central Europe redivivus', in Konrád, G. (ed.) *The melancholy of rebirth: essays from post-communist Central Europe, 1989–1994*. San Diego: Harcourt Brace, pp. 156–163.
Kundera, M. (1984) *The tragedy of Central Europe: the New York review of books*. Translated from the French by E. White, 26 April. Available at: www.nybooks.com/articles/1984/04/26/the-tragedy-of-central-europe/ (Accessed: 9 May 2022).
Lutz, H. (2015) 'Intersectionality as method', *DiGeSt. Journal of Diversity and Gender Studies*, 2(1–2), pp. 39–44.
Maclean, C. (2016) 'Friendships worth fighting for: bonds between women and men karate practitioners as sites for deconstructing gender inequality', *Sport in Society*, 19(8–9), pp. 1374–1384.
McNaughton, J.M. (2012) 'Insurrectionary womanliness: gender and the (boxing) ring', *Qualitative Report*, 17(17), pp. 1–13.

McRobbie, A. and Garber, J. (2006) 'Girls and subcultures: an exploration, in all', in Hall, S. and Jefferson, T. (eds.) *Resistance through rituals*. London: Routledge, pp. 177–188.

Murzyn, A.M. (2016) 'Heritage transformation in central and Eastern Europe', in Howard, P. (ed.) *The Routledge research companion to heritage and identity*. London: Routledge, pp. 315–346.

Nash, M. (2017) 'Gender on the ropes: an autoethnographic account of boxing in Tasmania, Australia', *International Review for the Sociology of Sport*, 52(6), pp. 734–750.

Oates, J.C. (1987) *On boxing*. The Ecco Press, Hopewell: New Jersey.

Oates-Indruchová, L. (2003) 'The ideology of the genderless sporting body: reflections on the Czech state-socialist concept of physical culture', in Segal, N., Cook, R. and Taylor, L. (eds.) *Indeterminate bodies*. London: Palgrave McMillan, pp. 48–66.

Országhová, K. (2021) *Field notes*. Unpublished.

Országhová, K. (2022) *Field notes*. Unpublished.

Paradis, E. (2012) 'Boxers, briefs or bras? Bodies, gender and change in the boxing gym', *Body & Society*, 18(2), pp. 82–109.

Podraza, A. (1997) *Central and Eastern Europe in the process of integration into the European Union*. Seattle: Unpublished.

Richards, C. (2013) *Teen spirits: music and identity in media education*. London: Routledge.

Schäfer, T. and Sedlmeier, P. (2009) 'From the functions of music to music preference', *Psychology of Music*, 37(3), pp. 279–300.

Smolík, J. (2015) 'The skinhead subculture in the Czech Republic', *Kultura-Społeczeństwo-Edukacja*, 7(1), pp. 91–103.

Smolík, J. and Novák, P. (2019) 'Roots of the Czechoslovak skinheads: development, trends and politics', *Human Affairs*, 29(2), pp. 157–173.

Tagg, P. (1989) 'An anthropology of stereotypes in TV music?', *Swedish Musicological Journal*, 71, pp. 19–42.

Tarlac, G. (2003) 'Turbo folk politics', *Balkan Reconstruction Report* 04/15. https://www.ceeol.com/search/article-detail?id=873

Tjønndal, A. (2019) ' "Girls are not made of glass!": barriers experienced by women in Norwegian olympic boxing', *Sociology of Sport Journal*, 36(1), pp. 87–96.

Volčič, Z. and Karmen, E. (2010) 'The Paradox of Ceca and the turbo-folk audience', *Popular Communication*, 8(2), pp. 103–119.

Xiaojiang, L. and Hui, L. (1989) 'Women's studies in China', *NWSA Journal*, pp. 458–460.

Zlatan, D. (2020) 'Fantasy, sexuality, and Yugoslavism in Lepa Brena's music', in Beard, D. and Rasmussen, L. (eds.) *Made in Yugoslavia*. London: Routledge, pp. 152–161.

Chapter 13

Gender Transgression in the (Trans)National Domain

Laura Serrano and Women's Boxing in Mexico

Marjolein Van Bavel

Laura Serrano's WIBF Lightweight victory over Deirdre Gogarty on April 20, 1995, turned her into the first female Latin-American world boxing champion (Serrano, 2009, p. 475). Yet, she was banned from entering the boxing rings at home in Mexico City due to the legal prohibition of women's boxing (1946–1998). After a moment of public fascination with female boxers in the post-revolutionary context of the 1920s and 1930s, boxing in Mexico had become construed as the ultimate sport of men (Van Bavel, 'La Chica Moderna', 2021). As men's boxing grew in popularity and women's boxing was prohibited, the sport increasingly became imagined as an expression of working-class masculinity and national identity, as it allowed for aspirations of upward mobility and transnational projections of Mexican virility (Allen, 2017; LaFevor, 2020; Moreno, 2009, 2011, 2015). In the 1990s, Serrano played an essential role in bringing the ban on women's boxing to an end as she challenged the patriarchal power system both symbolically, inside of the ring, and legally, outside of the ring (Van Bavel, 2022). Through a historical discourse analysis of Serrano's autobiographical text *La Poeta Del Ring* (2009) and of Mexican newspaper articles from the 1990s, this chapter examines the gendered ways in which the (auto-)portrayals of Laura Serrano both challenged and supported narrative myths about boxing in relation to transnational projections of Mexican virility.

A Puma and Poet in the Ring

Mexican boxers have typically been *mestizo* non-elite men who stem from tough working-class urban neighbourhoods or *barrios* which have long been imagined as plagued by vice, crime, and violence (Allen, 2017). In 1999, an article in the daily newspaper *La Jornada* cited several Mexico City Boxing commissioners in their agreement that 'before being boxers, they are human beings of low culture, with serious problems due to their environments as the vast majority stem from impoverished areas in which the consumption of alcohol and drugs are common' (Sepúlveda, 1999). As a highly disciplined activity that demands a commitment to rules and solid self-control to avoid physical damage, boxing was thought to have extraordinary virtues in terms of mental and moral development for boys and young men growing up in poverty and conflictive family situations. Boxing held the promise of shielding these men from the temptations of alcohol and drugs, and was conceived as a form of therapy that allowed individuals to leave vice and crime behind. Moreover, for a lucky few, boxing could even be a means out of poverty and a way of achieving the status of national hero.[1] Yet, the boxing commissioners warned that addiction continued to be a real problem for boxers, especially once they 'retired' after not achieving the fame and wealth they had hoped for, or – even more traumatic – when they did achieve it, but lost it all (Sepúlveda, 1999). Thus, alongside boxing's salvation narrative, the 'typical' narrative of the (male) Mexican boxer followed a 'rise-and-fall' arc. Stephen Allen has described how, going back as far as the 1930s, the life and career of the alcoholic boxer Rodolfo 'Chango' Casanova provided the example of 'a man from humble origins who rises to fame and fortune only to succumb to excess' as 'his apparent lack of self-discipline led to a life of abject poverty' (Allen, 2017, pp. 44–46).

For Serrano, boxing was not an escape from poverty or addiction but, rather, the result of her university education. Like many male boxers in Mexico, she was born into a working-class family living on the outskirts of Mexico City. Her father, Ranulfo Serrano Parra, and her mother, Ofelia García, sold *pulque* and *tamales* in the city's informal economy.[2] Despite these modest origins, she graduated as a lawyer at the National Autonomous University of Mexico (UNAM), where she had also taken up boxing in 1989 (Serrano, 2009, p. 465; *El Proceso*, 1995). As a law student, she had joined trainer Antonio Solórzano González's co-ed boxing classes at the university's *Ex-Reposo de Atletas* gym after coincidentally observing a young woman training to box on campus (*Gaceta UNAM*, 1997, p. 12; *El Proceso*, 1995, pp. 61–63). Since the 1940s, UNAM – the largest university of Latin America – provided Mexican youngsters from all walks of life with access to essentially free education, considering that tuition fees amounted to only a few pennies a year. As such, UNAM is seen as a quintessentially Mexican tool for self-development and social mobility. Sports form an important part of UNAM's project considering that the intellectual, social, and moral development of students has been linked to the integration of physical education and sports into a complete educational process. In the 1990s, the university's sporting infrastructure had developed into the biggest in Latin America, supporting 44,000 athletes across 42 sporting disciplines (*Gaceta UNAM*, 1997, p. 16). To this day UNAM's amateur and professional athletes – known as *pumas* – proudly wear the university's blue and gold colours and the *puma* emblem when they compete in the national and international domain.[3] Serrano, too, wore the UNAM uniform as she fought Deirdre Gogarty for the world title, thus publicly projecting the university's democratic discourse of self-advancement through discipline and hard work on the world stage (*El Proceso*, 1995, p. 61; Serrano, 2009, p. 475).

Although Serrano enrolled in discourses that connected boxing to self-discipline and self-advancement, she challenged misconceptions that framed Mexican (male) boxers as individuals of humble origins who lacked education.[4] For Serrano, her athletic career and education were intrinsically intertwined. Not only did she start to box as a student at UNAM, but she also described sport as a form of discipline that had impacted all domains of her life. It had made her well organised and taught her to work hard, which benefited her athletic activities and her studies (Hernández, 1995b, p. 46). Serrano argued that, while she had been involved in a variety of sporting activities from an early age, she had dedicated herself to boxing because she felt that it suited her character well: 'At times boxing is violent, aggressive, tough . . . but it also requires technique and intelligence' (*El Informador*, 1996a, p. 26). Although Mexican journalists throughout the twentieth century had described (male) fighters as 'scientific boxers' who fought intelligently, Serrano claimed an academically educated intelligence that simultaneously moved well beyond, but was also intertwined with her boxing intelligence (Allen, 2017, p. 95). In an interview with *El Universal* in May 1995, she reportedly said:

> Not only brute force is what gives us victory. You also must use skill. I am a technical boxer, with style. I always try to use intelligence. As a lawyer too: I consider myself idealistic, honest, and of firm convictions.
> (García and Velázquez, 1995, p. 5)

Besides emphasising her academic education as a lawyer, Serrano and journalists also referred to her love for literature and poetry. In symbiosis with her fighting style, this love for words earned her the nickname of 'Poet of the ring', which was originally given to her by her friend and journalist Jorge Sepúlveda Marín. Serrano did worry that this could damage her image as a fighter. In her autobiography, she wondered whether the nickname, rather than intimidate her rivals, predisposed them to assume that she was 'fragile, delicate, soft and weak'. Yet, she argued, 'who says that poetry is only that?' After all, there is also something like 'poetry in the fists, verses, pain' (Serrano, 2009, p. 457). These (self-)representations of Serrano explicitly challenge what ethnographer Loïc Wacquant has described as the misconception that boxers are 'near-illiterate' (1992, p. 222). Yet, Serrano's efforts to distance herself from suspicions of weakness indicate a need to balance her position as a lawyer and hobby poet with that of a serious boxer. Her position as a *female* boxer, too, asked for narrative work.

The Spectacle of Women's Boxing

For most of the 1990s, women fighters competed in underground circuits in Mexico City due to the official prohibition of women's boxing (Smith, 2014, p. 192). Looking back in interviews in *La Jornada* in 2013 and 2016, Serrano recalled how, at the time, women's boxing was still considered 'a grotesque spectacle'. Although women could win the respect of audiences with the quality of their fights, the public often mocked the female fighters as if they were a circus act. This was also the case during Serrano's amateur debut against María Elena Retana in the spring of 1990. Serrano recounted how this clandestine bout in the streets of the Mexico City neighbourhood of Tláhuac was followed – as happened more often – by a *batalla campal* whereby groups of women fought each other with their eyes blindfolded as the audience laughed, which Serrano felt made a mockery of her sport (Palma, 2013, p. A13). Pitched battles have long been a common trope in Mexican popular culture due to its importance in the Mexican sporting spectacle of *lucha libre* wrestling. However, Serrano's description of the blind-folded *batalla campal* strongly recalls the practice of Battle Royals (Van Bavel, 'Morbo, lucha libre', 2021, pp. 9–34). This prevalent form of fighting opened for boxing and wrestling shows in the U.S. South in the late nineteenth and early twentieth centuries. White promoters pitted three or more blindfolded African American men against each other in bloody free-for-all fights aimed at white audiences (Runstedtler, 2012, p. 15). In relation to these bouts, Andrew M. Kaye has argued that 'the more ferocious and ludicrous the action, the better'. Competitors would receive a small purse or 'scrabble on their hands and knees for coins thrown into the ring by the appreciative audience'. '[T]he drama was intended to rub off on its actors, destroying the dignity of the participants, and introducing them to the code of white supremacy' (Kaye, 2001).

Both in the racist Battle Royals and in the sexist *batalla campal*, otherness was employed as a commodity and comic interlude to uphold oppressive power dynamics. For women's boxing in Mexico too, this drew on a long tradition. Already in the 1920s and 1930s, the press coverage of women's boxing bouts suggested that women who acted out real violence on one another – made visible through bodily harm and the spilling of blood – caused both fascination and discomfort in Mexican audiences. Women's fighting was more readily accepted in the style of variety shows in which gendered contradictions were appeased through comedy as well as the framing of women's boxing as a voyeuristic and eroticised activity (Van Bavel, 2021b, La Chica Moderna'). As a boxer, Serrano upset female gender norms as well as the conventional narratives that, ever since the 1930s, had construed boxing in Mexico as an expression of virile national identity whereby strength, violence, and aggression were seen as legitimate and even 'natural' for men (Allen, 2017; Moreno, 2015).

Ridiculing female fighters served to appease anxieties. For decades, fears existed in Mexico that women who practised traditionally 'male' sports would become masculinised, thus losing their femininity and heterosexuality, which led to preoccupations about *marimachismo* or lesbianism (Santillán, Gantús and Gantús, 2010). Since the late nineteenth century and for much of the twentieth century, the feminine in Mexico has been understood as inherently tied up with the very nature of a woman's body and its potential for procreation. Although the 1980s and 1990s witnessed transformations in social norms for women and the increasing importance of gender equality policies, Mexican women continued to be imagined as 'naturally' nurturing, passive, and self-sacrificing, and were expected to realise themselves within their 'natural' roles as mothers and wives within the framework of the heterosexual monogamous family (Sanders, 2009). Women who displayed aggression and strength transgressed their supposedly physically and emotionally docile and 'motherly' nature (Tuñón, 2008). The development in women of aptitudes for a sport that was considered exclusively a masculine activity threatened the symbolic boundaries between male and female sport, as well as the broader constructions of masculinity and femininity as projected onto bodies.

Women boxers worked hard to receive recognition in a context that often withheld it based on gender stereotypes and discrimination. In an interview with the newspaper *El Informador* in 1996, Serrano argued that while men mostly came to watch women's boxing out of *morbo* (voyeuristic curiosity) rather than *afición* (sportive interest), women boxers served as examples to male boxers:

> Women show more dedication and heart in the ring. I have seen fights where men turn their backs to one another or drop-down while feigning excessive pain. On the other hand, we show more drive, and nobody surrenders a fight without first giving it their all, because we offer more heart, guts, and courage than men.
>
> (*El Informador*, 1996, p. 26)

A journalist from *El Informador* – reporting on a fight between Serrano and María Nieves García at the Arena Jalisco in Guadalajara on April 12, 1996 – agreed with Serrano's claims. While the main event – a bout between Manuel el 'Terremoto' Chávez Téllez and Francisco González – had been of low quality, Serrano and Nieves García had reportedly delivered the best fight of the evening. The female fighters had thrown rapid punches with great aim as they moved around the ring with agility. The article concluded: 'For many, it is unpleasant to watch two women punch each other, but no doubt exists that they know how to do it rather well within the framework of boxing technique and rules' (*El Informador*, 1996, p. 22). In *El Proceso* in 1995, Serrano even argued that women's boxing demanded more skill and marksmanship than men's boxing (*El Proceso*, 1995, pp. 61–63). Regulations for female boxers limited the allowed impact area on the body because hits to the breasts were outlawed due to longstanding worries that trauma to the mammary glands could cause breast cancer (Hargreaves, 1997, p. 38; Smith, 2014, p. 158). By emphasising the quality of women's boxing in terms of technique, dedication, and courage, Serrano was construed – by herself and voices in the Mexican press – as a serious athlete. Countering narratives that ridiculed women's boxing, these discourses projected women's boxing not only as equal, but as superior to men's boxing. Thus, Serrano claimed legitimacy as a fighter by taking part in 'serious' fights rather than the *batalla campal*, as well as through discourse which also involved conformation to expectations in national and gendered terms.

The Nation and the Feminine

On May 7, 1994, Serrano made her professional debut at the MGM Grand Hotel in Las Vegas against the reigning world champion, Christy Martin. She entered the arena wearing a *sarape* in the Mexican national colours and embroidered with the Virgin of Guadalupe (Serrano, 2009, pp. 473–474). The following year, she walked into her WIBF world title fight against Deirdre Gogarty as the traditional Mexican song the "Jarabe Tapatío" played, wearing a tricolour wrapper over her UNAM uniform (*El Proceso*, 1995; Serrano, 2009, p. 475). Through her international boxing performances, Serrano projected a public image immersed in Mexican nationalist sentiment. In doing so, she followed the common trope for male Mexican boxers who served as examples of working-class masculinity and as national heroes and who, through their performance of nationalism, took part in the transnational projection of Mexican virility. While women's boxing was still prohibited or relegated to a freak spectacle in the Mexican national context, Serrano claimed legitimacy as a boxer through her passionate and public adoption of the Mexican colours on the international boxing stage. By adopting the performance strategies of 'legitimate' national (and collegiate) heroes, Serrano sought to embody sporting seriousness.

Interestingly, while still prohibiting women's boxing, Mexican authorities also celebrated Serrano's world victory as a national achievement. The Mexico City Boxing Commission president, David García Estrada, acknowledged Serrano for her 'effort, quality and dedication'. He considered that she had 'made a sporting achievement that gratifies the country' and that her 'perseverance, preparation, and effort [were] a welcome example for the youth' (*El Informador*, 1995). In November of 1995, Serrano was lauded during the festivities in honour of the 85th anniversary of the Mexican Revolution. Together with other prominent (predominantly male) Mexican athletes, she was invited onto the stage that was mounted on Mexico City's main square, the *Zócalo* (*El Porvenir*, 1995, p. 4). Efforts by the Mexican authorities to link the performance of boxers to nationalism and the education of the country's populace were nothing new. The inclusion of a woman boxer in this discourse, however, was. Thus, Serrano was inscribed in what had historically been a highly male-gendered process, which simultaneously challenged the discursive construction that tied Mexican boxing and nationalism to masculinity. This caused unease, as exemplified by the continued efforts by the gatekeepers to the Mexican boxing sport to safeguard boxing as a male domain by upholding the ban on women's boxing in Mexico City.

To avoid what Judith Butler has called 'gender trouble' (that is, the upsetting of gender norms), women who engaged in the male-gendered activity of boxing needed to remain legible as appropriately gendered (Butler). This involves the symbolic and embodied balancing of their 'sporting' and 'feminine' bodies and the social roles and expectations projected onto them as athletes and women (Choi, 2000; Krane et al., 2004). According to Christy Halbert, women boxers have felt the need to show that besides 'tough enough', they were also 'woman enough' as they balanced 'a public identity that appears neither too masculine nor too feminine' (Halbert, 1997, p. 7). Female athletes have used various strategies, including identity and impression management, to be accepted as both athletes and women. For example, following her WIBF world title victory in 1995, the government-leaning daily newspaper *El Universal* described Serrano as wearing red lipstick and 'a touch of mascara' on her eyelashes and argued that she knew 'how to have a gentle gaze'. The article also quoted Serrano stating that she was 'romantic, tender, loving, and scrupulously feminine'. To the journalist's inquiry whether she felt that her involvement in boxing had masculinised her, Serrano responded:

> Many people think that when a woman steps into the ring, she loses her femininity and becomes a *marimacho* [i.e., tomboy]. But boxing does not mark her, nor does it make her different from other women. She retains her feminine essence even when she steps into the ring. Maybe she becomes more aggressive and violent, but she is still a woman.
> (García and Velázquez, 1995, p. 5).

The left-wing weekly news magazine *El Proceso* also quoted Serrano as stating that boxing did 'not quarrel' with femininity. Echoing discourses that had historically framed Mexican femininity around the concept of motherhood, Serrano was quoted as stating that several professional boxers were mothers. This was why, she argued, female boxers were subjected to medical examinations that test them for pregnancy, determine the health of their breasts, and ensure that they are not menstruating the day of their fights (*El Proceso*, 1995). The article argued that boxing had the reputation of attracting '*marimachas*' [lesbians] and inquired whether Serrano had a boyfriend. Her face reportedly lit up in smiles as she spoke of her journalist boyfriend, whom she refused to name. She said that she had dedicated several poems to him, some of which were quite erotic in tone (*El Proceso*, 1995).

Female athletes who compete in traditionally masculine sports have been expected to highlight their femininity and heterosexuality, which Jan Wright and Gill Clark have described as the notion of 'compulsory heterosexuality' (Wright and Clarke, 1999). Thus, Christine Mennesson argues, women's involvement in the traditionally 'male' sport of boxing leaves women in an ambivalent position: 'on the one hand, by definition, they challenged the existing gender order; on the other hand, they also reinforced the status quo by displaying traditional modes of femininity' (Mennesson, 2000, p. 21). Consequently, the discourses surrounding Mexican women's boxing tapped into conventions that continued to construe Mexican womanhood as intrinsically associated with a supposed 'friendly' female nature, as exemplified through heterosexuality and motherhood.

Nevertheless, Serrano's efforts to balance her identity as a serious boxer with that of her as an 'appropriately' gendered woman helped to claim acceptability for women's boxing, which opened new possibilities for women and allowed for the imagining of a Mexican female boxer. Serrano was represented by herself and journalists as the embodiment and integration of both the identities of fighter and woman. For example, an article in *El Proceso* argued that while Serrano was 'a very cheerful *muchacha* [girl]' who 'smiled constantly', the reader should not be fooled by 'her friendly side', considering that 'in her eyes, one can also see the hardness that one must possess as a fighter'. The article contrasted Serrano's friendly and non-threatening way of carrying herself with how her body language transformed the moment she entered the boxing ring (La Redacción, 1995, *El Proceso*). Moreover, in *Fem* magazine, displaying the legacy of second-wave feminism, Serrano's traditionally female attributes were positively appreciated:

> Her anxious, apprehensive, slightly childish gaze is transformed in that 4 by 4-meter space. . . . Watching her train, she moves around in the ring with the skill and beauty that only good technique allows, hitting and avoiding blows. This makes that *chica enamorada* [girl in love] disappear for a moment, the one who smiles when she tells us about her journalist boyfriend, whom she hopes to marry in December of 1996. But that is precisely what makes us admire her more; she is like any other woman, with dreams and the desire to have a partner and a family, who is dedicated and for whom her boyfriend is part of 'my mind, my heart . . . he completes me.
> (Hernández, 1995)

Serrano and journalists reassured the public of her 'acceptable femininity' by way of affirming her desire to marry a man and to have a family. However, her passion for boxing also stood in the way.

The Vice and Price of Boxing

Serrano's autobiography includes a poem (*The Poet of the Ring*, Serrano, 2009, p. 460) which speaks to conventional boxing narratives that emphasise strength, courage, blood, and sweat in relation to self-discipline and self-advancement. The poem reveals her dreams for success, fame, happiness, love, and a comfortable life. Yet, her involvement in boxing did not necessarily bring her these things. In her autobiography, Serrano recounts how boxing cost her several romantic relationships. Emphasising her inability to give up boxing as if it were an addiction, Serrano described how a boyfriend asked her to quit: 'I stopped for seven months, which seemed like seven years to me', but 'maybe my love was not big enough to keep up my boxing abstinence'. The complaints from another boyfriend – to whom she became engaged – that she preferred money and boxing over him did not withhold her from moving to Las Vegas to pursue her boxing career. In the end, Serrano wrote, 'there was no wedding' (Serrano, 2009, p. 501). In 1995, in the monthly feminist magazine *Fem*, Serrano even referred to boxing as '*mi amante*' [my lover], thus comparing her pursuit of boxing – even if 'my boyfriend gets angry' – to being romantically unfaithful (Hernández, 1995a). This resonates with MMA fighter Heather Hardy's description of boxing in 2019 as her 'bad boyfriend', saying that even though boxing treated her poorly – through its low financial revenues, physical injury, and institutional violence – it continued to be her true love (Crews and Lennox, 2020, pp. 107–108).

That Serrano prioritised herself and her passion over her romantic partners meant that she transgressed feminine archetypes tied to the concept of *abnegación*, which construed the ideal Mexican woman as a self-sacrificing mother and wife (Sanders, 2009, p. 1547). This held great emancipatory potential. Serrano embodied and vocally stressed the potential of women to carve out new roles for themselves. When *El Universal* described boxing as a risky profession, especially for women, Serrano responded: 'Women are just as capable as men to carry out any activity. Her feminine condition is not a limitation. That is why we must not marginalise ourselves' (García and Velázquez, 1995, p. 5). Hernández Carballido, in the feminist magazine *Fem*, argued that, thanks to Serrano, old barriers had started to come down 'little by little', to which Serrano responded: 'I am flattered that they say that I have opened spaces for women in this sport. I did not do it on purpose, but women's boxing has come to be seen differently with my performance' (Hernández, 1995, pp. 46–47). In *El Universal*, Serrano also stressed that she had not intended to modify social behaviours. Rather, it had been 'sheer stubbornness and the desire to conquer a space for my own freedom and independence' (García and Francisco, 1995, p. 5). Nevertheless, the national visibility that Serrano provided through her involvement in women's boxing in the international domain, as well as her efforts to lift the legal ban on women's boxing in Mexico City, opened the doors for women's boxing in the Mexican capital. It did come at a personal price.

In her autobiography, Serrano recounts how she gave up her steady job as a lawyer at the criminal court at the *Reclusorio Oriente* prison to pursue a career in professional boxing (Serrano, 2009, p. 471). However, the low financial revenues in women's boxing forced her to rely on the economic support of her family (Hernández, 1998a). Her professional debut and world title victory, respectively, earned her 1,500 and 2,000 dollars, which – considering that she only fought once a year – were annual incomes from which various costs were still deducted (Serrano, 2009, p. 475; *El Informador*, 1996b, p. 26; Hernández, 1998). She was denied state and private sponsorship, even though she had approached a beer company, a sportswear shop, and a bookshop (Serrano, 2009, p. 454, 464). Yet, Serrano continued to box because – she emphasised – it truly was her passion and *vicio* [that is, addiction or vice] (Hernández, 1995, pp. 46–47; Serrano, 2009, pp. 454–455). Thus, Serrano enrolled herself in narratives that had long since connected boxers to excess. Rather than boxing being presented as a potential route out of addiction and poverty, for Serrano, boxing was construed as addiction itself, which not only thwarted her romantic relationships but also diverted her from her path towards social mobility as a lawyer.

Thus, Serrano's involvement in boxing followed the same 'rise and fall' arc that Allen had described for male Mexican boxers. Just as male boxers' access to wealth and social status was generally only temporary – keeping them in their place in the working-class margins of Mexican society – women's involvement in boxing did not provide a happy ending. Although Serrano held two world championship titles and one intercontinental championship title, and had been the first Mexican and Latin American woman to become a world boxing champion, she was never able to make a living out of professional boxing. Neither was she ever given the official opportunity to fight at home, as the Mexico City Boxing Commission continued to boycott her for her role in bringing the capital's prohibition of women's boxing to an end (Van Bavel, 2022).

Conclusion

Having grown up in a working-class family living in a *barrio* at the foot of the *Ajusco* mountain in Mexico City, Serrano shared characteristics with most (male) Mexican boxers. As she became a world boxing champion, she was inscribed – by herself, authority figures, and journalists – in dominant boxing narratives connected to nationalism, discipline, and self-improvement, which had long been a male preserve. Yet, she also inscribed herself in UNAM's narrative of self-advancement and emphasised her intelligence and love of poetry. As an academically educated lawyer, she challenged the misconception of boxers as 'near-illiterate'. In a context in which boxing was still considered a highly male gendered activity – due to its connection to notions of Mexican masculinity and nationalism – and women's boxing was not taken seriously, Serrano worked to claim herself simultaneously as a serious boxer and as an 'appropriately' gendered woman. Together with journalists, Serrano appeased gendered anxieties and construed boxing as an acceptable activity for women by emphasising that it was not in contradiction to the 'natural' role of women as mothers and that she, as a serious boxer, was also an 'appropriately' gendered woman in a heteronormative sense. Serrano also inscribed herself in narratives that linked the lives of boxers to vice. While for men, this has mostly meant a struggle with alcohol and drug addiction, Serrano construed her passion for boxing itself as her *vicio*, as an addiction and selfish pursuit that cost her a steady job and romantic relationships. Serrano's construction of boxing as her *vicio* not only served as a counternarrative to boxing's salvation narrative, but also allowed her to enrol in the dominant boxing myth that tied boxers to vice and decline, thus framing herself as a true boxer. This chapter has shown the social expectations placed on Mexican women in the 1990s and how Serrano, through her boxing and self-portrayals, both affirmed and subverted dominant gender norms, thus providing an insight into the complexity and plurality of gender performance within rigid and oppressive heteronormative readings of femininity.

Notes

1 All translations by author. Sepúlveda Marín, J. 'Los púgiles no admiten su adicción y para los autoridades es inexistente', *La Jornada*, September 1999, p. 15. Available at: www.jornada.com.mx/1999/09/15/dep-pugiles.html (Accessed: 3 June 2022).
2 *Pulque* is an alcoholic beverage made from the fermented sap of the maguey plant. *Tamales* are steamed corn-dough dumplings. La Redacción (1995) 'Con su campeonato mundial, Laura Serrano espera abrir las puertas al boxeo femenil en Mexico', *El Proceso*, 8 May 1995, pp. 61–63. Palma, E. (2013) 'Laura Serrano: el difícil inicio del boxeo femenil en México', *La Jornada*, 4 May 2013, p. A13.
3 In 1968, the university's stadium even hosted the Olympic Games. See: Castañeda, L. (2012) 'Choreographing the metropolis. Networks of circulation and power in Olympic Mexico', *Journal of Design History*, 25(3), p. 287.
4 As illustrated in the autobiography by the powerful secretary of the Mexico City Boxing Commission from 1953 to 1985: Barradas Osorio, R. (1989) *El Box Fuera del Ring. Lo Blanco y Negro del Boxeo Professional en México*. Mexico City: Rafael Barradas Osorio, p. 7.

Bibliography

Allen, D.S. (2017) *A history of boxing in Mexico: masculinity, modernity, and nationalism*. Albuquerque: University of New Mexico Press.
Arbena, L.J. (1991) 'Sport, development, and Mexican nationalism, 1920–1970', *Journal of Sport History*, 18(3), pp. 350–364.
Barradas, O.R. (1989) *El Box Fuera del Ring: Lo Blanco y Negro del Boxeo Professional en México*. Mexico City: Rafael Barradas Osorio.
Castañeda, L. (2012) 'Choreographing the metropolis: Networks of circulation and power in olympic Mexico', *Journal of Design History*, 25(3), pp. 285–303.
Choi, P.Y.L. (2000) *Femininity and the physical active woman*. London: Routledge.
Crews, S. and Lennox, P.S. (2020) *Boxing and performance: memetic hauntings*. London: Routledge.
El Informador (1995) 'Inicia la CBDF los estudios para evaluar el box femenil', 7 May 1995.
El Informador (1996a) 'Función de box en honor de la abuelita Bejines', 12 April 1996.
El Informador (1996b) ' "El 'Terremoto" Chávez ganó fácil en el primero', 13 April 1996.

El Porvenir (1995) 'Impresiona public a "Rocket' y Karim"', 21 November 1995.
Gaceta UNAM (1997) 'La UNAM cuenta con la infraestructura deportiva más grande de América Latina', *Gaceta UNAM*, 3106, 2 June 1997, p. 16.
García, R. and Francisco, O.V. (1995) 'Laura Serrano: "Aún en el ring conservó mi esencia femenina"', *El Universal*, 9 May 1995.
Hernández, C.E. (1995a) 'De Atletas: Deportes no femeninos. Machismo o Falta de Costumbre', *Fem*, June 1995, p. 48.
Hernández, C.E. (1995b) 'De Atletas. El boxeo: Un deporte, un arte . . . es passion: Laura Serrano García. La mejor deportista mexciana de 1995', *Fem*, December 1995.
Hernández, C.E. (1998a) 'El boxeo femenil . . . un desgaste fuera del ring', *Fem*, March 1998.
Hernández, C.E. (1998b) 'Abajo del *ring*, los golpes más duros para las boxeadoras', *La Jornada*, 25 April 1998.
Hernández, M. (2022) 'La UNAM, motor incontenible de cambio y movilidad social: Graue', *Gaceta UNAM*, 12 January 2022.
Halbert, C. (1997) 'Tough enough and woman enough: Stereotypes, discrimination, and impression management amongst women professional boxers', *Journal of Sport and Social Issues*, 21(1), pp. 7–36.
Hargreaves, J. (1997) 'Women's boxing and related activities: introducing images and meanings', *Body & Society*, 3(4), pp. 33–49.
Kaye, M.A. (2001) ' "Battle blind" Atlanta's taste for black boxing in the early twentieth century', *Journal of Sport History*, 28(2), pp. 217–232.
Krane, V., Choi, P.Y.L., Baird, M.S., Aimar, M.C. and Kauer, J.K. (2004) 'Living the paradox: Female athletes negotiate femininity and muscularity', *Sex Roles*, 50(5–6), pp. 315–329.
LaFevor, C.D. (2020) *Prizefighting and civilization: a cultural history of boxing, race, and masculinity in Mexico and Cuba, 1840–1940*. Albquerque: University of New Mexico Press.
La Redacción (1995) 'Con su campeonato mundial, Laura Serrano espera abrir las puertas al boxeo femenil en Mexico', *El Proceso*, 8 May 1995.
Matthew, C.G. (2002) *The Romance of democracy: compliant defiance in contemporary Mexico*. Berkeley, Los Angeles and London: University of California Press.
Mennesson, C. (2000) ' "Hard" women and "soft" women: The social construction of identities among female boxers', *International Review for the Sociology of Sport*, 25(1), pp. 21–33.
Moreno, H. (2009) 'Boxeo, Peligro y Masculinidad', *Revista de Investigación Social*, 5, pp. 41–59.
Moreno, H. (2011) 'El Boxeo Como Tecnología de La Masculinidad', *La Ventana*, 33, pp. 152–196.
Moreno, H. (2015) 'Género, Nacionalismo y Boxeo', in Serret, E. (ed.) *Identidad Imaginaria: Sexo, Género y Deseo*. Mexico City: Universidad Autónoma Metropolitana, pp. 55–91.
Palma, E. (2013) 'Laura Serrano: El difícil inicio del boxeo femenil en México', *La Jornada*, 4 May 2013.
Runstedtler, T. (2012) *Jack Johnson, Rebel Sojourner: boxing in the shadow of the global color line*. Berkeley, Los Angeles and London: University of California Press.
Sanders, N. (2009) 'Mothering Mexico: the historiography of mothers and motherhood in 20th-century Mexico', *History Compass*, 7, pp. 1542–1553.

Santillán, E., Gantús, M. and Gantús, F. (2010) 'Transgresiones femeninas: Futbol. Una Mirada desde la Caricatura de la Prensa, México 1970–1971', *Tzintzun. Revista de Estudios Históricas*, 52, pp. 141–174.

Sepúlveda, M.J. (1999) 'Los púgiles no admiten su adicción y para los autoridades es inexistente', *La Jornada*, 15 September. Available at: https://www.jornada.com.mx/1999/09/15/dep-pugiles.htm (Accessed: I3 June 2022).

Serrano, G.L. (2009) 'La Poeta Del Ring', in *9 Estampas de Mujeres Mexicanas Tomo II*. Mexico City: DEMAC, pp. 452–510.

Smith, M. (2014) *A history of women's boxing*. Lanham: Rowman & Littlefield Publishers.

Tuñón, J. (2008) *Enjaular los Cuerpos: Normativas Decimonónicas y Feminidad en México*. México City: El Colegio de México.

Van Bavel, M. (2021a) 'Morbo, *lucha libre*, and television: The ban of women wrestlers from Mexico City in the 1950s', *Mexican Studies/Estudios Mexicanos*, 37(1), pp. 9–34.

Van Bavel, M. (2021b) '*La Chica Moderna* and the virile sport of boxing: women boxers, gender politics, and identity construction in Mexico in the 1920s and 1930s', *The International Journal of the History of Sport*, 38, pp. 345–367.

Van Bavel, M. (2022) 'The commission knocked out cold: Laura Serrano and the end of the Mexico City prohibition of women's boxing in the 1990s', *Gender & History*, pp. 1–18.

Vázquez, J.M. (2016) 'Laura Serrano pagó el precio de ser la pionera en el boxeo femenil', *La Jornada*, 2 April 2016.

Wacquant, L.J.D. (1992) 'The social logic of boxing in Black Chicago: Toward a sociology of pugilism', *Sociology of Sport Journal*, 9, pp. 221–253.

Wright, J. and Clarke, G. (1999) 'Sport, the media and the construction of compulsory heterosexuality: a case study of women's Rugby union', *International Review for the Sociology of Sport*, 34(3), pp. 227–243.

Afterword: Boxing and Cultural Value

The powerful narratives through which boxing is understood are insufficiently challenged in popular and academic encounters with the sport. This volume invites a multidisciplinary approach to respond to this dilemma. Its diverse range of authors question the cultural value of boxing and present alternative readings of how individual boxing identities manifest, and how boxing communities are valued otherwise. As Löic Wacquant's frequently cited remark observes, boxing is a sport about mattering, in every sense of the word: '[a] boxer in the ring is a being who screams, with all his [sic] heart, with all his [sic] body: "I want to be someone. I exist"' (Wacquant, 2005, p. 148). This volume explores the complicated relationship that individual boxers navigate – not solely in their roles as competitive athletes and ambassadors for boxing, but also as representatives of their respective countries, communities, and broader socio-cultural identities. This collection has demonstrated that, '[a]ll boxers negotiate power relations daily not just amongst themselves but in relation to preconceived gender norms' (Heiskanen, 2014, p. 29), ethnic and racial stereotypes, and the responsibilities attributed to elite-level athletes. Authors have confirmed the wide-ranging (and historical) practices of discrimination in boxing, as well as the exploitation and exclusion experienced by individuals and community groups, particularly those residing within difficult political and socio-economic conditions. The gradual movement towards including women in boxing, for example, is indeed cause for wide-scale celebration – as are the commitments made to improving the experiences of female participants in boxing post-2012 Olympics. However, whereas female boxers at all levels of the sport are beginning to escape Oates' reductive remarks about how women in boxing 'violate' the stereotype of 'nurturer', the overwhelming 'masculine and misogynistic doxa' of the sport remains (Paradis, 2012, p. 85). Female fighters continue to be 'pitted against male fighters' (Heiskanen, 2014, p. 29), against each other, and also against patriarchal restrictions that increase their individual labour whilst simultaneously diminishing their cultural value and commercial worth.

But as several contributors have shown, the ritualistic training practices of boxing creates a space for dialogue and reinvention wherein individuals and communities can explore their senses of self. Independent and collective action in and through boxing is powerful – it has the capacity to transform the daily experiences of its participants. For Supriya Chauduri, 'Boxing is not a symbolic act' or 'social tool of 'empowerment'. Rather, for Muslim women and girls in India, boxing 'is a means . . . for this community and its members . . . for a construction of selfhood'. As chapters from Országhová, Easterling and Hanson, and Crews indicate, within boxing gyms themselves and through associated community (social) spaces, there is scope to move within the stronghold of popular dominant narratives in boxing that gives way for practices towards social justice to emerge. Such movement(s) in boxing indicate alternative forms of 'athletic achievement and personal development', affirming the body as a potential 'site for personal empowerment, reinvention of identities, and social rehabilitation' (Heiskanen, 2014, p. 29).

Our collective critical intervention in the narrative resources (scholarly and popular) available for defining and attributing *cultural value* to boxing bodies and communities expands the space for invention and movement in and through boxing, narrative, and culture. The space created for this reflexive work to materialise is vital as a means of continuing to respond to dynamic changes in cultural heritage, national histories, and diverse performances of identity in boxing. The long-term aim for this project is maintaining the generous and critical manner in which the various authors included in this volume explore the socio-political narratives that are mapped onto individual boxing bodies and groups. Opposing the commonly held view that boxers are isolated individuals struggling and striving to succeed, this volume presents opportunities to *resist* and *reject* 'individualist aspiration in favour of collective' gain (Boddy, 2008, p. 134). The focus on intersectionality as it relates to both boxing practices and scholarly methodology, and the celebratory awareness of the quality of relationality and community that are always already present in boxing, provide a critical starting point for addressing the urgent concerns facing boxing today – be they culturally, geopolitically specific, historical, or systemic. Sports media and scholarship have only recently started to respond to the global dilemma of COVID-19 and its impact on athletic communities, sporting events, and businesses (Lewandowki, 2022). This collection is a timely introduction to methodologies and perspectives that offer a step towards addressing the seismic, global ramifications that the pandemic has had on boxing, as well as broader sports and leisure communities, events, and activities.

For boxing, the COVID pandemic represented the financial demise of the already uncertain and unstable business model of professional boxing. The trickledown effect has meant these crises are felt most deeply at amateur and grassroots levels. For Boddy, Joe Louis is an example of a boxer whose status was often used to 'harness support for political struggles' (Boddy, 2008, p. 134). However, alongside other such individuals celebrated in this book, several authors gesture towards the various ways in which their community groups posit platforms and practices for negotiating the fraught relationships between the personal, public, and political narrative identities in boxing, which we can learn from. Examples outlined by Chauduri, Országhová, Easterling and Hanson, and Barrett et al. indicate the potential to imagine alternative futures for boxing and its longstanding troubles. The robust research practices presented by Schneider, Crews, and Van Bavel, on the other hand, provide critical accounts of boxing histories, which otherwise suggest ways of accelerating our progression out of the nebulous and reductive binds that boxing and its associated (regulated and regulatory) bodies are caught within. Collectively, this collection works to disrupt hegemonic and persuasive narratives of boxing, offering up counternarratives as a means to interrogate the problematic legacy of seductive depictions of boxing, which continue to plague commercial and cinematic depictions of the sport in the public lens. This series begins by seeing boxing otherwise, understanding boxing bodies outside of the myopic narratives that haunt popular notions of the bodies, identities, and practices that populate the sport. Whilst for Oates there is 'nothing fundamentally playful' about boxing (Oates, 1987, p. 18) because it is not a game, it is life (Oates, 1987, p. 19), this volume celebrates a particular type of playfulness found within the critical engagement with the sport and its under-researched areas.

Bibliography

Boddy, K. (2008) *Boxing: a cultural history*. London: Reaktion Books.
Heiskanen, B. (2014) *The urban geography of boxing: race, class and gender in the ring*. Oxon: Routledge.
Lewandowki, D.J. (2022) *On boxing: critical interventions in the bittersweet science*. Oxon: Routledge.
Oates, J.C. (1987) *On boxing*. New York: Harper Collins.
Paradis, E. (2012) 'Boxers, briefs or bras? Bodies, gender and change in the boxing gym', *Body and Society*, 18(2), pp. 82–109.
Wacquant, L.J.D. (2005) 'Men at work', in Gattuso, J. (ed.) *Shadow boxers: sweat, sacrifice & the will to survive in American boxing gyms*. Milford, New Jersey: Stone Creek Publications, pp. 145–148.

Index

Note: Page numbers in *italics* indicate a figure or photo and page numbers in **bold** indicate a table on the corresponding page.

Abdul-Jabbar, Kareem 168
Achebe, Chinua 150
Adams, Nicola 11, 16, 20n5, 132
addiction 195, 202–204; *see also* drug abuse
Afghanistan 67
Africa 148–154, 159–160; combat sports 151; diaspora 107; East 153; pre-colonial 150; sub-Saharan 17; wrestling and fighting contests 150
African Boxing Union 153
African Confederation Boxing Championship 17
aggression 46, 66, 79, 83, 119, 129, 181, 197–198
Ali, Laila 116, 137–138
Ali, Muhammad 116, 148, 179
amateur boxers 1, 12–13; female 13
Amateur International Boxing Association (AIBA) 1
American Women's Continental Championships (Guayaquil, Ecuador) 17
#Andthenew 132–136
Andy Capp cartoons 27
anti-communist ideology 185
antifascist 75; machismo 76; movement 76
anti-Muslim violence 64
anti-sexism 76–78
Araujo, Adriana 17
Aristotle 56–57
art project 4, 105–114
Asia 17, 58, 64

Association Internationale de Boxe Amateur (AIBA) 2–3, 20n1, 20n3, 20n6; Women's World Championships 59; *see also* International Boxing Association (IBA)
athletes: amateur 195; Black 5, 11, 150, 152; female 9–13, 20n4, 89, 91, 94, 128, 132–134, 137–139, 142, 200; lesbian 20n5; male 9, 11–12, 14, 91, 138; professional 122, 131, 195; white female 134; *see also* women athletes
athleticism 11, 120, 133, 142
Australia 4, 42, 130, 136, 140, 148; Canberra 42
authenticity 2, 24–37, 134, 168

Balkans 180, 187–188
Banerjee, Asit 61, 67
Bangladesh 63
Barthes, Roland 179
batalla campal 197, 199
Battle Royals 197
Belgium 90
Bend it Like Beckham 167
Bengal Amateur Boxing Federation (BABF) 58–59, 61
Bharatiya Janata Party (BJP) 64
Bieber, Justin 179, 181, 183–184, 190–191
biological sex 83
Black women 11, 16; negative stereotypes of 11

body(ies) 77–82; athletic 129; boxing 2, 4–5, 30, 72, 75, 144, 179, 208–209; cis male 81; female 75, 80–84, 96, 120, 128, 134–136, 138–139, 144, 187, 190; female athletic 154; female-presenting 77, 129; feminine 80, 184, 200; gendered 183; hyperfeminine 132; image 65, 119; labouring 186; legitimate 30, 55–56; male 80, 179; male athletic 66; male-presenting 129; marginalised 179; masculine 1; non-binary 75, 81; nonconforming 75; non-masculine 81; non-white 75; othered 187; political 164–168; racialised 179, 190; -/sex positivity 140; as sexualised objects 190; shaming 143; as social and political tool 120; sporting 55, 200; trans 75, 81; transgressive practices 187; vulnerability of 81–82; white 152, 181; white middle-class feminine 187; women's 81, 120, 198
bodybuilder, competitive 130, 136
body confidence 83, 134
Bollywood 64, 167, 170, 173–174
Bourdieu, Pierre 31, 55–58, 61, 68–69; see also habitus
boxers: amateur 1, 12–13; Black 150; brain damage in 27; champion 4, 13, 40; competitive 40, 186; male 13–14, 16–19, 21n7, 47, 63, 79, 98, 120, 133, 183–184, 189, 191, 195, 203; professional 33, 89, 116, 121, 130, 133, 135, 143, 200; punch-drunk 27; traditional 27; white 47; see also female boxers; women boxers
boxing 55–69; amateur 9, 12, 59, 88, 124, 164, 180; as art form 106; bodies 2, 4–5, 30, 72, 75, 144, 179, 208–209; commercial 1; and cultural value 47, 207–209; culture 1, 116, 120, 179; drama of 164–165, 167, 169, 171, 175, 197; as empowerment 69, 92, 94, 97–98, 116, 124n1, 129, 142, 189, 191, 208; and gender 182, 185; gym 2–3, 5, 29, 33, 35, 43–44, 47–48, 72, 74–75, 77, 79–80, 87, 95, 105, 108, 114n6, 123, 179–189, 191, 208; hearts and beats 179–191; history of, in Zimbabwe 150–154; identity(ies) 2–3, 5, 24, 29–35, 47, 116–124, 129, 172, 180, 182, 207; in India 58–59; narratives 1, 33, 133, 137, 140–141, 164, 167–168, 201, 207, 209; practice 1–2, 4, 73, 78, 81, 151, 208; ring 2, 10, 61, 65, 116, 156, 170, 172, 194, 201; as ritual performance 167, 169; sites 3; spaces 3, 5, 31, 44, 49, 119, 179–181, 186–187, 190–191; tag team match 28; traditional 18, 25, 27–29, 31–33, 36, 55; white collar 26; women-centred approaches in 89, 92, 94–95, 98; see also boxing clubs; celebrity boxing; crossover boxing; female boxing; females in boxing; feminist boxing; influencer boxing; international boxing; Muay Thai boxing style; professional boxing; trans boxing; women in boxing; women's boxing; YouTuber boxing
Boxing! 2, 9, 12–15, **14**, 17–19, 20n2, 20n3; coverage of females in **14**
boxing clubs 3, 40–53, 58, 61, 66, 89–90, 92, **92**, 105–114, 118, 139, 169; boxing coaching and leadership 44–47; culture and ethos 47–49; funding and impact 50–51; Norwegian 89, 92, **92**
Boxing Federation of India 59
Boxing Ladies 62, 65
BoxRec 27
BOXXER 128, 135, 145n9
Brækhus, Cecilia 'The First Lady' 89
brain damage, pathologised 27
Brena, Lepa 181, 187, 189; 'Jugoslovenka' 181, 187
Bridges, Ebanie 'Blonde Bomber' 4, 130–137, 139–144
Bulgaria 180, 187
bullying 43, 49, 143
burqa 60, 62, 67

212 Index

Burqa Boxers 61, 67–68
Butler, Judith 74, 82, 119, 164, 187, 200

capital: bodily 172, 175; cultural 24, 55, 65; economic 30–31, 33; financial 55; physical 120; political 31; reputational 31; social 30–31, 43–44; socio-economic 30; symbolic 31; *see also* celebrity capital
Carrillat, François 3, 25, 30–32, 34
celebrification 31, 37n6
celebrity 31, 130, 149, 155–156, 184; identity 37n6; *see also* celebrity boxing; celebrity capital; micro-celebrity
celebrity boxing 26
celebrity capital 30–35; *see also* celebrity capital life cycle
celebrity capital life cycle 30–35; *see also* celebrity capital life cycle framework (CCLCF)
celebrity capital life cycle framework (CCLCF) 3, 25, 30–32, 34–35; redemption/resurgence stage of 34
celetoid 31, 37n5
Central Eastern Europe (CEE) 179–184, 189–191; socialist experiment in 186
Chan, Jackie 170
change agents, men as 92, 94, 97–98
cheating 1
Chieng, Jennifer 17
Chinembiri, Proud 'Kilimanjaro' 148, 153
Chopra, Priyanka 64, 70n3, 167, 172–175
Christian faith 169, 173
Chungneijang, Mangte *see* Kom, Mary
Citizenship Amendment Act 64, 69–70n2
coaches 1, 3, 12, 18, 40, 44–45, 48–52, 56, 105, 169; boxing 20n3, 20–21n6, 40–41, 44–45, 48, 89, 91–92, **92**, 94–97, 109, 114n6; community 44, 52; female 15–16, 21n7, 45, 89–90, 92, 94–95, 97; gender quotas for 94, 96–98; head 89, 94–97; international 90, 93; main 96; male 48, 91, 95–97; in Norway 87–98, **92**; women 89–90, 94–96; women boxing **92**, 95–96; *see also* coaching
coaching 19, 41, 44–47, 50, 61, 89–90, 93, 95–97, 105, 110
co-authorship 4, 106, 109–111, 113
collaborative practices 32
colonialism 151
colourism 173
combat sparring 95
combat sports 19, 72–84, 110, 136, 150–151
Commonwealth countries 17
Commonwealth Games 59
community(ies) 1, 3–5, 40, 55–69, 91, 105–107, 109–110, 140, 142, 158, 165, 174, 207–209; Anglo-Indian 58; Armenian 58; athletic 4, 208; Black 111; boundaries 60; boxing 27, 44, 48, 95, 97–98, 134, 145n9, 180–181, 187, 207; -building 1, 4, 106; centres 27, 105, 109; deprived 40–53; failed 158; global 130; groups 207; Hindu 63; identity 60; impoverished 62; indigenous 151; international 166; Kom 165; local 43–45; marginalised 42, 44, 62, 179; masculinity 76; minority 63; Muslim 60, 63; Nigerian Igbo 150; poor 154; rural 118; sport 75; underprivileged 159; urban 42; working-class 121; *see also* community gyms
community gyms 72, 78, 82; feminist 75; transfeminist 75–77
conditioning 58
corrupt judging 2
COVID-19 pandemic 62, 92, **92**, 208
criminal activity 43, 49
criminal justice system 43
crossover boxing 25–26; *see also* influencer boxing
cultural imperialism 168
culture: African American 107; critique of boxing 1; gang 45; mainstream 189; masculine patriarchal 186; skinhead sub- 185–186, 191n3; sub- 76, 185–186; tasteless low 190; tasteful high 190;

Index

working-class 179, 185, 191; see also boxing culture; sport cultures
Cyrus, Miley 183
Czechoslovakia 185, 191n3
Czech Republic 5, 180, 185

Daily Star, The 139, 142
Dalits 168
David and Goliath 169–170
DAZN platform 26–27, 32, 37n2, 130
de Beauvoir, Simone 74
deprived communities 40–53; local deprivation rates and participation 41–44
determinism: socioeconomic 56
Devi, Laishram Sarita 59, 64
'Diriyah Champion' belt 32
discrimination 60, 112–113, 173–174, 207; ethnic 42; gender 11, 19, 98, 132, 152, 198; gender-based 98; racial 42, 152
divas 187–191
'double binds' 129, 132, 144
drama, of boxing 164–165, 167, 169, 171, 175, 197
drug abuse 1, 158
Dundee, Angelo 1, 132

England 3, 40–41, 43, 47–49, 58, 90, 130, 145n9; Home Office 51
England Boxing 40, 43, 145n9
ethnicity 16, 18, 49, 55, 167, 182
evaluative practices 32

Fatima, Zainab *8*, 61–63, 66, *104*
female athletes see women athletes
female boxers 2, 4, 75–76, 84, 89, 91, **92**, 95–98, 116–117, 121, 128–139, 142–144, 152, 154, 166, 183–191, 194, 196, 198, 200, 207; amateur 13; athletic abilities of 142; bodies of 75; depictions of 133; entertainment value of 142; feminisation of 18; gains for 128, 142; images of 21n7, 184, 191; Mexican 201; opportunities for 89, 139; in print media 9–20, 21n7; professional 143; regulations for 198; (re)presentations of 3, 13–18; responsibility of 138; Serbian 189; sexualisation of 18; side-lining of 154; South American 17; status of 139; stereotypes of 132; visibility of 19, 130; work of 134, 136; see also female boxing
female boxing 118, 128, 134, 140–141; bodies 4–5, 144; coaches 16, 92, 94–95, 97; competitions 14; identities 129; officials 91; see also females in boxing; feminist boxing
female empowerment 134, 138
female referees 16
femininity(ies) 4, 74, 80, 83, 87, 119–120, 123, 131, 134–136, 142–144, 150, 172, 182, 184–187, 189, 191, 197–198, 200; acceptable 136, 201; construction of 19, 72, 182, 186; forms of 136, 144; hegemonic 122; heteronormative 204; hyperbolic 188; images of 191; infantile 184; male 184; Mexican 200; misconceptions of 4; negotiation of 185; performance of 132–134; range of 187; representation of 190; traditional 201; unacceptable 136; working class 185–187
feminism 4, 67, 72, 79, 134, 136; narratives of 134; neoliberal 189; 'physical' 83; popular 67, 140, 142, 144; second-wave 201
feminist approach/perspective 72, 78–79, 81
feminist boxing 72–84
feminist methodology 117–118
feminist movement 77
feminists 73; anti-porn 143; sex-positive 143
feminist studies/cultural studies 4, 98, 117
field theory 31
fight mode 13, 15, 18
'Fight of the Century' 152
financial management 159
Foreman, George 148
Fortin, Ariane 13
Foucault, Michel 169
funk 106–107, 111–113
Fury, Tommy 32, 34
Fury, Tyson 'Gypsy King' 1, 130

gender 55–69; -based 10, 60, 98; binary 110, 150, 182; and boxing 182, 185; categories 56, 76; cis- 129; construction of 11, 72–73, 76, 150; difference 11; discrimination 11, 19, 98, 132, 152, 198; disparities 10–11, 21n7; equal 12, 17–18; equality 87–88; equity 11, 15–16, 18, 91, 97; expression 111, 113–114, 138; feminine 80; heteronormative 77; hierarchy 10–11; identity(ies) 182, 184, 186, 188, 191; ideologies 121; images of 190; inclusivity 12, 18; inequality 117; inequities 10; listening to 181–182; marker 119; and music 108, 182; myth of 111; -neutral 12, 16, 186; -nonconforming 110; norms 9, 74, 77, 83, 117, 124, 142, 184, 187, 190, 197, 200, 204, 207; order 19, 120, 154, 187, 201; performance 4, 12, 191, 204; performance of 117, 119–120, 122–123; performativity 187; prefixes 14–15, 17–18; quotas for coaches 94, 96–98; regime 120, 123; relations 122; relations of power 120; roles 10, 19, 78; segregation 109; stereotypes 5, 198; traditional 117; transgression 194–204; variance 5; -variant individuals/persons 4, 106, 113; *see also* 'gender trouble'
gendered: advertisements 11; anxieties 203; appropriately 201, 203; assumptions 129; barriers 91; bodies 183; boxing bodies 184; coverage 12; experience of music 191; hierarchies 10; identity(ies) 93, 184; images 184; limitations 143; male- 199–200, 203; norms 5; patterns of participation in sports 19; patterns of reporting 11; perceptions 184; postures 73; practices 190; recruitment processes 97; relation to sounds 182; reporting 13–14; representation of female athletes 20n4, 194; restrictions 129; social order 3, 19; sport dichotomies 123; sports media 10–11; stereotypes 95; system of athletics 106; ways of listening 187
'gender trouble' 200
generative practices 32
globalisation 2
Global South 17–18, 91
global sport 2, 27, 55
Gogarty, Deirdre 194–195, 199
Gore, Lesley 140
Gujarat riots 64

habitus 55–58, 61–63, 66, 68–69, 185; pugilistic 58, 63, 66, 69; social 56
Hanson, Nolan 4, 105–114
Hearn, Eddie 130, 134–135, 141
Hemingway, Ernest 27
heroes 1, 150; cultural 148; film 167; martial arts 170; national 199; of the ring 168, 172; sporting 159
heroism 172; masculine 25
heteronormative 9, 75, 77, 83, 142, 154, 203–204
heterosexuality 154, 191, 197–198, 200–201
'heterotopia' 169
hijab 20, 60, 67
Hindu 63–64, 166, 171
hip-hop 179, 188
Huggins, Jennifer 17
Hungary 180

IBF 4, 37n1, 130
identity(ies): activist 123; boxing 2–3, 5, 24, 29–30, 47, 116, 124, 129, 172, 180, 182, 207; branding 175; celebrity 37n6; class 187; community 60; construction 91, 182; crisis 25; ethnic 18; female 129, 137, 144; formation 25, 37, 120, 151; gender 182, 184, 186, 188, 191; gendered 93, 184; group 24; heroic 34; individual 30; male gender 184; and music 182; national 4, 172, 194, 197; normative gender 182, 191; performances 173, 184; personal 37; pro-producing narratives 179; public 46, 200; quasi-liminal 26;

racial 18; rebellious 123; redeemed 34; regional 180, 188; religious 93; rewards 35, 37, 47; salvaged 34; social 16, 19, 24; socio-cultural 46, 207; socio-political 164–165, 167; work 3, 24, 30, 35–36; working-class 186–187; see also narrative identity
Ilicic, Jasmina 3, 25, 30–32, 34
inclusivity 4, 18, 47–48, 107
India 5, 58–61, 63–64, 67, 69, 70n4, 165–169, 171, 173–174, 175n2, 208; Bengal 58–61, 64; Bihar 60; boxing in 58–59; Delhi 9, 13, 64; Kolkata (formerly Calcutta) 3, *8*, 55, 58–60, 62, 65–66, 68, 70n4, *104*; Manipur 5, 59, 61, 64, 164–171, 173–175; Muslim women boxers of Kolkata 59–63; Partition 59–60, 63; politics, community, and nation 63–65; Uttar Pradesh 60
Indian Amateur Boxing Federation (IABF) 59, 61
Indian blockbuster 164–175
Indianness 173
individualism 4, 49, 128–144
influencer boxing 3, 24–37, 37n2
Influencer Championship Boxing Championship (ICB Championship) 32
Influencer Fight League (IFL) 32
Instagram 26, 130, 134, 136
International Amateur Boxing Association 59
international boxing 47, 94, 98, 199; see also International Boxing Association (IBA); International Boxing Hall of Fame
International Boxing Association (IBA) 9–10, 12–13, 15–20, 20n1, 20n2, 20n3, 20–21n6, 21n7, 88, 90, 93; Women's Commission 15
International Boxing Hall of Fame 1
International Olympic Committee (IOC) 1, 15–16, 121
Ireland 15, 42, 47, 90, 116–119, 121–124, 132; Dublin 42; national Olympic team 11
Italy 3, 47, 72, 76; Milan 75–76; Naples 72, 82–84

Jay-Z 179
Jeffries, James 152
Johnson, Jack 152
Johnson, Samuel 68
Joshua, Anthony 1
juju 152, 157

Kendra Lust 140
Kidderpore School of Physical Culture (KSOPC) *8*, 56, 61–63, 66–67, *104*
Kinahan, Daniel 1
kinship 4, 128–144
knockout 87, 90, 175
Kom, Mary 5, 13, 15–16, 59, 64, 164–175; biopic *Mary Kom* 165, 171, 173–174; Manipuri autobiography 164–175; *Unbreakable* 64, 165, 171
Kom, the 165–166, 168, 175
KSI (Olajide Olayinka Williams Olatunji) 25–29, 32, 35, 37n2, 37n4
Kumar, Omung 166, 168, 171, 173, 175n2

Latin America 5, 17, 195, 203
leaderism 77
leadership 19, 41, 44–47, 49, 61, 88, 95, 97
Lee, Bruce 167–170
legitimacy 2, 9–10, 12, 25, 27–28, 30, 32, 81, 199
Le Sberle, Community Feminist Gym 72, 75–77, 81–84
lesbian 20n5, 119, 200; lesbianism 197
Li, Jet 170
Liebling, A. J. 28–29
Lipa, Dua 183
Lorde, Audre 112
Louis, Joe 208–209
lucha libre wrestling 197

machism 77
machismo 76; mari- 197
Madison Square Garden 117, 134
Madonna 140
manhood 116, 150
marginalisation 10, 64–65, 91, 98
marimachismo 197
Marshall, Savannah 131, 134–135, 143, 145n9, 145n16

martial arts 51; Anglo-Saxon 175; Chinese 167, 169; cinematic/film 170; *see also* mixed martial arts
Martin, Christy 137–138, 199
Martland, Harrison 27
masculine privilege 12
masculinity(ies) 3, 5, 19, 72, 74, 76–77, 80–81, 83, 87, 117, 119–120, 150–151, 172, 184, 187, 191, 199; community 76; construction(s) of 19, 72, 182, 198; dominant 79–80; female 77, 80; hegemonic 3, 72, 74, 77, 79–81, 119; heroic 45, 132; heteronormative 9; hyper- 120; male 185; markers of 79; Mexican 203; militant 77; narratives of 181; religion of 66; respectable 76–77; traditional 184; white 142; working-class 194, 199
mass media 9–10
Matchroom 37n2, 128, 130, 134
Mauss, Marcel 56–57
Mayer, Mikaela 143–144, 145n16
media 2–3, 5, 10–11, 14, 117, 129, 131, 128, 140–141, 159–160, 181; attention 128, 131; boxing 135; commentaries 5, 138; coverage 3, 10–11, 13, 16, 19–20, 20n5, 128; effects 19, 20n4; focus 129, 132; frenzy 143; images 11–12, 134, 180; influence 141; interest 140; investment 19; landscape 133–134; local 119; mainstream 20, 130, 142; narratives 142; outlets 131; platforms 139, 142; popular 145n15; practices 10; print 9–20; support 133; traditional 2–3, 26; visibility 31–32; *see also* mass media; social media; sport(s) media
mediatisation 65, 68, 168, 172
Mehrajuddin Ahmed 59, 61–63
Meiteis 166, 168, 173
men 1, 10–11, 13–14, 16–17, 20, 25, 48, 57–58, 62–63, 65–66, 72, 79, 80, 82, 87, 89, 92–97, 116, 118–121, 135, 150–151, 156, 172, 182, 186, 188, 190, 194–195, 197–198, 202–203;
African American 197; Black 152; as change agents 94, 97–98; marginalised 30; media coverage of 21n7; non-elite 194; white 117; young 116, 195
Merleau-Ponty, Maurice 57
#metoo 138
Mexican Revolution 199
Mexico 91, 114n4; Mexico City 194–197, 199–200, 202–203, 204n4; women's boxing in 194–204
micro-celebrity 25, 31, 36
Milošević, Slobodan 188
Misfits Boxing promotional company 26, 37n2
misogyny 67–68, 120, 138, 142–144, 207
Mitra, Payoshni 63–66; *The Bold and the Beautiful* 65–66
mixed martial arts 19, 21n11, 26
mixed training 79, 83
moral disposition 57
motherhood 167, 171–172, 200–201
Mother India 171, 175n2
Muay Thai boxing style 19, 110–111
muscularity 119–120
music 26, 112, 117, 140, 175n2, 179–191, 191n1; and athletic activity 181; Black 112; dance 2; halls 28; and identity 182; skinhead 181, 185, 187, 190–191, 191n3; and social interactions 182; *see also* funk; pop-folk; pop music; turbo-folk music
Muslims 60, 63–64, 69–70n2
Muslim women boxers in Norway **92**
Muslim women boxers of Kolkata 3, 55–56, 59–63, 65; work of representation 65–68
mythology 153, 165; Graeco-Roman 172; Hindu 171
myths 111, 131, 165, 179–181, 186–187, 191, 196; boxing 180, 204

Nandakumar, Anusha 62, 66; *Boxing Ladies* 66
narrative(s): boxing 1, 33, 133, 137, 140–141, 164, 167–168, 201, 207, 209; of change

135; conventional 197, 201; counter- 204, 209; cultural 27, 30; dominant 116, 131, 142, 148–160, 203, 208; of failure 158–159; of feminism 134; fighting 170; hegemonic 209; historical 150–151; identity-producing 179; mainstream, of combat sports 72–84; of masculinity 181; media 142; myopic 209; normative gender identities 191; personal 209; political 209; popular 132, 134, 208; post-socialist 186; of poverty 159; practices 31; public 25, 28, 209; of redemption and salvation 34; resources 1, 3, 24–25, 27, 30–31, 34–37, 48, 208; self-sacrifice 137; socio-political 208; of struggle 55–69, 186; trailblazer 135; tropes 1; working-class 186; *see also* narrative identity
narrative identity 3, 25, 36–37, 209
Nasr, Ariel 67; *The Boxing Girls of Kabul* 67
national affiliation 55
National Autonomous University of Mexico (UNAM) 195–196, 199, 203
national hero 135, 167, 195, 199
nationality 18
national teams 3, 14, 16, 18, 87; gender quotas for coaches on 94, 96–98
Netflix 130, 166
norms 75, 151, 169; appropriate music preference 187; binary gendered 5; conservative 56; deconstruction of 83; expected 49; gender 9, 74, 77, 83, 117, 124, 142, 184, 187, 190, 197, 200, 204, 207; gendered 5; gender equality 19; global diffusion of 21n9; religious 69; social 198; socio-cultural 5; traditional 117
Northern Ireland 42, 156; Belfast 42
Norway 42, 87–89, 91–92, 94, 97; development of women's boxing in 88–90; Muslim women's boxers in 47, **92**, 93; *see also* Norway Female Box

Norway Female Box 3, 87–98, *90*
Norwegian Boxing Association 89–90, 92–93, **92**, 98

Oates, Joyce Carol 27–28, 65, 116–117, 119, 121, 132, 136, 190, 207, 209
'Occupy' movement 76
O'Connell, Shannon 140, 143
Olympics/Olympic Games 1–2, 12, 14–16, **14**, 20–21n6, 59, 87, 91, **92**, 98, 118–119, 121, 128, 130–131, 133–136, 143, 153, 169, 204n3; 2028 2; Helsinki (1952) 59; London (1948) 59; London (2012) 11, 15–17, 67, 87–88, 121, 123, 128–129, 145n9, 166–168, 207; Paris (2024) 20; Rio (2016) 17, 20, 87, 130; St. Louis (1904) 99n1; Tokyo (2020) 1, 87
OnlyFans 139–142
organised crime 1
organised sport 55
Orientalism 173–174
Orlík 181, 185–186, 190, 191n3
otherness 174, 197

Pakistan 47–48, 63–64
Paradise, Justine 33
patriarchy 67; patriarchal nationalism 189; patriarchal values 137
Paul, Jake 24, 26–27, 32–35
Paul, Logan 26–27, 35
physical culture 186
physical enquiry 1
physical practices 3, 25, 30, 34–37, 128
Piper, Adrian 106–109, 114n1
Poland 180
political agency 64
political statement 1
political symbol 165, 167–168, 170–171, 175
political symbolism 164–175
pop-folk 188–191
pop music 25, 179, 188
popular culture 24–25, 169, 179, 188
poses 18; active 12, 14–15; classic boxing 18; fight 14; passive 10, 12–13; suggestive 10
poverty 42, 66–67, 148–149, 153, 155–159, 179, 189, 195, 203

218 Index

power relations 93, 121, 207
Premier Boxing Champions (PBC) 109, 114n3
prize fighting 27, 42
professional boxing 1, 24, 27–28, 37n2, 42, 58, 63, 90, 116–117, 120, 128, 135, 202–203, 208; women's 116, 122–124
professional wrestling 28
promoters 27, 122, 128, 130, 132, 134, 138, 141–142, 159, 165, 197
public art 108, 114n2
pugilists 20, 149, 154, 156, 180
punch-drunk boxer 27

Qamar, Mohammad Ali 59

race 16, 18–19, 55, 73, 133; *see also* racism
racism 64, 171, 173–174, 185, 191n3, 197; racist ideology 151, 185
Raghuram, Alka 61, 67–68; *see also* Burqa Boxers
'rags-to-riches' 5
rappers 179
reality television shows 25
redemption: quest for 24–37; self- 158
relative deprivation 42
Rhodes, Frank 109
Rhodesia 151–153
ring girl 135–136
Ring Heavyweight Champion 37n1
role models 5, 52, 62, 92, 94–96, 118, 144, 150, 157, 166, 170; women 92, 94–96
Romani people 185
Roy, Paresh Lal 58–59
'Rumble in the Jungle' 148

Sachar Committee Report 60
Said, Edward 173
Sassu, Alice 67
Scandinavia 88–89
segregation: gender 109; racial 152
self-affirmation 65, 68–69, 182
self-defence 82–83
selfhood 64, 69, 208
selfishness 128–144, 204
self-managed 78; movement 76
Serbia 180, 187–189
Serrano, Amanda 117, 123, 134

Serrano, Laura 5, 194–204; *La Poeta Del Ring* 194; and nationalism 199–201; price of boxing 201–203
sexism 57, 76–77, 120, 135, 142, 154, 197; anti- 76–78
sex positivism 140, 143
sexual assault 33, 96
sexuality 49, 112, 131, 142–144; hetero- 191, 197, 200–201
sexual orientation 20n5, 80
sex work 25, 61, 82, 140
Shabnam, Razia 61–63, 66–68, *104*
shared narrative resources 1, 3, 24–25, 30, 36–37
Shields, Claressa 131–135, 137–138, 143, 145n9, 145n16
Shields, Clarissa 16
showmanship 36, 116
Sibanda, Monalisa 154
skinhead: music 181, 185, 187, 190–191, 191n3; subculture 185–187, 191n3
Sky Sports Boxing 128
Slovakia 5, 180, 187
social biography 159; method 148, 154–155
social control 150–151
social engagement 4
social group 24–25, 37
socialisation 57, 152
socialism 186
socialist ideology 186
socialist society 186
social justice 208; movement 117
social media 25, 72, **92**, 117, 130–131, 135, 138–144, 145n9; stars 25, 37n4; *see also* social media influencers (SMIs)
social media influencers (SMIs) 26, 30–33, 36
social mobility 60, 149–150, 154, 159, 190–191, 195, 203
social networks 47
somateque 72
soundscapes 5, 179, 182, 186, 190–191
South Africa 149–150, 152
South America 17
South Calcutta Physical Culture Association (SCPCA) 61, 67
South Korea 91

Soviet Union 180
spaces 65, 68–69, 73, 75–82, 84, 87, 95, 106, 110–111, 113, 117, 123–124, 124n1, 136, 151, 164, 168–169, 201–202, 208; accessible 169; bodies and 77–82; boxing 3, 5, 31, 44, 49, 119, 179–181, 186–187, 190–191; community 208; cultural 116, 120, 124n1, 188, 191n3; domestic 81; gym 83; habitus and 68–69; local 169; male 77, 119; male-dominated 136; masculine 132; mental 188; physical 66, 68; political 73; private 173; public 60, 77, 81, 152; safe 82, 94; music in 179–191; social 56, 58, 61–62, 68–69, 116, 120, 124n1, 208; sports 77; training 186
sport cultures 10, 12, 119
sporting personality 160
sports: amateur 58, 128; female 198; global 2–3, 27, 55; individual 155; international 153; male 198; masculine 94, 200; Olympic 14–15, **14**, 134; professional 122, 155; team 12, 143, 155; *see also* combat sports; sport cultures; sporting personality; sports entertainment; sports media
Sports Authority of India 59, 67
sports entertainment 27–28, 31, 36
Sports Illustrated 137, 149
sports media 9–10, 19, 66, 128, 132–134, 208; gendered 10–11; imaging women athletes in 11–12
Stallings, L.H. 106, 111–112
stereotypes 2, 11, 13, 66, 83, 110, 116, 132, 140, 143, 173, 175n3, 179; ethnic 207; gender 5, 184, 198; gendered 95; negative 11; 'nurturer' 207; racial 207; religious 45; social 45; trailblazer 135; visual 67
Steward, Emanuel 114n6
stick fighting 82, 84
subaltern 65, 168–169; groups 190
Sugden, John 28–30, 42–43, 90
Sweden 90

Taliban 67
Taylor, Katie 4, 15–16, 116–124, 130–134, 143, 145n7; disguised as a boy 118–120; lead advocate for and presence in women's boxing 121–122; recognisable face in women's professional boxing 122–124
#Teamskankystripper 143–144
Te Ciacco gym 72, 75, 82–84
TikTok 33, 134
'Times Up' 138
Tinago, Langton 'Schoolboy' 148, 153
trailblazer trend 132–134, 145n6
trans athletes 110
trans boxing 4, 105–114
trans fighters 111
transformative purpose 2
trans individuals/persons 4, 111
(trans)national domain 194–204
transphobia 112–113
Trattles, David 65–66, 70n4; 'The Boxing Ladies' 65, 70n4
Trinidad and Tobago 91
turbo-folk music 179, 181, 187–189, 191; *see also* pop-folk
Twitter 26, 130, 136, 140, 143
Tyson, Mike 149

UK, the 42, 130–131
Ultimate Fighting Championship (UFC) 26
underdog 169
United States (US/U.S./USA) 1, 16, 19, 42, 91, 107, 122, 132–133, 152, 197

victim support 47
Virgin Mary 75

Wacquant, Loïc 2, 4, 29–30, 42, 49, 58, 66, 90, 116, 164, 196, 207
Wasserman Boxing 26–27, 37n2
WBO Heavyweight Champion 37n1
Weber, Max 57
Weller, Joe 25
white supremacy 197
WIBF 5, 194, 199–200
Wilder, Deontay 'Bronze Bomber' 130
wildness 181, 190
With this Ring 64
womanhood 119, 165, 172–173, 201

Index

women athletes 9–10, 13, 67, 89–91, 94, 96, 98, 122, 128, 132–134, 137–139, 142, 200; body images of 65; imaging of, in sport media 11–12; representation of, in sport media 10–11, 20n4; sexualisation or feminisation of 10; white 134; worth, status, and legitimacy of 10

women boxers 3, 9–10, 13, 15–20, 59, 62, 64–64, 68, 72, 79, 87, 89, 93, 95, 98, 119, 121, 123–124, 187, 191, 198–200; Afghan 67; amateur 15–16; Black 11, 16; feminisation of 13, 17; imaging of 13; Indian 62, 64–65, 70n4; media coverage of 19–20; Muslim 3, 55–56, 59–63, 65, 70n4; sexualisation of 13, 17; trivialisation of 13; *see also* female boxers

women in boxing 3, 13, 19, 87–98, 119–120, 128, 135–137, 139–140, 142, 144, 154, 207; around the world 90–91; empowerment of 87–98; *see also* women's boxing

women of colour 16, 134

Women's Amateur World Boxing Championship (Ningbo, China) 167

women's boxing 128–144; in Mexico 194–204; as spectacle 196–199

Women's International Boxing Association (WIBA) 154

women's rights activism 12

Women's World Championships: 2012 16–17; Delhi (2006) 13; Ningbo (2008) 15; Podolsk, Russia 15; Astana, Turkey (2016) 17–18

World Boxing Association (WBA) 32, 121; WBA Heavyweight Super Champion 37n1; WBA Heavyweight World Champion 37n1

World Boxing Championship: 2022 122; Delhi (2007) 9; Turkey (2002) 173

World Boxing Council (WBC) 32, 109, 114n4, 149, 153–154; WBC Heavyweight Champion 37n1

World Series of Boxing 19

Yahoub, Kheira Sidi 17
YouTube 20n3, 20–21n6, 26, 28, 33, 130, 140–141, 185
YouTuber boxing 26; *see also* influencer boxing
Yugo-nostalgia 5
Yugoslav wars 188

Zaire (now Democratic Republic of the Congo) 148
Zareen, Nikhat 59, 64
Zimbabwe 5; history of boxing in 150–154; Mbare 148, 151, 153, 155, 158; post-colonial 148–160
Zvenyika, Alfonso 'Mosquito' 5, 148–160; boxing fame and the life of the celebrity 155–156; contemporary iteration of 157–159; downfall of a boxing legend 156–157; early years 155; incarceration 157; Mosquito Boxing School of Excellence 158; takeaways from 159